LEARNING
IN THE
FIELD

For our daughters—

Dara Tomlin Rossman, Tamara Beth Rossman,
and Bethany Alexis Rallis—

who have taken us "into the field" in ways we could
never have imagined. Their questions and answers,
their criticisms and affirmations—the challenges
and joys they bring to our lives—have helped us
grow as researchers, authors, and people.

Also, for the men who support us in our work—

David and John—

without whom we may not have taken risks and grown.

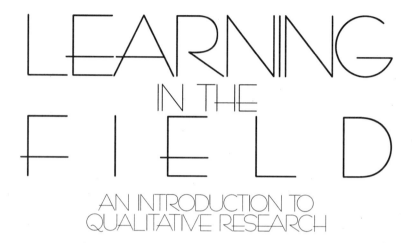

LEARNING
IN THE
FIELD

AN INTRODUCTION TO
QUALITATIVE RESEARCH

GRETCHEN B. ROSSMAN & SHARON F. RALLIS

SAGE Publications
International Educational and Professional Publisher
Thousand Oaks   London   New Delhi

For information:

SAGE Publications, Inc.
2455 Teller Road
Thousand Oaks, California 91320
E-mail@sagepub.com

SAGE Publications Ltd.
6 Bonhill Street
London EC2A 4PU
United Kingdom

SAGE Publications India Pvt. Ltd.
M-32 Market
Greater Kailash I
New Delhi 110048 India

Printed in the United States of America

Library of Congress Cataloging-in-Publication Data

Rossman, Gretchen B.
   Learning in the field: An introduction to qualitative research /
by Gretchen B. Rossman and Sharon F. Rallis.
      p. cm.
   Includes bibliographical references (p.   ) and index.
   ISBN 0-7619-0352-6 (cloth : acid-free paper). — ISBN
0-7619-0353-4 (pbk. : acid-free paper)
      1. Social sciences—Research—Methodology. 2. Qualitative
reasoning. I. Rallis, Sharon F. II. Title.
   H62.R667 1998
   300'.72—dc21   97-33901

98 99 00 01 02 03 04 8 7 6 5 4 3 2 1

Acquiring Editor:	Peter Labella
Editorial Assistant:	Renée Piernot
Production Editor:	Sanford Robinson
Production Assistant:	Denise Santoyo
Typesetter/Designer:	Danielle Dillahunt
Indexer:	Teri Greenberg
Cover Designer:	Ravi Balasuriya
Print Buyer:	Anna Chin

Contents

Preface   xi

1. Qualitative Research as Learning   1
    What Is Qualitative Research?   5
    Characteristics   7
    Ways of Using Research   11
        Instrumental Use   12
        Enlightenment Use   13
        Symbolic Use   14
        Emancipatory Use   15
    Three Qualitative Research Strategies   16
        Descriptive Cultural Studies   17
        Evaluation or Policy Studies   17
        Action Research   18
    Habits of Mind and Heart   18
    Overview of the Book   20
    Further Reading   22

2. The Researcher as Learner   23
    The Reflexivity of Qualitative Research   26
        Paradigms   27
        Subjectivity Versus Objectivity   28
        Status Quo Versus Radical Change   33
        Four Paradigms   34
    Perspective in Practice   37

95995

The Self at Work: Reflexivity 38
Establishing Perspective 40
Trustworthiness 43
Standards for Practice 45
Ethics 48
Politics 53
Using the Habits of Mind and Heart 54
Further Reading 56

3. Planning the Research 58
Do-Ability 61
Want-to-Do-Ability 62
Should-Do-Ability 62
What Is a Research Proposal? 63
Major Qualitative Research Genres 66
Critical and Postmodern Assumptions 66
Ethnographies 67
Case Studies 70
Phenemenological Studies 72
Conceptual Framework 74
Use of the Literature 74
Introduction 75
The Topic 76
Statement of the Research Problem or Issue 77
Purpose 78
Significance 80
Overview Questions and Subquestions 81
Limitations and Delimitations 84
Design and Methodology 84
Overall Strategy and Rationale 85
Site or Population Selection 85
Data Gathering Procedures 87
Data Management and Analysis Procedures 88
Using the Habits of Mind and Heart 88
Further Reading 90

4. Entering the Field 91
Preparation 94
Intended Involvement 96

Degree of Involvement   96
Portrayal of Involvement   98
Approach and Negotiations   101
Time   101
Introduction and Invitation   102
Written Permission   103
Expectations and Relationships   104
Reciprocity   105
Organizational Gatekeepers   108
Using the Habits of Mind and Heart   111
Further Reading   112

5. Gathering Data in the Field   113
Decisions About Gathering Data   117
Depth or Breadth   118
Prefigured or Open-Ended   119
Ebb and Flow   120
Systematic Inquiry   120
Data About the Research   121
Data About the Process and Yourself   122
Generic In-Depth Interviewing   124
Types of Interviews   124
Social Group Identities   126
Follow-Up Questions   128
Specialized Forms of In-Depth Interviewing   132
Ethnographic Interviewing   132
Phenomenological Interviewing   133
Interviewing "Elites" or "Experts"   134
Focus Group Interviewing   134
Interviewing Children   135
Observing People, Actions, and Events   136
Taking Field Notes   137
Making Raw Field Notes Usable   138
Examples of Field Notes and Interview Transcripts   139
Anthony's Field Notes   139
Ruth's Field Notes   141
Marla's Interview Transcript   142
Studying Material Culture   145

Using the Habits of Mind and Heart   147
Further Reading   147

6. Issues That Arise in the Field   **149**
"How Do I Prepare to Gather Data?"   151
"How Can I Get Comfortable in the Field?"   153
"What Are the Data?"   157
"How Do I Turn Sights, Sounds, and Objects Into Data?"   159
"I'm Bilingual. What Language Do I Use?"   161
"How Can I Change My Research Plan?"   163
"What Do I Reflect on?"   163
"How Do I Leave the Field?"   165
Using the Habits of Mind and Heart   166

7. Analyzing and Interpreting Data   **168**
Decisions About Analysis   172
Ongoing Analysis Versus Analysis at the End   172
Structured or Open-Ended Analysis   174
Analysis Related to Qualitative Genre   174
Generic Analysis   176
Organizing the Data   177
Familiarizing Yourself With the Data   178
Generating Categories, Themes, and Patterns   178
Coding   180
Searching for Alternative Understandings   181
Writing the Report   182
Strategies for Analyzing Interview Data   183
Analyzing Ethnographic Interview Data   183
Analyzing Phenomenologic Interview Data   184
Analyzing Narrative Data   184
Strategies for Analyzing Field Notes From Observations   186
Strategies for Analyzing Material Culture   187
Using the Habits of Mind and Heart   188
Further Reading   189

8. Presenting the Learnings   **190**
Presentation   193
Audience and Purpose   194

Possible Formats   195
    Voice   197
Organizing the Report   200
    Chronology   200
    Life History   200
    Thematic   201
    Composite   201
    Critical Events   202
    Portraits   202
Using the Habits of Mind and Heart to
    Generate Useful Knowledge   203

Epilogue   **205**

Appendixes: Introduction   **207**

Appendix A: Ruth's Data and Analysis   **209**

Appendix B: Marla's Data and Analysis   **225**

Appendix C: Anthony's Data and Analysis   **240**

References   **258**

Index   **263**

About the Authors   **271**

•◆•

Preface

This book is intended as an introduction to qualitative research. During our combined years of teaching students about this fascinating enterprise, we have used excellent texts—several could supplement this one. We have found, however, that beginning students do not always connect well with the organization of these texts nor with the examples provided. We were challenged to create a book that we could use in our own teaching and that, we hope, others would find valuable. Our purpose was to simplify the complexity of qualitative research and make it accessible to newcomers to the trade. To accomplish this, we have made several decisions, reflected in the style and organization of the book.

Many texts are written in a style that beginners find difficult to grasp. This style creates a sometimes insurmountable distance between the author, as an expert on qualitative research, and the reader. Examples are too exemplary; beginners cannot identify with them. They suggest, moreover, that beginners are not yet ready to do strong, ethical qualitative research. We thought that beginners might more easily relate to the work of other beginners. We decided to create three characters—Ruth, Marla, and Anthony—as students in an introductory qualitative research course. We created them as students to reflect our belief—expressed throughout the book and in its title—that research is a process of learning. The characters are composite portraits of students we have taught and researchers we have known. Each chapter begins with a vignette depicting the characters' conversations after class. Through their dialogue, we introduce the puzzles and tensions that beginning students encounter. The dialogues forecast the content of each chapter. Throughout the book, we use their evolving research projects as examples in addition to those from our own work and from the work of our students throughout the years. We hope this makes the struggles and excitement of doing qualitative research vivid and real.

We struggled with the voice to use in the narrative. We did not want to create unnecessary distance between you, the reader, and us, the authors. We decided to use "we" when we refer to ourselves specifically and "the qualitative researcher" to show general principles or guidelines. We directly address you, the reader, throughout the text, as a way of engaging you in the narrative. This issue of voice is an important one for qualitative research because it reveals your stance about inclusion and distance in research and the written text.

The organization of the book further reflects decisions we have made. In the evolution of our understanding of qualitative research, we have come to see the distinction between interviewing and observing—the mainstays of qualitative research—as somewhat artificial. You cannot interview without observing—taking note of physical environment, body language, and subtle cues about feeling and reflection. We therefore blur the boundaries between these data gathering techniques, presenting them together in one chapter. A few other qualitative research texts take a similar stand, but it is unusual.

We end each chapter with a section on the habits of mind and heart of qualitative researchers. This construct captures the important ways of thinking and feeling that are integral to doing competent, ethical qualitative research. These include a comfort with ambiguity, a deep respect for the experiences of others, sensitivity to complexity, humility in making claims for what you have learned, and thinking that is creative, analytic, and evocative. In these sections, we use the habits to suggest a perspective on the puzzles and tensions raised in the vignettes.

We include footnotes throughout the text. These serve various purposes. Sometimes they are directed at you, the reader, for amplification of a point. Other times, they direct you to further information. At still other times, they explicate our thinking about a complex topic. We also include a list of references for further reading at the end of each chapter. These are intended for those of you who want to delve deeper into the subject.

Chapter 1 provides a description of qualitative research and describes four ways of using research: instrumental, enlightenment, symbolic, and emancipatory. Our belief is that, to be ethical, research should be useful to various audiences for various purposes. We then present three generic qualitative research strategies: descriptive cultural studies, evaluations or policy studies, and action research. Chapter 2 defines the qualitative researcher as a learner and discusses reflexivity as a central aspect of becoming a competent researcher. We discuss the assumptions undergirding all inquiry, specifically qualitative research. These assumptions shape your perspective—your stance—as the learner in a research project. We discuss trustworthiness as a set of considerations to help ensure that your study is ethical, sound, and rigorous.

Chapter 3 details the complex thinking that goes into planning and designing a qualitative project. Three considerations are paramount: do-ability (feasibility), want-to-do-ability (interest), and should-do-ability (ethics and politics). In planning their projects, our characters consider how they link to the major qualitative research genres: ethnography, phenomenological studies, and case studies. The elements of a qualitative research project design are discussed, with examples from our characters showing how they weigh alternatives and make informed decisions.

Chapters 4, 5, and 6 describe the processes of gathering data in the field. Chapter 4 discusses entry and access: preparing for fieldwork, negotiating with participants, expectations and building relationships, and reciprocity. Chapter 5 provides details on gathering data through the primary techniques of talking with people (interviewing); paying attention to actions, activities, and interactions (observing); and collecting artifacts—material culture—to provide insight into the phenomenon you are studying. Chapter 6 presents questions that frequently arise during data gathering.

Chapter 7 discusses the often opaque processes of analyzing qualitative data. We present six phases of generic analysis and then offer strategies for analyzing interview data, field notes, and material culture. The six generic phases are organizing the data, immersing yourself in the data, generating categories and themes, coding, searching for alternative understandings, and writing the report. These phases mirror elements of the creative process: immersion, incubation, insight, and interpretation.

In Chapter 8, we discuss various modes for presenting what you have learned in the project. Although we offer ways of organizing and writing a formal report, we encourage the reader to consider alternative modes—for example, multimedia presentations, newsletters, and oral presentations. Here, we revisit the notion of voice as fundamental to representing what you have learned in your research in useful, ethical, and thoughtful ways.

We conclude the book with three appendixes that develop the preliminary data analysis of our characters. Each character's study is briefly described, samples of their data are presented, followed by preliminary analytic memos that they write to help deepen their interpretations.

We cannot end without giving thanks and appreciation to those who have had a major influence on the ideas, form, and style of this book. First are the many students we have taught throughout the years; we have learned much from them. Karen Campbell-Nelson challenged the separation of interviewing and observing; her clear articulation of this artificial dichotomy crystallized our thinking on this issue. Others reviewed early drafts of the chapters: Jane Crudden, Tim Lannon, Bob McCarthy, and David Stevens. The work of several students appears as examples throughout the text. We do not reference their work directly but acknowledge them here: Janice Barclay, Judy Chu, Daria Fisk, Tim Knowles, Meta Reid, and Samona Jo Tate, among others. Colleagues also gave us important feedback as did the five anonymous reviewers.

Our daughters provided sustained support and direct assistance. Bethany Rallis worked through many of the ideas in conversations walking along the Narragansett Bay; Dara Tomlin Rossman and Tamara Rossman spent one marathon weekend reviewing and making suggestions for revisions on the manuscript. Their insights and fine editing comments are reflected throughout the book. Our characters would not be quite so real without the litmus test of their readings.

Finally, our editor, Peter Labella, has been a constant source of ideas, support, and encouragement as we worked through issues of voice, organization, and purpose. With a gentle hand and much cheerleading, he has guided this project to completion.

CHAPTER ONE

◆

Qualitative Research as Learning

❦

Ruth, Marla, and Anthony gathered up their notebooks and walked toward the classroom door. Their first class in Introduction to Qualitative Research had been confusing . . . and exciting.

Ruth turned to Anthony, "So . . . what did you think?"

"Just great! A piece of cake!" Anthony replied with irony in his tone. He continued, "Actually, I don't think it will be so bad. Just find some place where I can talk with folks, hang around for a while . . . then write it all up."

Marla mumbled under her breath, "I don't think it's all that simple, Anthony."

"I don't, either," added Ruth. "I'm concerned about what doing a 'small scale' project means. I don't think it'll be a 'piece of cake.' I mean, how do I start? And how much is enough?"

Anthony shrugged his shoulders, "Anyone want a cup of coffee? Maybe we can sort it out."

"Sure, sure," Marla and Ruth answered in unison. "Maybe the student union's still open."

As they walked across the parking lot toward the student union, they were quiet with their own thoughts. Professor Kent had talked about characteristics and different strategies for doing qualitative research. Kent had also mentioned producing knowledge and using the results as well as a whole raft of

1

other considerations. The three students were anxious about their first qualitative research course at the university.

"Well, have you got it all solved?" Anthony asked while juggling three cups of coffee as his backpack slipped down a shoulder.

"Oh, yeah, we've got it wired!" answered Ruth. "After all, Kent told us that the purpose is learning, so not to worry. In truth, I haven't a clue how to sort it out. I'm still not even sure what 'qualitative research' is."

Anthony jumped in, "I think it's very different from the stats class I had last year. Here we have to spend a lot of time 'in the field,' observing and stuff. Remember how Kent kept saying that? Like a mantra: 'in the field, in the field.' To me, that means we have to go find some group or organization or place . . . whatever . . . where we can study the people there."

"No, no!" interrupted Marla. "I don't want to feel like I'm putting people under a microscope. That's not what I want to do! I want to spend time with them, learning about what's going on, what they think and feel. I think that's what qualitative research is all about."

Ruth hesitated, "I'm just not sure yet. I got the sense that we're to understand what's happening . . . or how people think, by watching and listening. But, when is it really research? Won't people say I just went out and heard—or saw—what I wanted to hear or see? What about being objective? Isn't research supposed to be objective?"

"I always thought so," said Anthony. "And that's just what I'm going to try to do in this project. I'll figure out just what I want to know, go and gather the data, and I'll be done."

"Pero, what if you find out that there's much more going on? What if it doesn't all fit into your neat little package?," probed Marla.

Anthony paused, but only for a moment: "Well, let's see what the readings say on all this."

"My guess right now is that there's probably several approaches that are all ok," Marla suggested. "I just can't tell the difference between them yet, but Kent says they are all systematic inquiry."

"Yes," answered Anthony, "but Kent used terms I've never heard before. I know I want to look at program effectiveness but I don't know where that fits."

"Doesn't 'effectiveness' make it an evaluation question?" interjected Marla. "I mean, didn't Kent say evaluation was research, too?"

"Well, I remember him saying there is evaluation and policy something, and action research, and something about descriptive studies," said Ruth. "I think I'll just do basic research . . . that seems easier."

"I guess you missed the rest of what Kent said. We don't really do basic research—only the guys in white coats do that," laughed Anthony.

"Ok, but what about all those uses, like instrumental and symbolic? Are they different?" asked Ruth. "I don't see how I can have any control over how anyone will use my work."

"The point is that the terms are new and . . . it feels like learning a whole new language, at least for me," Marla pointed out. "I feel I need to know more before I can begin to do it—like I need more vocabulary before I can speak."

"Didn't Kent say that we can only learn by doing it?" groaned Anthony. "How do we do it, if we can only learn how to do it by doing it? Whoa . . . !"

"I bet other people in class feel just like we do," said Marla. "They probably are wondering just what this is all about and are worried, too. But I'm glad to have met you two and talked a bit. It's helping . . . I think!"

Systematic inquiry, naturalistic inquiry, instrumental, interpretive, evaluation, enlightenment, emancipatory, and iterative—Marla, Ruth, and Anthony are students who have just encountered the confusing array of terms that comprise the vocabulary of qualitative research. The terms represent various processes, uses, and perspectives of qualitative research as well as specific approaches to gathering, analyzing, interpreting, and writing up data. Many of the terms and differences in approaches are specialized and subtle. Each, however, helps explicate the following central themes of this book:

1. Research should be undertaken to generate knowledge.

2. The researcher is the learner, continually and consciously making decisions that affect the questions pursued and the direction of the study.

3. Research is a process of conceptualizing, designing, conducting, and writing up what is learned; it is recursive, iterative, messy, tedious, challenging, full of ambiguity, and exciting.

We begin this chapter by introducing three students whose learning and studies will lead you through the complex, often confusing, but exciting world of qualitative research. Next, we address the question of what qualitative research is, describing its goals and common features.

Then we examine what qualitative researchers actually do in the process. We end the chapter with an overview of the rest of the book.

We offer Marla, Ruth, and Anthony as three students in an introductory qualitative research course who learn as they study and participate in the qualitative research process. They illustrate different perspectives and starting points, but each experiences the tensions and satisfactions of framing questions, listening, watching, reading, and writing. Marla is an experienced health care professional who, early in her career, helped build a clinic in a Central American village. She sees herself as an activist and hopes to improve the U.S. health care system for poor women, so she has enrolled at the university to receive a master's degree in public health. Although she is not certain about the specific aspect of health care that she wants to attack, she is sure that the recipients of the care should take part in posing the questions. Her greatest concern is how the people in her study are affected by it, so she envisions involving the study participants in seeking the answers and determining how the answers are used. Her experiences as a Latina in the United States have taught her that collaboration is more effective than competition for changing any existing system, so she is attracted to a form of research she has heard about called **action research.** The possibility that research can be coupled with action appeals to her proactive nature. Self-assured and optimistic, she believes the world can be changed for the better.

Anthony is returning to the university for an advanced degree in public policy. Upon graduation from college, he volunteered as a community development worker on issues of water quality and housing. When funding for this project was cut, he applied for a legislative internship in Washington, D.C., to serve as staff on a joint committee on arts and education. His interest in **evaluation and policy studies** springs from these experiences: He learned firsthand, when his project's funding was cut, the effects of policy decisions on community members and their advocates. He hopes that his work can inform the policy-making process through the provision of more effective, thoughtful, and detailed information.

The youngest of the three, Ruth is an undergraduate majoring in psychology. She is an avid athlete. At the university, she has been goalie for the lacrosse team and often works out in the gym early in the morning. For the past several years, she has worked at a summer camp for children with disabilities. She enjoys working with children, especially through athletics, and has designed a 3-day wilderness course for deaf children. She volunteers one afternoon a week at a local elementary school. Ruth's major requires that she take an introductory research course. She has chosen qualitative research because she believes it will be a way to explore the lives of the children with whom she works. Ruth's interests in their lives led her to a **descriptive cultural study**.

All three feel some anxiety and doubt, but each will grow in clarity, insight, and accomplishment. In their own unique ways, they will make sense of the course and the professor, of the literature, and of their chosen topic. Ultimately, they master the skills and habits of mind and heart of competent and ethical qualitative researchers. They produce knowledge that is useful in addressing recurring social issues.

WHAT IS QUALITATIVE RESEARCH?

Qualitative research begins with questions; its ultimate purpose is use.[1] To inform the questions, the researcher collects data—the basic units or building blocks of information. Data are images, sounds, words, and numbers. When data are grouped into patterns, they become information. When information is put to use or applied, it becomes knowledge. The process is analogous to building a house. Like data, cinder blocks are not useful by themselves, but they can come together to make a wall. Like information, the wall can be used to build a house. Both the researcher and the builder start with questions and end with a product to be used. Their questions are seldom simple, however, and use takes complex forms. Some uses are intended; some are not. We take on the issues of multiple use later in this chapter.

Qualitative researchers seek answers to their questions in the real world. They gather what they see, hear, and read from people and places and from events and activities. They do their research in natural settings rather than in laboratories or through written surveys. Their purpose is to learn about some aspect of the social world and to generate new understandings that can be used by that social world. As qualitative researchers, they become part of the process, continually making choices, testing assumptions, and reshaping their questions. As the inquiry process grows from curiosity or wonder to understanding and knowledge building, the researcher is often transformed. In many cases, the participants are also changed.[2]

Qualitative research has two unique features: (a) the researcher is the means through which the study is conducted, and (b) the purpose is learning about some facet of the social world. Both these characteristics are integral to a view of learning that sees the learner as a constructor of knowledge rather than a receiver of it. From this perspective, the learner accumulates data, not reality itself but rather representations of reality. The learner transforms these data, through analysis and interpretation, into information. When put to practical use, through judgment and wisdom, to address recurring social issues, information becomes knowledge.

The transformation of information into knowledge is an active learning process: Qualitative researchers are learners and qualitative inquiry provides the detailed and rich data for this learning process. The learner—the researcher—makes choices that shape and are shaped by the emerging processes of inquiry. This notion of the interrelatedness of purpose and process underlies the central themes of this book.

Traditionally, basic research has been distinguished from applied: Basic research generates theory and produces knowledge for its own end, whereas applied research informs action and enhances decision making. Basic research is judged by the explanations it provides, whereas applied research is judged by its effectiveness in helping policymakers, practitioners, and the participants themselves make decisions and act to improve the human condition. The term *basic research* has been borrowed from the natural sciences; our position is that applied and social scientists rarely engage in basic research. Because social scientists depict some aspect of the human condition, they do social research that is quintessentially applied.

Qualitative inquiry as a form of research is rooted in empiricism; that is, the doctrine that knowledge is obtainable only by direct experience with the physical senses. Perhaps one of the first qualitative researchers was Aristotle, who made sense of the world by watching and listening. He proposed that ideas are concepts derived from experience with actual objects, beings, and events. Aristotle taught that nothing exists in our minds that we have not first perceived with or experienced through our senses. We then use our reason to organize and imbue those experiences with meaning—to make sense of the sensory experiences. For example, we group or categorize what we have seen or heard into categories based on characteristics of sights and sounds (Gaarder, 1994).

Qualitative research is a broad approach to the study of social phenomena; the approach is naturalistic, interpretive, and draws on multiple methods of inquiry (Denzin, 1994). That is, qualitative research is conducted in natural settings rather than controlled ones; it assumes that humans use what they see and hear and feel to make meaning of social phenomena, and it relies on a variety of data gathering techniques. Historically, qualitative research has been associated with various social science disciplines: cultural or social anthropology, qualitative sociology, history, and organizational behavior, and so on. It has clear roots in certain philosophical traditions, notably phenomenology (questioning the structure and essence of lived experience) and hermeneutics (questioning the conditions that shape interpretations of human acts or products).

These well-established approaches to qualitative research draw on theoretical bodies of knowledge that are traditionally associated with the formal, academic world. Recently, researchers have begun to use approaches to analyzing text[3] that derive from literary criticism and cultural studies; others conduct studies that espouse explicitly ideological positions such as feminist or critical theory studies. These "newer" approaches challenge the assumption that knowledge is generated exclusively through the traditional academic disciplines. The project of these researchers is to validate alternative sources of knowledge; they often write about giving voice to those previously excluded from formal, academic discourse, such as women and people of color.

In Chapters 2 and 3, we more fully describe the various traditions that have shaped qualitative inquiry, and we discuss the assumptions driving these various approaches. For now, we depict what the different members of the qualitative research community have in common. What are the characteristics of qualitative research? What perspectives do qualitative researchers share? What stances do qualitative researchers typically take? How do they go about their work?

CHARACTERISTICS

There are eight characteristics common to qualitative research. First, qualitative researchers[4] are oriented toward the **natural world**—they gather data about sensory experience: what people (including themselves) see, feel, hear, taste, and smell. As noted previously, qualitative research shares this focus on the empirical world with quantitative forms of inquiry. Qualitative research, however, stands in stark contrast to the experimental laboratory conditions of traditional psychology, the probabilistic sampling of a survey researcher, or the quasi-experimental design that uses control groups to compare "intervention effects." Qualitative research developed in part as a critique of the artificial settings of the laboratory, searching for ways to systematically understand people's lived experiences. Doing research in the field—rather than in the laboratory or through a mailed questionnaire—became an important, complementary, and legitimate approach to social science. Qualitative researchers go to the people; they do not extricate the people from their everyday worlds (Table 1.1).

Second, qualitative researchers work in the field, face-to-face with real people. They try to understand how people make sense of their worlds through **multiple methods that are interactive and humanistic:** talking, looking, listening, and reading. These are known more formally as the primary techniques of interviewing, observing, and gathering documents. They talk with the people, they watch and listen as folks go about their everyday tasks, they read documents, and they look at physical space, clothing, tools, decorations.

Third, qualitative researchers value the messiness of the lived world; they make a sustained **focus on context** integral to their work and assume that a detailed understanding of human experience is gained by exploring these complexities. Again, this stance is distinct from experimental conditions in which the messiness of everyday life is controlled through processes of randomization and standardization. This respect for context draws qualitative researchers to look at social worlds *holistically*, as interactive, complex systems rather than as discrete variables that can be measured and manipulated statistically. They describe and interpret rather than measure and predict.

Historically, qualitative researchers have tried to be as objective as possible in studying the lives of people, just like their quantitative counterparts. As the field evolves, however, it is becoming clear that the researcher herself is critically important in conducting the study. Because the researcher enters the world of the participants, she may shape that world in significant ways. A fourth characteristic of qualitative research,

TABLE 1.1 Characteristics of Qualitative Research

Qualitative research
  Takes place in the natural world
  Uses multiple methods that are interactive and humanistic
  Is emergent rather than tightly prefigured
  Is fundamentally interpretive

The qualitative researcher
  Views social phenomenon holistically
  Systematically reflects on who he or she is in the inquiry
  Is sensitive to his or her personal biography and how it shapes the study
  Uses complex reasoning that is multifaceted and iterative

---

then, is that the researcher **systematically reflects** on how she affects the ongoing flow of everyday life.

The researcher does more than affect ongoing social life: his *weltanschauung*—worldview—shapes the entire project. From early curiosity all the way to writing the final report, the researcher's personal biography is the lens through which he sees the world. Gender, race and ethnicity, age, sexual orientation, politics, and beliefs all affect the qualitative project. Reflecting on who you are and how that affects the research has thus become important. The fifth feature of qualitative research, then, is an **exquisite sensitivity to personal biography**. Unlike the allegedly objective social scientist, the qualitative researcher values his unique perspective as a source of understanding rather than something to be cleansed from the study. Marla, for example, knows she will draw on her experiences working with poor people. Anthony will recollect working in projects that received negative evaluations. Ruth will need to be alert to any latent biases she may harbor in favor of children who are talented athletes. This sensitivity is a simultaneous awareness of self and other and of the interplay between the two, captured by the term *reflexivity* (discussed further in Chapter 2).

Qualitative researchers try not to impose a rigid a priori framework on the social world; they want to learn what constitute important questions about the participants' lives from them. No formal hypotheses are cast prior to the study but, as noted previously, qualitative researchers do bring predispositions and guiding questions. This conceptual framework, however, can be—and most often is—changed, modified, and refined once in the field as other, perhaps more important, questions are discovered. In addition, the specific data gathering actions can be altered, depending on what makes sense for the setting, the participants, and the researcher's growing knowledge about the project. This sixth element is the **emergent nature** of qualitative research.

These emergent aspects have been historically defined as resting on principles of inductive logic. Rather than reasoning from theory to a test of its applicability, qualitative researchers have traditionally been described as reasoning from the particular to more general statements. Our stance is that this characterization of qualitative researchers as inductive rather than deductive oversimplifies and trivializes the complexity of any research, especially qualitative research.[5] Qualitative researchers often begin a study with a well thought-out conceptual framework that focuses and shapes their actions, but this framework, as noted previously, is flexible. We argue that all inquiry proceeds through a complex nonlinear process of induction, deduction, inspiration, and just plain old hard thinking. This seventh feature of qualitative research, then, is a reliance on **sophisticated reasoning that is multifaceted and iterative**, moving back and forth between the parts and the whole (Figure 1.1).

Finally, qualitative research is **fundamentally interpretive**. In contrast with quantitative approaches, which attempt to control and predict, qualitative research focuses on description, analysis, and interpretation. The qualitative researcher assumes that understanding (analyzing and interpreting) and representing (interpreting and writing about) what has been learned are filtered through her own personal biography that is situated in a specific sociopolitical, historical moment. Through this lens, the researcher tries to make sense of what she has learned; the researcher interprets the world that she has entered. Field notes and snippets of interview transcriptions do not speak for themselves; they must be interpreted in ways that are thoughtful, ethical, and politically astute. The resulting "tale of the field" (Van Maanen, 1988) is, ultimately, the researcher's story about the stories people have told her (Geertz, 1983).

To recap, qualitative research is a complex field of inquiry that draws on many diverse assumptions but embraces a few common characteristics and perspectives. A qualitative research project takes place in the field, relies on multiple methods for gathering data, and calls on the researcher to be pragmatic, flexible, politically aware, and self-reflective. It is fundamentally interpretive and emergent, characterized by a stance

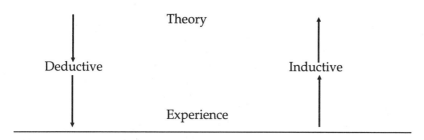

Figure 1.1. Deductive and Inductive Reasoning

of openness, curiosity, and respect on the researcher's part. On the practical side, qualitative research is labor-intensive, time-consuming, frustrating, and challenging. There are no formulaic rules to follow, only guiding principles gleaned from direct experience, including reading the literature and studying with others and the actual doing. It is also exhilarating, deeply moving, and can change the researcher's world-view.

WAYS OF USING RESEARCH

Anthony, Ruth, and Marla embark on qualitative studies because they want to learn something about their social world. Marla begins with a hunch she wants to explore; she suspects that the health care system does not adequately address women's issues. More specifically, she is puzzled about something she has seen: She noticed that women visiting a clinic where she once worked only came for initial visits and seldom returned for follow-up. Ruth, in contrast, is simply curious about children with various types of disabilities. She asks: What are their lives like? Anthony wants to know how decision makers use information. He is particularly interested in how they use evaluations to make funding decisions. Each one begins with a question, a curiosity, and an intriguing puzzle. Use is built into the questions both Marla and Anthony ask. Ruth soon recognizes the potential for her descriptions of children to be extraordinarily useful for many audiences.

The ultimate goal of qualitative research is to transform data into information that can be used. Usefulness, however, is not a simple

TABLE 1.2 Uses of Research

Instrumental use	Knowledge is applied to specific problems
	Provides solutions or recommendations
Enlightenment use	Contributes to general knowledge
	Enhances understanding
	Offers heuristic insight
Symbolic use	Provides new ways of expressing phenomena
	Crystallizes beliefs or values
Emancipatory use	Offers ways to take action to transform structures and
	practices for the better

unitary concept. We suggest four perspectives for thinking about use: the instrumental, the enlightenment, the symbolic, and the emancipatory (Table 1.2). These perspectives serve as lenses to understand how the results of a particular study may be used. Different audiences might use the same written report in different ways—for example, one instrumentally and the other symbolically. A qualitative researcher cannot dictate or control the uses that various audiences may make of her study. The researcher, however, does need to be aware that the study will be used, one way or another, and sometimes those uses are different from the ones she intends.

Instrumental Use

People commonly think of use as *instrumental*—that is, intended use by intended users (Patton, 1990). Specifically, concrete information is applied to a particular problem. A problem exists or a goal is sought; research is conducted to determine a best solution or approach to reach the goal. For example, a private school hires a research firm to discover why enrollment has dropped or a service agency surveys its community to identify unmet needs. The findings of research, then, are developed into knowledge—plans to implement in practice. Knowledge generation and knowledge utilization are directly linked.

This perspective on use is linear and assumes a rational decision-making process; decision makers have clear goals, seek direct attainment of these goals, and have access to relevant research knowledge. As Patton (1990) notes, instrumental use usually requires planning for use before the data are even collected. The researcher works with the intended users to develop relevant questions from which the data collection techniques and analysis strategies flow. Evaluation and policy studies, practitioner inquiry, and action research are all candidates for instrumental use if the researcher and user work together to produce technical knowledge. For these reasons, Marla's and Anthony's studies are likely to be used instrumentally.

Enlightenment Use

In our experience, the links between knowledge generation and utilization are seldom clear and direct. Research findings often serve to *enlighten* the user (Weiss, 1979). Knowledge accumulates, contributing to a gradual reorientation of the user's thought and action. Specific information cannot be identified as the basis for a particular decision or action. Moreover, one piece of information may contribute to several decisions. We imagine this model of use as a pool of accumulated knowledge into which the user may dip when making a decision.

From the enlightenment perspective, users base their decisions on knowledge, but the specific information is not important. Weiss (1980) describes knowledge as providing a background of working understandings and ideas that "creep" into decision deliberations. Policy actions are not decided in a clear-cut, brisk style with obvious connections among problems, people, and alternative choices. Instead, policy "accretes" (Weiss, 1980). Research findings become part of the general culture, incorporated into accepted concepts, beliefs, and values that naturally influence any decision making in that arena.

Detailed findings become generalizations that eventually are accepted as truths and come to shape the ways people think. Rein (1970) cites the example of a series of controversial and threatening reports about conditions in a mental hospital. The reports were not used by the hospital staff, perhaps because the staff themselves were criticized. The information was, however, picked up by health care advocates. The result was a gradual change in the operation of mental institutions in general. Rein's point is that although the information was not used in an instrumental sense, it did shape the policy-decision arena. The research findings were initially not compatible with the decision makers' values or goals. Findings may challenge existing beliefs and work their way into public consciousness. The result is an overturning of established values and patterns of thought (Weiss, 1979). Similarly, Ruth's descriptive study of children with disabilities could serve to enlighten education officials.

Research findings as accumulated knowledge also serve to improve practice through enhancing understanding of that practice. Accumulated knowledge can build practitioners' understandings of the principles behind their procedures. Whole language instruction is an example of a practice that has been enlightened by research knowledge. Many teachers held the philosophy and practiced the approach long before they heard the label. As they read the emerging literature on whole language, they came to understand the principles behind what they were doing. This knowledge, in turn, enhanced their teaching. In parallel fashion, if Anthony is able to identify and label a particularly effective element in the program he evaluates, that knowledge is likely to improve it.

Symbolic Use

Research also offers a variety of *symbolic uses* of knowledge (Rallis, 1980; see also Bolman & Deal, 1991). Findings become knowledge by encouraging users to reconfigure old patterns and to see familiar pictures in new lights. Explanation and understanding are important human needs. Maslowe (1970) notes that human beings tend to look for patterns and create narratives that make sense of the world and its phenomena. Research can address this need by offering symbolic explanations that groups of people can share. Qualitative research can sort and explain, making complex and ambiguous experiences or beliefs comprehensible and communicable to others.

Ordered beliefs may represent a synthesis of cultural feelings and thus help to legitimize events or actions within that culture. The conduct and completion of Ruth's study can, in and of itself, serve to foster public acceptance of children with disabilities. Research results may also serve to surface deeply disturbing actions that a culture publicly masks. Tracey Kidder's *Old Friends* (1993) provides an example: His rich descriptions of residents of a nursing home are evocative of aging in America.

Furthermore, because qualitative research directly involves the participants, the process generates stories. Folks talk—often underground—about the study and the routines involved in its conduct (see, for example, Van Maanen's *Tales of the Field*, 1988). This "talk" becomes part of cultural knowledge that offers new and often satisfying interpretations of familiar events. These interpretations become myths—stories that offer explanations and reveal shared understandings.

Instances of symbolic use have appeared in several studies we have conducted.[6] In an evaluation of a federally funded compensatory education program, school personnel used ambiguous findings to applaud mediocre programs. They appeared to reason that, because an evaluation was completed every year, the program must be legitimate, and it must be good, whatever the actual results. After completing studies of cardiopulmonary resuscitation training, we heard stories about our research routines. Participants told these stories, time and again, as explanations for the way things were done in the training and as support for the training's continuance. It is not uncommon to see an organization's leader proudly point to a fat evaluation report sitting on a shelf. The very existence of such a report is valued. These and other experiences illustrate how important the symbolic uses of research knowledge can be to organizations and individuals.

As researchers, however, we feel obligated to ensure that the symbolic use does not preclude other uses. Once, we evaluated a school restructuring initiative. The goals and objectives of the program were admirable, but little or nothing was happening to implement them. Program staff were talking but not acting. Our formative evaluation reports revealed the problem, but the program manager simply thanked us, checked off that required evaluations had been completed, and filed them away. Because we felt that the program had potential to make a difference for children and because the program consumed a substantial number of federal dollars, we wanted more than superficial symbolic use in this case. We took steps to end the study. Fortunately, a new manager was coincidentally appointed, and she established a strong and productive relationship with us.

Emancipatory Use

Another use of research is *emancipatory*. The researchers (usually including the participants) hope that the process of inquiry, action, and reflection and the knowledge they generate will transform some aspect of society to "free" or empower the participants. The research—process and results—becomes a source of empowerment both to the individual's immediate daily life and to change structures that dominate and oppress. The participants are not generating knowledge simply to inform or enlighten an academic or social science community. They are collaboratively producing knowledge to improve their work and their lives. Participants do the research about their own settings; the person in the official researcher role serves to facilitate. Emancipatory use grows out of Paolo Freire's (1970) *web of praxis*—the belief that the reflection and action implicit in knowledge can free practice. Freire viewed research as a form of social action. His research in the 1960s and 1970s on Chilean literacy involved members of oppressed communities in identifying issues of vital importance to their communities. These collaborative discoveries became a foundation for literacy instruction and for community empowerment. The two purposes of the research were to help participants acquire literacy and to help them improve their lives.

Today, participatory action research and feminist studies offer examples of hoped-for emancipatory uses. The women who come to collaborate with Marla in her study become savvy in using clinic services regularly. At the same time, they realize that they avoided the clinic because of sustained and pervasive patterns of subtle discrimination against them because of language, gender, and poverty. Their discoveries empower them to try to change these patterns for other women. In this light, the research of Marla and her collaborators is emancipatory.

In summary, researchers' questions lead them to collect data. They arrange these data into meaningful patterns. The information becomes knowledge through its instrumental, enlightenment, symbolic, or emancipatory application and use or all of these. The qualitative researcher, then, is in the business of generating knowledge that can serve the society studied, whether through immediate impact on a decision, through shaping people's understandings of a complex topic, through interpreting and reinterpreting the meaning of events, or through actions that empower the participants.

THREE QUALITATIVE RESEARCH STRATEGIES

The questions that a researcher pursues are shaped, in part, by the overall qualitative strategy adopted. Although there are many, we focus on three strategies: **descriptive cultural studies, evaluation or policy studies,**

TABLE 1.3 Qualitative Research Strategies

Evaluation or policy study	Describes, analyzes, and informs decision making about social programs
Descriptive cultural study	Describes social phenomena and contributes to understanding about them
Action research	Changes existing programs or practice and describes and analyzes what happens

and action research (Table 1.3).[7] These strategies share a common goal of generating useful knowledge, but their primary purposes vary. Each strategy suggests instrumental, enlightenment, symbolic, or emancipatory use. Descriptive cultural studies are, more often than not, used to enlighten. Evaluation or policy studies typically serve instrumental uses. Action research tends to be emancipatory. All three may serve symbolic uses. The strategy chosen, however, does not determine use.

Descriptive Cultural Studies

Ruth wants to understand better the lives of children with disabilities. For her, understanding comes through describing their lives so she chooses to perform a descriptive cultural study. She soon discovers, however, that description is seldom neutral. She develops rich interpretive narratives depicting the children's activities, feelings, and the people with whom they interact. She explores their struggles, triumphs, courage, and ordinariness. Ideally, the result is a compelling story about the world the researcher has explored.

Evaluation or Policy Studies

Seeking to influence or inform decision making or planning, Anthony chooses evaluation or policy studies. He is hired as a consultant to evaluate the several different activities of a community arts program. The funding agency wants to know if the program is accomplishing its goals of creating experiences of the arts for a wider audience. Evaluation research provides formative or summative[8] information that describes and assesses the effectiveness of a program. Policy studies provide information that helps governmental, institutional, or organizational authorities develop programs or make policy decisions. As in Anthony's case, evaluators or policy researchers are usually contracted by an organization or agency to conduct the study and prepare a report.

Action Research

Marla's questions, which emphasize stakeholder participation and change in practice, lead her to action research. As will be shown, she and the women's group in her project use their results to try to bring changes in access to health care for women living in poor urban settings. Action research is "the study of a social situation with a view to improving the quality of action within" (Elliot & Keynes, 1991, p. 69). Practitioners may study their own practice to understand it better to improve it, or groups may undertake a project to understand better and improve their environment. In the former, individuals explore their own practice to improve what they do. In the latter, collective, collaborative, and self-reflective inquiry is undertaken by the participants. Their purpose is to promote social change by transforming structures through the influence of the information collected. We elaborate these three strategies throughout the book as Ruth, Anthony, and Marla design and conduct their studies.

HABITS OF MIND AND HEART

Marla, Ruth, and Anthony are setting out to generate knowledge by learning in the field. They will design studies; collect, analyze, and interpret their data; and present their findings. The process is an active one, and it is not simple. They will face one decision after another for which few prescribed rules exist. Their tasks are not tightly specified, and they have few explicit steps to follow because knowledge creation is not straightforward and linear. They learn by doing.

By definition, knowledge is iterative; it builds on itself. Therefore, the research process is *heuristic—a discovering experience.* Heuristic inquiry, from the Greek for "discover," implies personal insight and tacit knowing (Polanyi, 1962). Tacit knowing is deep inner understanding; it is unarticulated knowledge that derives from experience. Out of this knowing come the hunches that drive the questions we do articulate. Qualitative research recognizes the heuristic aspect of knowledge creation and works with deeply subjectivist assumptions, as will be discussed in Chapter 3.

As they learn in the field, Marla, Ruth, and Anthony must be exquisitely conscious of the contexts surrounding their individual studies. They will come to know that each interprets his or her data from a particular perspective, standpoint, and situation. They will learn that each researcher can only report his own discoveries or represent what he believes to be the perspectives of the people he studied. They will not attempt to be "objective" by seeking the one "true" answer for their studies. Their processes, then, are hermeneutic, leading each to choose from among possible answers.

Ultimately, they will stop asking for a rulebook and learn to trust the process. They will seek meaning in the rich descriptions they create from what they see, hear, and read. They will learn to suspend disbelief and to cope with ambiguity. Their initial questions shape early data collection; this reshapes the questions, which, in turn, call for further data. Their decisions cascade, and data form patterns of information that can become knowledge. They learn by doing.

Marla, Anthony, and Ruth start with curiosity; the first step in qualitative research is to want to discover something. They will need to be perceptive and to develop competence in the basic skills required: interviewing, observing, analyzing, interpreting, and preparing an engaging presentation of what they have learned. They face, however, a conundrum: They need to know everything about qualitative research to do it, but they can best learn how to do it by doing it! What will help them through this conundrum are certain sensibilities rather than specific skills. The skills are what they learn by doing; the sensibilities enable this doing. These sensibilities include the following:

- Comfort with ambiguity
- Capacity to make reasoned decisions and to articulate the logic behind those decisions
- Deep interpersonal or emotional sensitivity
- Ethical sensitivity of potential consequences to individuals and groups
- Political sensitivity
- Perseverance and self-discipline
- Awareness of how many data are enough

As our characters work in the field, these sensibilities become *habits of mind and heart*—unconscious actions that make them proficient and ethical qualitative researchers.

Anthony, Marla, and Ruth are students in an introductory qualitative research class. They will conduct small-scale studies as a course requirement. Their individual curiosities lead them to questions that will shape their study designs. These three students will move through the research process of designing a study; collecting, analyzing, and interpreting data; and reporting their findings. The depth of these learning experiences will be guided and shaped by their habits of mind and heart.

In this chapter, we have described qualitative research as an emergent, interpretive, holistic, reflexive, and iterative process that uses interactive and humanistic methods. It is conducted in the real world. Qualitative researchers are learners who are systematic and rigorous while sensitive to ways their own life histories are shaping their projects. As learners, they generate knowledge that various audiences use instrumentally, to enlighten, symbolically, to empower, or all of these. Qualitative researchers use strategies such as descriptive cultural studies, evaluation and policy studies, and action research. Fundamentally, they practice certain habits of mind and heart that enable them to operate in this ambiguous and uncertain world competently and ethically.

OVERVIEW OF THE BOOK

The project of this book is to introduce you to qualitative research. In this chapter, you have read about the characteristics of the process, use of the products, strategies for conducting, and the qualitative researcher's habits of mind.

In Chapter 2, our focus falls on the person doing the research. As a learner, you, the researcher, make assumptions about what you know and what you accept as the truth. Ethics, politics, and the trustworthiness of findings are not divorced from the assumptions that undergird your study. This chapter presents you as a constructor of knowledge and explores the worldviews within which researchers operate.

Chapter 3 examines how a question turns into a design for a study. We show how you develop a conceptual framework from an idea and question and then how you design a study. We describe how choices for methodologies and designs draw from the various qualitative research traditions.

Chapters 4, 5, and 6 deal with data collection, analysis, and interpretation. Texts on qualitative research usually separate data collection into chapters on the two primary techniques: observation and interviewing. Because we find that separation artificial, and because researchers also use other techniques, we create different distinctions. Chapter 4 discusses access and introduction to the research site or participants. Chapter 5 demonstrates how data are collected through looking, asking, listening, and reading. Chapter 6 discusses several questions that often arise during fieldwork. Chapter 7 considers how you make sense of what you have collected; how do you analyze and interpret your data? Finally, if the research is to be used by anyone other than yourself, the information must be presented so that appropriate audiences can access and understand it. Chapter 8 discusses how you connect with audiences for the research through various ways of reporting the information.

To present the process of data analysis in some detail, we offer appendixes that develop the analysis undertaken in each character's study. These appendixes present samples of data and describe the analytic process each character goes through. They end with preliminary analytic memos that Marla, Ruth, and Anthony write. Our purpose here is to make concrete the specific actions and writing that help move the analytic process along.

NOTES

1. Use takes many forms. We are concerned that expending resources in the historic knowledge production function that results in reports sitting on shelves and articles languishing unread in academic journals should be balanced by research conducted with explicit goals of use. Research should be conducted with the goal of improving the human condition, whatever form that takes.

2. Historically, those researched have been referred to as subjects, respondents, and informants. We choose the more inclusive term *participants*, reflecting our subjectivist assumptions (discussed in Chapter 3).

3. Text refers to more than written words. Construed quite broadly, it embraces all utterances or artifacts of a culture. Writ somewhat smaller, it means the authored words—written and oral—available for analysis.

4. We struggled with the "voice" to use throughout the text. Using "qualitative researchers" places some distance between us, the authors, and them, the researchers, although we certainly place ourselves with them (otherwise, we would not have written this book). Using "we" to refer to qualitative researchers, however, creates distance between you, the reader, and us, the authors. We have chosen to use the term qualitative

researchers to avoid distance between you and us. When we use the term *we*, we are referring to ourselves. To avoid sexist language, we alternate between "he" and "she" when we refer to "the researcher."

5. The distinction between deduction and induction may well be an example of the Western proclivity for dichotomizing the world. One of our colleagues uses the term *specious bifurcations* to refer to the false dichotomies that imprison understanding of the world.

6. We choose not to give citations to our own work in these examples because the stories are "notes from the underground" and revealing the sources would be unethical.

7. We use this as an inclusive term rather than a specialized one, stipulating that participatory research, which is explicitly ideological, be included along with other forms of action research.

8. Formative information is used to improve the program; summative information contributes to a final decision about the value and effectiveness of the program in producing the intended changes.

FURTHER READING

Use

Eisner, E. W., & Peshkin, A. (Eds.). (1990). *Qualitative inquiry in education: The continuing debate.* New York: Teachers College Press. (See Part IV, "Uses of qualitative inquiry," pp. 301-364)

Green, J. C. (1990). Knowledge accumulation? Three views of the nature and role of knowledge in social science. In E. G. Guba (Ed.), *The paradigm dialogue.* Newbury Park, CA: Sage.

Lindblom, C. E., & Cohen, D. K. (1979). *Usable knowledge.* New Haven, CT: Yale University Press.

Patton, M. Q. (1996). *Utilization-focused evaluation* (3rd ed.). Thousand Oaks, CA: Sage.

Descriptive Cultural Studies

Erickson, F. (1986). Qualitative methods in research on teaching. In M. C. Whittrock (Ed.), *Handbook of research on teaching* (3rd ed., pp. 119-161). New York: Macmillan.

Van Maanen, J. (1988). *Tales of the field: On writing ethnography.* Chicago: University of Chicago Press.

Evaluation and Policy Studies

Chelimsky, E., & Shaddish, W. R. (Eds.). (1997). *Evaluation for the 21st century: A handbook.* Thousand Oaks, CA: Sage.

Weiss, C. H. (1998). *Evaluation: Methods for studying programs and policies.* Upper Saddle River, NJ: Prentice Hall.

Action Research

Kincheloe, J. L. (1991). *Teachers as researchers: Qualitative inquiry as a path to empowerment.* New York: Falmer.

Stringer, E. T. (1996). *Action research: A handbook for practitioners.* Thousand Oaks, CA: Sage.

Chapter Two

The Researcher
as Learner

"Oh, sure! I'm supposed to come up with a research question by next class! I know I want to evaluate something, but I don't even know what it could be," Anthony complained to his companions.

"For me, it's pretty clear," Ruth said. "What I want to know more about is, what's it like to be a kid with disabilities? That's my question!"

"Is that all? I guess if I were asking that question, I'd want to know about the programs . . . in schools, for example," responded Anthony. "I'd ask things like . . . who are the kids who participate? What do they think about the program? How do they react? When I interned in Washington, people had to ask questions like that."

"So . . . you haven't said what your question is, Marla," noted Ruth.

"That's because I'm not exactly sure yet. I'm interested in women's health issues, especially poor women's health. But should I start with what issues they—the women—have? I think there is already a lot written on that, so maybe I should take one issue and ask something about that. Like about women's access to health care services. Or to hospitals. Or their follow-up to service. What do I want to know, specifically? I'm just not sure," Marla replied.

"Actually, Marla, I think I'm in the same boat," said Ruth. "I know I want to find out about those kids but that's too broad. How do I narrow it?"

"We have to start somewhere," Marla laughed. "For me, the women themselves will help me narrow down my question."

"Kent expects us to do an actual study, beginning to end, soup to nuts. Maybe I should just describe the kids," said Ruth.

"Pero, how will you describe them? I think there are a lot of different ways to describe something. Will you tell it like a story or a report? Will you tell it like you see it or from the kids' point of view?" Marla questioned.

"Yeah. . . . This could be really interesting. What do you suppose is involved in doing an actual study?" asked Ruth. "I've got a topic, how do I pick the kids? How do I get them to talk to me? And. . . is describing enough?"

"How will you know that you aren't just hearing what you expect to hear?" wondered Anthony. "Talking to people just doesn't seem enough."

"And talking to people can get pretty personal . . . . I want to respect my subjects, whoever they are," Marla said. "And their questions may differ from mine . . . theirs might be the real questions. I even feel weird about calling them 'subjects'. . . subjects of what? Subject to what?"

"Whoa! I don't know about you but I don't even have a setting yet," Anthony said. "I need to find a real evaluation I can do. I heard the grad assistant say some agency was looking for graduate students to evaluate their community arts program. I'll check that out. . . . But even so, if we just talk with folks, how will we know they are telling the truth? As an evaluator, I'll need to be careful that I get a full picture of what's happening. I don't know yet how I can be sure that my findings are true."

"Yeah. Kent talked a lot today about knowing the truth. Epistemology? Did you two understand that?" Ruth asked.

"Well, the whole discussion pushed me to think about how I know what I say I know . . . and what I will take for evidence. That's my take on it," Marla answered.

"I didn't really get all that stuff about assumptions. Is that what you mean by 'beliefs'?" Ruth asked.

"I think so," explained Anthony. "What's our perspective on our projects. What do we think about the topic right now. Like you said, Marla, how will Ruth describe the kids? Whose point of view will she take? And what does she think about the kids right now? We know you've worked with deaf kids, Ruth, but what about a kid with muscular dystrophy?"

"I guess for me one thing to think about is why I want to make a difference for the women," interjected Marla. "Once I know something that I think needs changing, I want to change it. But I have to make sure that it's not just me taking over—you know how I love to take charge!"

"I'm not the activist you are, Marla," observed Anthony. *"But I still don't think I'll be able to just drop it when I'm finished. I realize that I'm going to be spending a lot of time doing this work. At the very least, I'll want to share what I learn with them."*

"And you think that'll be easy? What if your findings aren't all rosy? Do you really think everyone wants to hear the truth about what they do? You're going to have to think about how you can give them feedback," said Ruth.

"I guess I'm still hung up on what the 'truth' is. I'm getting the story from them, aren't I? Why wouldn't they want to hear it when I tell it back to them?" asked Anthony.

"I know. I can see myself getting pretty involved with those kids, but feedback? I don't know how I'll do that," pondered Ruth. *"I guess each of us is going to have to figure out for ourselves how we'll deal with our participants."*

"Well . . . isn't that ethics?" commented Marla. *"To me, being ethical is creating ways people can participate. Why do the study if you don't intend to see the results used in some way?"*

"Even more basic," added Ruth, *"How do I relate to my participants while I'm studying them?"*

"Yeah. I'm still grappling with what's my role in the study," said Anthony. *"I'll be the evaluator, but how do I make sense of what I'll be seeing and hearing?"*

Ruth, Marla, and Anthony have begun to grapple with the many facets of learning about qualitative research. They are considering the questions they want to ask; they are thinking about designs (setting, participants, and ways of gathering data); and they are flirting with their perspectives—the ways they think about research in general and their projects specifically. These are all significant topics to ponder and make decisions about. The challenges they face, at this early stage, are to incorporate new information from class, juxtapose this with assumptions they hold about truth and the social world, and think through their perspectives on these research projects.

All this entails reflection on their own *personal epistemologies*—the ways they understand knowledge and the construction of knowledge. This is, after all, what research is about: the creation of new knowledge or understandings, as discussed in Chapter 1. We construe this as a journey during which our characters learn; they create knowledge. They undertake these projects because they want to learn more about their topics. As they do their projects, they will construct knowledge. They will do so in trustworthy ways—ones that are consistent with formal standards for research and that are sensitive to ethics and politics of the setting. This chapter discusses these important ideas: Researchers are learners; they have assumptions; and these assumptions shape how they go about doing their projects and have implications for trustworthiness.

THE REFLEXIVITY OF QUALITATIVE RESEARCH

Qualitative methodologists often refer to the researcher as the "instrument" of the study. We find this an unfortunate metaphor because it evokes an image of an antiseptic enterprise—one in which the researcher is merely a tool. Instead, we find it useful to frame Marla, Ruth, and Anthony as the learners: They will construct an understanding of their topics through the questions they ask, the contexts they study, and their personal biographies.

Qualitative research is quintessentially interactive, as discussed in Chapter 1. What does this mean? The researcher is involved, face-to-face, with participants in the study. In experiments or surveys, for example, participants interact with standardized sets of procedures or written questionnaires; they have little or no direct contact with the researchers. Qualitative studies, as should be clear, take the researcher into the field, into complex and varied interactions with the participants. This implies that the knowledge constructed during a qualitative study is essentially interpretive: The researcher makes meaning (interprets) what he learns as he goes along. Data are filtered through the researcher's own unique ways of seeing the world—his lens or worldview. Given this interpretive nature of qualitative research, the researcher's personal biography shapes the project in important ways. It is crucial, therefore, that researchers develop an acute sensitivity to who they are in their work.

These reflexive capacities and their abilities to question and explore will shape our characters' journeys. Also important will be their familiarity with and use of the methodological literature—the learnings of those who have undertaken qualitative research before them and written about it. As they engage with course materials, critique them, and build their own understandings of that literature, they grow to appreciate the traditions and standards for the practice of qualitative research. As they conduct their projects, they develop competence in the qualitative skills of seeing, listening, reading, and making sense of their perceptions.

Because you construct the study and because you ask the questions, becoming aware of your perspective (your assumptions) with its built-in interests, biases, opinions, and prejudices is an ongoing task. Data do not speak for themselves; they are interpreted through complex cognitive processes. You discover patterns that turn those data into knowledge. Try, therefore, to be exceptionally careful to articulate the conceptual framework you use to interpret the data. You will develop an "intellectual identity, one that includes a theoretical as well as a methodological orientation" (Lareau, 1989, p. 213). Rather than pretending to be objective, state and make clear who you are and what assumptions drive the study. You will need to become clear about your orientation and the approach, boundaries, and limitations of the project. All this depends on some fundamental assumptions that, explicitly or implicitly, shape your study.

Paradigms

In the field, talking with people, observing their everyday worlds, and learning about what matters to them is what qualitative researchers do. What undergirds this work? What is the intellectual orientation of qualitative research in general? How does it differ from quantitative research? The perspective of qualitative research is grounded in assumptions about social science and the social world—assumptions about small things such as, What is knowledge, anyway? What is acceptable as evidence? What is the nature of human action in the world? and What characterizes the social structures and processes that researchers want to learn about? To encourage you to begin to think about these questions, we turn to a discussion of research paradigms and the assumptions that shape them. Getting clear about the assumptions undergirding your work is important for establishing the intellectual traditions to which it connects. Implicit in these assumptions, moreover, are standards for judging your research. Different assumptions imply different standards for what constitutes good research, as we discuss under Trustworthiness.

Philosophers and sociologists of science have attempted to understand and describe the complexity of thought that guides definitions of "science." They have used the concept of *paradigm*[1] to capture the idea that definitions of science (whether natural or social) are the products of shared understandings of reality—that is, worldviews (complete complex ways of seeing and sets of assumptions about the world and actions within it). Used this way, the concept has a grand scope, describing whole worlds of thought. It is more easily grasped when thought of in everyday ways as the perspectives that Ruth, Marla, and Anthony—and, by extension, you—bring to research projects. For example, we know that Marla believes that the social world can be improved; Anthony assumes that decisions can be based on data; and Ruth believes that mental health depends on physical well-being.

Burrell and Morgan (1979) developed a typology of paradigms in sociology that has proven useful in provoking thought and reflection about some deep assumptions that undergird approaches to research. We present their work as a guide to help you think about where you stand on some basic questions and to begin to situate yourself along two continua of assumptions, one about research and the other about the social world.[2]

Subjectivity Versus Objectivity

In the vignette at the beginning of this chapter, Anthony asks a rhetorical question about knowing if participants are telling the truth. Although he may not yet fully realize it, he is asking a fundamental question about assumptions he and his peers make about the construction of knowledge and about what that knowledge is—what is "the truth" and how do we know it? Assumptions that relate to these questions are captured by the *subjectivity and objectivity continuum*. Think about what you believe is truth. How do you know something is true? How do you trust what someone says to you? When you ask a friend or colleague, "how do you know that?," what do you take as evidence that convinces you? What is the relationship between the knower and the known or the learner and what he or she learns? What do you believe about the nature of reality? How do people act in that reality? What do

TABLE 2.1 Assumptions About Social Science

Subjectivist Assumptions	*Objectivist Assumptions*
Contextual dependency	Generalizing tendency
"Working understandings"	"Universal verities" or laws
Getting close to the subject	Systematic protocol and technique
Focus on understanding subjective experience	Focus on testing hypotheses
Comparative logic	Logic of probabilities
Case study designs	Experimental or quasi-experimental designs
Researcher as "instrument"	Reliable instrumentation
Interpretive analysis of data	Statistical manipulation of data
Data in the form of words	Data in the form of numbers

these beliefs imply for doing research—your methodology? The continuum appears as follows:

subjectivity ⟵⟶ objectivity

Where our characters position themselves depends on answers to important sets of questions. Table 2.1 summarizes the polar extremes of the continuum.

These extreme anchor points form two fundamentally different conceptions of the work of social science. Although the tendency is toward subjectivist assumptions, qualitative projects can be found at several points along the continuum. Early ethnographic studies, in particular, rested on assumptions that were objectivist.

The Nature of Knowledge and Knowing

What are your assumptions about what constitutes truth and how you know it? Subjectivists hold that the very notion of "truth" is problematic. They argue that, except for certain principles about the physical world, there are few truths that constitute universal knowledge; rather, there are multiple perspectives about the world. An objectivist, by contrast, asserts that there is a truth about a particular circumstance that can be determined. Your question, then, follows: In doing research, will you search for Truth—with a capital T—or truths—multiple perspectives?

Questions you can ask yourself include the following: How do I learn about something? What do I take as "evidence" to support a point? Do I accept what I read and hear, or do I examine it critically, based on my own experience? From an objectivist position, Anthony might argue that knowledge is tangible and "hard"; legitimate evidence comes in formal documents, the opinions of experts, clearly argued logic, and, often, numbers. With more subjectivist beliefs, Marla might argue that knowledge comes in multiple forms, many quite personal, including dreams, intuitions, and spiritual and transcendent experiences.

Another question invites you to think about where you believe knowledge can appropriately be produced and who can legitimately engage in that creation.[3] Subjectivist views hold that knowledge about the social world arises from many quarters; important understandings are evident in novels, the arts and the media, and in formal social science reports and articles. A poem or drawing is as legitimate a portrait of life experiences as a research report. An objectivist would see such knowledge as soft, unscientific, and idiosyncratic. By extension, subjectivist assumptions argue that much knowledge production in the social sciences has privileged formal academic knowledge, thereby excluding other ways of knowing. Therefore, those with subjectivist assumptions seek to create spaces where marginalized voices can be heard. On the one hand are assumptions that objectivity is possible and desirable as the goal of social science inquiry; on the other hand, subjectivist assumptions challenge this notion, asserting that understanding lived experience, the researcher's and those whose lives she studies, is the legitimate project of inquiry.

An example may help clarify this point. Marla, Ruth, and Anthony leave class confused about what qualitative research is and, specifically, are concerned about procedures they do not really understand but will have to follow. Part of their discussion centers on the reality of the class experience and what Professor Kent did or did not say and mean or did not mean. Debate about what Kent did or did not say—the actual words—would suggest a more objectivist conception of reality: Anthony asks if Kent said they had to have a plan for dissemination. Did Kent say specifically if this was required or not? Ruth's response is a subjectivist stance: She probes for Kent's meaning and searches for a broader interpretation. An objectivist stance implies that reality—in this case, what went on in the classroom—is fact based. A subjectivist stance suggests that an understanding (interpretation) of reality is formed through personal experience, interaction, and discussion.

The Nature of Reality

This facet of the subjective-objective dimension explores beliefs about reality—which is no small task. This question is important because social science, whatever its methodologic guise, seeks to learn about social phenomena—reality as people understand it. To help locate yourself on this continuum, ask the following questions: Do I believe that reality is of an objective nature? Is it "out there," independent of human perception, and therefore something that I can learn about without direct experience? Does it exist independently of my perception? In contrast, do I believe that reality is the product of my individual experience and understanding? Is reality constructed through my subjective experience and intersubjective understanding?

Objectivist assumptions hold that reality exists independent of human cognition and that the work of social science is to discover important facts and processes that constitute that reality. The processes are out there, waiting to be uncovered. Subjectivist assumptions, however, argue that humans construct understandings of reality through their perceptual and interpretive faculties. Social processes are created by human interpretation; they do not constitute reality per se but are concepts that describe it. Another example may help.

In one of their qualitative methods classes, our characters were discussing this point. Ruth asked where Chaos Theory (Gleick, 1987) would fit along this continuum, asserting that chaos, as a principle of social organization, exists. Almost in one voice, other students dissented, countering that Chaos Theory is a social construct that helps us better understand reality. They argued that chaos did not exist "out there," waiting for Gleick to discover it. Because she claimed that chaos exists, Ruth could be viewed as holding objectivist assumptions about reality, whereas those disagreeing may well have more subjectivist assumptions.

The Nature of Human Agency

This facet of the subjective-objective dimension focuses on assumptions about our relationship to the world we live in. You might ask yourself the following: Do I assume that people respond mechanistically, in a predetermined manner? Are we conditioned by external circumstances such as social forces? Are we more creative, exercising free will and agency in shaping our environments and everyday lives? Objectivists assume that human actions are predictable and, hence, controllable. They believe that splicing social phenomena into variables and causal models is not only possible but also desirable. From this perspective, Anthony would assume that if a particular intervention worked with one population, it should work with others. In other words, he would believe that predicting outcomes is possible. Subjectivists, however, hold that human agency is crucial for shaping everyday lives and larger social patterns. They maintain that unpredictability is the hallmark of human action; the goal here is to describe and interpret how people make sense of and act in their worlds. Here, Anthony would argue that what works in one setting may or may not work in another; he would be more intrigued with understanding what makes an intervention work in a particular setting.

Methodology

The assumptions made in the previous three categories have implications for the methods you choose to conduct your work. Different assumptions incline you toward different methods. Although none of our characters will do quantitative projects, "pure" objectivist assumptions would incline a researcher toward control-group designs, standardized instrumentation, and quantitative analysis of data. The purpose of research deriving from these assumptions is to generate laws or "universal verities"—to generalize from the research sample to larger populations, making predictions about behavior.

The kind of project you do will likely be based on the subjectivist assumptions of most qualitative research. This will incline you to focus on small case studies, firsthand knowledge of the social world, and interpretive analysis of data. Research guided by these assumptions moves toward "working understandings" of the subjective world rather than general predictive laws. In reflecting on your personal epistemology, you will need to consider another continuum of assumptions about society.

Status Quo Versus Radical Change

The second continuum describes models of society, again encouraging you to probe your beliefs about important theoretical questions. This second dimension posits that, when you investigate social phenomena—when you conduct social research—you do so with some model or theory about society. Often, these theories operate at the meta-cognitive level; your task is to get more clear about where you stand—your theoretical orientation to social research.

Think about your political stance about the social world. Do you view society as essentially orderly or as characterized by oppression and domination? On the one hand are researchers who focus on explaining the "underlying unity and cohesiveness" (Burrell & Morgan, 1979, p. 17) of society; on the other hand are those who search for understandings of "deep-seated structural conflict . . . [and] modes of domination" (p. 17). These two perspectives view society in quite different ways. Beware of dichotomizing these views, however; as with the objectivist-subjectivist dimension, think about these two orientations along a continuum that looks as follows:

The two orientations at the extremes represent alternative conceptions of society and social processes. A focus on the status quo, the predominant model of social science, presumes that society is basically well-ordered and functionally coordinated. Researchers espousing this perspective explain why society holds together in predictable ways and, indeed, assume that prediction is possible. They believe that inquiry into social processes holds the potential for improving social and organizational life; research will help fine-tune social functioning to better meet the needs of the system or the individual. This is the exemplar of instrumental use (described in Chapter 1).

In contrast is an orientation about radical change, which assumes that social processes deprive individuals and systems of important satisfactions. Deeply embedded in society are contradictions—structures of domination and oppression—that imprison individuals and systems in

TABLE 2.2 Assumptions About Society

The Status Quo Orientation Is Concerned With	The Radical Change Orientation Is Concerned With
The status quo	Radical change
Social order	Structural conflict
Consensus	Modes of domination
Social integration and cohesion	Contradiction
Solidarity	Emancipation
Need satisfaction	Deprivation
Actuality	Potentiality

both subtle and explicit ways. Those espousing this perspective strive for the radical transformation of society (emancipatory use). Often explicitly political in purpose, radical change researchers tend to be idealistic—they see the possibility of transformation. The contrasts between these two conceptions of society are presented in Table 2.2 (Burrell & Morgan, 1979, p. 18).

As you learn more about Anthony, Ruth, and Marla, you will see these orientations about society reflected in their work. Marla embodies the radical change perspective through her drive to involve participants and to do research that has the potential for empowerment. At the start of her study, Ruth is only concerned with the status quo: She thinks she will simply describe the children's lives. In the course of her journey, however, her descriptions take on an explicitly political agenda as she becomes dedicated to the lived experiences of children with physical disabilities.

Four Paradigms

When the two continuua are crossed, the result is four paradigms[5] that capture important sets of assumptions that shape research about the social world. These assumptions often operate at the tacit level.[6] The four paradigms are provided in Table 2.3.

Each paradigm carries a set of assumptions about the nature of social science and about the nature of society. We offer a brief description of the four paradigms next. While reading the following sections, consider

TABLE 2.3 Four Paradigms

	Subjectivist	*Objectivist*
Radical change	Radical subjectivism	Radical objectivism
Status quo	Interpretivism	Positivism

research that you have read or conducted yourself; try to analyze the assumptions driving these efforts and situate them in one of the paradigms. Qualitative researchers operate predominantly in the interpretivist paradigm, although their work can also operate in the positivist and radical subjectivist paradigms.

Positivism

Research conducted within the positivist paradigm has dominated the social sciences. Although there is diversity here, much of the work takes a fundamentally rational view of the social world. Assuming a rational and ordered social world, with an orientation toward the status quo, the project has been to explain and improve organizational functioning. Research methodologies represent the attempt to apply methods derived from the natural sciences to social phenomena, assuming an objectivist epistemology. Experimental and quasi-experimental designs predominate with randomization the sine qua non of sampling procedures. Researchers operationalize variables that are then measured and analyzed quantitatively. Much research within this paradigm is pragmatic in purpose and instrumental in use.

Interpretivism

The interpretive paradigm holds status quo assumptions about the social world and subjectivist assumptions about epistemology. Interpretive research typically tries to understand the social world as it is (the status quo) from the perspective of individual experience; the locus of understanding shifts from the positivist's focus on the objective observer to an interest in subjective worldviews. Prediction is seen as an undesirable goal because with prediction likely comes social control; rather, the goal is to generate "thick description" (Geertz, 1983) of the actor's worldviews. Humans are viewed as creators of their worlds; thus, agency in shaping the everyday world is fundamental to the paradigm. Research methods typically rely on humanistic methods—face-to-face interactions, whether in the form of in-depth interviews or extended observations or some combination.

At the top of the matrix are two other paradigms that make very different assumptions about the social world than either positivism or interpretivism. Influenced heavily by the writings of Karl Marx, work in both the radical subjectivist and radical objectivist paradigms assumes a conflictual society. Society is viewed as being composed of oppressive social structures and domination by powerful and hegemonic groups. Work here often tries to liberate or emancipate, either directly or by dissemination, and severely critiques much positivist and interpretive work.

Radical Subjectivist

Radical subjectivists view individual consciousness as the agent to empower, transform, and liberate groups from dominating and imprisoning social processes. Research and theorizing in this paradigm rely on the notion of "false consciousness," a concept that asserts that human agency is constrained by "ideological superstructures" (Burrell & Morgan, 1979, p. 32). Radical change occurs at the individual level, transforming social relations at the "local" level. Research is typically conducted using the humanistic methods found in the interpretive paradigm. One significant difference between the interpretive and the radical subjectivist paradigms is the researcher's stance: The radical subjectivist researcher is explicitly participatory in the research project, sharing the initiation, conduct, analysis, and writing with those studied. The theoretical framework guiding radical subjectivist research derives from critical theory and postmodern perspectives.

In their original work, Burrell and Morgan (1979) did not anticipate the enormous growth, during the past 15 years, in the critical perspectives represented by feminist theory, research focusing on race and ethnicity, participatory action research from international development work, and current theorizing focusing on sexual orientation. Discussion of these important critical standpoints is largely absent from Burrell and Morgan's work. We argue, however, that much of this current work can be usefully seen as holding subjectivist and radical change assumptions.

Radical Objectivist

Rather than focusing on individual human consciousness, the radical objectivist paradigm analyzes the power relations embedded in political and economic structures. Radical social change is viewed as arising from crises in these basic social systems, leading to more equitable distributions of power and wealth. Although there is diversity within this paradigm, research tends to rely on large-scale data gathering that is often represented quantitatively.

In summary, Burrell and Morgan's (1979) work, although asking questions you might not typically ask of yourself, is useful for understanding the broad sweep of social science research and for beginning to situate various qualitative traditions—as well as our characters' and your own work—along the continua and within the paradigms. We introduce a cautionary note here, however. Given our subjectivist assumptions, we view the concept of paradigm as just that: a concept. It is not reality "out there"; it is a heuristic trope that many have found valuable in organizing what is a complex array (a cacophony at times) of research claiming to contribute to understanding the social world. Think of the categories in Table 2.3 as having mushy and permeable borders.[7]

Using the previous theoretical discussion, you can begin to understand better where qualitative researchers situate themselves—the assumptions they make, the beliefs they hold about what is important work to do, and the orientations they bring to their work. These considerations, you recall, are important for explicating the theoretical and methodological perspective you take in your work. Because qualitative research is fundamentally subjectivist and interactive, reflecting on your perspective is crucial. How do you go about doing this besides asking some of the questions posed previously? What do you think about as you begin to conduct a study? What do you construe as your relationship with the participants in your study? What do you bring to the work?

PERSPECTIVE IN PRACTICE

The qualitative researcher needs to be constantly aware of his separateness from those he is researching. The researcher needs to know who he is and what he is doing in the setting. This self-awareness allows the researcher to distinguish his sense-making from the sense-making of those he is studying. Anthropologists have labeled the researcher's perspective the *etic*, or outsider, perspective. They refer to the perspective of the participants as the *emic*, or insider, perspective. Because fully representing the subjective experience of the participants (the emic perspective) is an unachievable goal,[8] qualitative researchers strive to represent clearly and richly their understanding of what they have learned (the etic perspective). What they write is interpretations (their own) of participants' understandings of their worlds (the participants' interpretations). Our characters hope that participants will see themselves in their portrayals, but they recognize that this may not be fully achieved and take responsibility for the interpretations they put forward. They are scrupulous, therefore, to identify that it is their own understanding, shaped by their perspective, what they have learned, and how they choose to write it up.

The Self at Work: Reflexivity

The personal biography of the researcher and the roles she takes influence the research—both the sense she makes of the setting and how people she studies make sense of her. Whether the researcher has chosen to participate in the setting, as has Marla, or is trying to be less obtrusive, the very fact of her presence changes the context. Hammersley and Atkinson (1983, p. 15) state, "There is no way in which we can escape the social world in order to study it." Put simply, a relationship always exists between the researcher and those being researched. This relationship and the researcher's reflections on it comprise a phenomenon called *reflexivity* that is central to understanding the practice of qualitative research.

The word reflexivity has as its root *reflexive*, which means "capable of turning or bending back" (Brown, 1993, p. 2522). The term has its origins in the Latin word *reflexus*, which means "a bending back," from which we also derive the English use of reflex to mean an automatic response produced in reaction to an action or event. When used in the context of social science, reflexive means that a method or theory "takes account of itself or especially of the effect of the personality or presence of the researcher on what is being investigated" (p. 2522).

Reflexivity in the setting begins with you, the researcher. As you observe or interview, you react to the participant's words and actions. They trigger thoughts, hunches, working hypotheses, and understandings of the setting and the participants. You generate constructs or identify patterns drawn from your theoretical orientation and cultural knowledge to describe and explain the actions you observe or words you hear. These constructs or hypotheses begin as unexamined reflexes in reaction to what you see or hear.

Reflexivity, however, also involves the study's participants. The participants react to you; theirs is also an unexamined reflex. By your mere presence, you become a part of their social world; therefore, they modify their actions accordingly. The more you appear to be like members of this world or the longer you remain a part of this social world, the less your presence may affect the everyday routines. In one sense, you become an integral part of the social world. The way participants react to you is a part of their repertoire, their recurring actions in their world. Reflexivity, in this sense, is the package of reciprocal reactions between the researcher and the participants in the setting.

The root word has another important meaning. It also denotes reflection and introspection. When thinking about research and the writing of a report, reflexivity means that an author or text "self-consciously refer[s] to itself or its production" (Brown, 1993, p. 2522). In qualitative research, reflexivity captures both these meanings: the reactions that naturally occur because an outsider enters and interacts with the setting and the capacity to reflect on those reactions. Both meanings are crucial. As you reflect on your initial reactions, they grow into an examined and rigorous *representation* of an etic perspective.

In our view, qualitative researchers need to be acutely aware of both meanings: *reflex*, as in unexamined reaction, and *reflect*, as in the turning back of thoughts. Both words—reflect and reflex—originate from the same Latin root. For a human being, to reflect is to contemplate. We see the researcher's reflection as an essential component of his or her role. The researcher reacts, but, most important, he contemplates those reactions.

Reflexivity is an interactive and cyclical phenomenon rather than a linear one. Both "seeing is believing" and "believing is seeing" are true. The qualitative researcher is open to the interplay of what is considered fact and opinion. He asks, "What sense do I make of what is going on or of this person's actions?" This is the etic perspective. At the same time, the researcher asks, "What sense do the participants make of what *they* are doing? What is the individual's sense of his or her own actions?" These questions seek the emic perspective. Although the researcher cannot actually get into the participants' mind, he can search for evidence of their worldviews. Overlaid on these ongoing emic and etic processes is the set of questions about what you are doing—your actions—and how they are perceived.

The objectivist deals with reflexivity by assuming that it can be controlled; hence the scientist's struggle for objectivity. Objectivists admonish the researcher to eliminate all bias, to remain disinterested. Qualitative researchers, however, assume that objectivity is elusive. Recognizing that reflexivity is present in social interactions, they focus on understanding and explaining the effects of reflexivity. This makes their inquiry systematic and rigorous. Delamont (1992) cautions us to be "constantly self-conscious about [the qualitative researcher's] role, interactions, and theoretical and empirical material as it accumulates. As long as qualitative researchers are reflexive, making all their purposes explicit, then issues of reliability and validity are served" (p. 8).

To ensure that data collection is systematic, qualitative researchers begin by being explicit about their purposes and by being themselves. For us, being ourselves means that we have articulated our perspectives or frames of reference toward the topic—that is, we know our beliefs and values and our assumptions and biases relative to that topic. We are clear about our theoretical and methodological orientation; we consider past experiences that might influence our views. In short, we try to be aware of and vigilant about the baggage we carry into the inquiry.

Establishing Perspective

You can take several deliberate steps to establish your perspective. Think about the issues presented previously; this can help. Read widely about the subject and about social science theories that inform the subject. Voracious reading is crucial to establishing a perspective. To avoid reinventing the wheel, read material directly about the subject and, whenever available, contrasting viewpoints. Read relevant theories. To illustrate, we found the knowledge built from reading on inclusive education proved especially valuable in establishing our orientation for a court-ordered evaluation of inclusive education (Rossman, Rallis, & Uhl, 1996). The reading made us aware of the scope and complexity of inclusive classrooms, including the legal, political, and economic issues that could arise. We decided the most useful information we could provide would be on educational issues; we therefore focused on the educational experiences of children in inclusive classrooms.

The next step in establishing perspective is to ask yourself how you *feel* about the subject. More often than not, you have an opinion about the worth or value of what you are studying. Try not to let this opinion prevent you from "seeing" clearly and widely in the settings; remain open to the views of others. For example, Anthony may not enjoy modern dance, but he may still evaluate the community arts program, which includes modern dance; he is not being asked to critique the performance itself. As long as he remembers that he is tracking the audience's attention and satisfaction, his personal dislike of modern dance does not have to interfere. Drawing on the paradigms discussed previously, a subjectivist Anthony recognizes that multiple perspectives—a range of appreciation—are possible. Still, he must be vigilant to ensure that he does not read his lack of enthusiasm into the audience's reactions.

As we will discuss in Chapter 3, having a compelling interest is important. For example, Anthony may want to see the community arts program succeed. He will take care to produce thick descriptions that explore all aspects and angles of the program. Because he does not hold objectivist assumptions about an independent reality, he cannot claim to report only hard facts, but he does aim to discover the social construct—the culture—of the program. As another example, several years ago we studied the introduction of teacher assistance teams into schools (Rallis, 1990). Our reading about the concept and its goals and objectives convinced us that effectively functioning teams could profoundly improve the way schools work. We could easily have served as advocates for the program. Instead, even before we entered the schools to see how teams functioned in practice, we reminded ourselves of our roles as evaluators. We focused on describing what we saw, identifying specific strengths that could be replicated and problems or weaknesses that should be addressed. In this way, our evaluation was able to improve what we saw as an inherently good program.

Perhaps most important, Anthony—and you—will need to be sensitive to the subtle differences between compelling interest in a subject, advocacy, and out-and-out bias. Qualitative researchers are careful to check their feelings for bias or prejudice. If they encounter a study about which they feel so strongly that they cannot avoid passing judgment, they often consider and clarify their motivations. They may decide not to become involved in the study. Once we refused to do an evaluation of an early childhood program that claimed to teach 3-year-olds to read because we felt our goal would be to debunk the program. In another example, should Ruth find she has no patience for children whose physical disabilities preclude being athletic, her clear bias would prevent her from discovering the realities of these children's lives.

Your perspective is also related to your role. Depending on the strategy (evaluation or policy study, action research, or descriptive cultural study), the design calls for particular actions and seeking information in particular forms. Marla's role allows her to participate in the work of the clinic because she has chosen action research. Because she is working in the setting, she has direct access to an emic perspective. As an evaluator, Anthony's role is to provide information to program policymakers and funders who will make decisions about program directions, services to be offered, and resource allocations. He seeks data that can inform decisions, and he is guided by program purposes, audience needs, and program impact. His role in evaluating the community art program is not to critique the displays but to gather data on the community's use of facilities and events: Who attends what activities? When and why do they attend? What do they think of displays and performances? Do folks appreciate certain aspects more than others? What problems are encountered? What are the unexpected costs? His role is also to communicate the resulting information to the decision makers so they may use it. In each case, the qualitative researcher has the responsibility to make clear for the study participants what role he or she intends to take.

Finally, because the qualitative researcher is learning and constructing, and because she is *reflectively reflexive* while doing so, her inquiry is subjective. It is not, however, unsystematic. The researcher is meticulous about her documentation and recording, both of what she sees and of what processes she uses. The researcher's process should be deliberate and conscious; her decisions and actions should be explicated and displayed so that others may understand how the study was done and can assess its adequacy. Just as the researcher collects and displays her

her data, she collects and displays data about her own research decisions and actions and their development. How does the researcher define her terms? What assumptions has she made? What does she do and why? What decisions has she made? What are the parameters of the study? What preconceptions and prejudices does she bring? What problems does she encounter?

It is better to err on the side of telling more details about research design and experience than to give too few. Whenever possible, keep a log of the process. It is helpful to allocate time shortly after any data collection for processing the observation or interview or record review, even if it means that you sit in the car or stand on a street corner noting the day's events. In our work, we appreciate fieldwork done as a team so that we can drive together; the ride offers a time to critique the experience collaboratively.

Documenting your intellectual and methodological journey is crucial for establishing the soundness of the study. Getting clear about your perspective helps establish the intellectual integrity of the project. It places boundaries, describes assumptions, and details the process. All these go far to establishing the trustworthiness of the project, to which we turn next.

TRUSTWORTHINESS[9]

The trustworthiness of a qualitative research project is judged by two interrelated criteria. First, does the study conform to *standards for acceptable and competent practice?* Second, has it been *ethically conducted* with sensitivity to the politics of the topic and setting? We say that these are interrelated because it is our stance that a study can meet accepted standards for practice but, if not ethically conducted, falls short in integrity.[10]

As described in Chapter 1, we believe that the purpose of a study should be use: to contribute in some way to understanding and action to improve social circumstances. For a study to be useful, however, readers—potential users—must believe and trust in its integrity. It must have credibility to users, whether these are other researchers, policymakers, practitioners, or the participants themselves. Each group assesses the study's integrity using different criteria. Other researchers judge the conceptual framework and rigorous use of methodology. Policymakers ask if the study addresses important policy concerns and how the results help them make policy and program decisions. Practitioners think about ways the results shape their everyday work. Participants judge how ethically and sensitively their words and perspectives are portrayed. Each group, to varying extents, considers whether the study was well conceptualized, implemented in sound ways, and written up with care and rigor.

Standards for judging the value of research projects used to be clear and uncontested: Reliability, validity, generalizability, and objectivity were the historic criteria and are still used in quantitative research. If instrumentation is reliable, the study is valid in its conclusions. It is then generalizable to a defined population. If the study meets all these conditions and was conducted objectively, it is judged competent. With the development of qualitative research and the critical and postmodern perspectives, however, ideas about what precisely constitutes good research have become blurred. Is a novel research? If you participate fully, have you biased your inquiry? Is just talking with people sufficient?

Our position is that appropriate standards depend on the assumptions you make about inquiry and how consistently these assumptions are played out in the project. This determines the *integrity* of the project—its wholeness and its coherence. Integrity, however, also implies *soundness of moral principle*—the ethical dimension that constitutes the second element of trustworthiness. Explicating both the theoretical and methodological orientation and the ethical standards that have guided your project is crucial. You must convey both to the reader of any written report. Standards for practice and ethical positions may vary, depending on the assumptions you have made. There are, however, some anchor points about both elements to help you and our characters along. In what follows, we first discuss standards for practice and then turn to the sometimes thorny ethical considerations involved in doing qualitative research.

Although it seems daunting at this point, Ruth, Marla, and Anthony begin to consider the worth of their projects. How can they judge the quality of their work? How can they ensure that their projects will be well-conducted? What standards do they use? How do they deal with ethical situations? The questions they ask one another, and themselves, focus on figuring out what constitutes trustworthy, ethical practice.

Standards for Practice

All research, no matter what its paradigmatic roots, should respond to legitimate questions that readers pose. As noted previously, these questions focus on the accuracy of what is reported (its truth value), the methodology used to generate the findings (its rigor), and the usefulness of the study (its generalizability and significance). We discuss each in turn.

What Is the "Truth Value" of This Work?

Qualitative researchers pursue multiple perspectives about some phenomenon; they search for truths, not Truth. They typically assume that reality is an interpretive phenomenon, and that meaning is constructed by participants as they go about their everyday lives. The qualitative researcher's task is to render an account of participants' worldviews as honestly and fully as possible. This rendition of what has been learned, however, is also an interpretation—the researcher's. Interpretations of interpretations. In judging the truth value of a project, readers depend on how adequately multiple understandings (including the researcher's) are presented and whether they "ring true" (have face validity).

Several strategies help establish the truth claims of qualitative research. One is to design the study so that data are gathered over a period of time or intensively rather than in a one-shot manner. A second is sharing your interpretations of the emergent findings with participants, often called "member checks" (a decidedly infelicitous term!). A third strategy is designing the study as participatory or action research from beginning to end, thereby ensuring that the truth value of what you discover and report is intimately linked to participants' understandings. A fourth is to triangulate—that is, draw from several data sources, methods, investigators, or theories to strengthen the robustness of your work. Using a colleague or peer as a critical friend also strengthens the value of what you conclude and report. Judicious and modest writing about your perspective—your personal biography with its interests, potential biases, strengths, and unique insights—helps the reader explore how and in what ways you as the researcher have shaped the project and the findings you report. Finally, a stance of humility in the claims you make establishes that you understand the conditional and approximate nature of knowledge about complex social phenomena. Contextualizing your findings to the specific setting and participants also tells the readers that your conclusions are bounded by time and space.

How Rigorously Was the Study Conducted?

Another criterion readers use for judging research is whether it has been rigorously conducted. From an objectivist perspective, this has meant that results are replicable because the instrumentation used for data gathering is reliable: If the study is repeated, will the results be the same? Achieving the same results depends on the reliability of the instrumentation: If used again, it will yield the same results. From subjectivist assumptions, however, this notion of replicability becomes difficult. The purpose of qualitative research is not to immaculately replicate what has gone before; in fact, such replication is impossible, given the dynamic nature of the social world and given that the researcher is not *an instrument* in the experimental sense. As Merriam (1988) notes,

> Because what is being studied [in qualitative research] is assumed to be in flux, multifaceted, and highly contextual, because information gathered is a function of who gives it and how skilled the researcher is at getting it, and because the emergent design of a qualitative . . . study precludes a priori controls, achieving reliability in the traditional sense is not only fanciful but impossible. (p. 171)

Instead, for qualitative studies, this historic concern shifts to a consideration of how thoughtfully and dependably the researcher conducted the study—it focuses directly on implementation. Was the study well conceived and conducted? Are decisions clear? Was sufficient evidence gathered and presented? Was the researcher rigorous in searching for alternative explanations for what was learned? Are differing interpretations put forward and assessed?

Rather than judging whether replication would yield the same results, this standard for practice assesses the extent to which an outsider would concur with the results of the study, given the data collected and displayed. Can someone else understand the logic and assumptions of the study and see the reasoning that resulted in the interpretations put forward? Are these interpretations sound and grounded in the data? Is the process of analysis clear and coherent?

One strategy to help ensure that your qualitative study is rigorously conducted is to make your position clear, a demand we have stressed throughout this chapter. Another is to rely on multiple methods for gathering data, thereby enhancing the complexity of what you learn in the field. A third is to document assiduously the process of gathering, analyzing, and interpreting the data. Erickson (1986) refers to this as the *natural history of the inquiry.* Keep a log or journal. Write interim analytic memos. These all serve to document the intellectual odyssey of your study and help you establish its rigor to readers and potential users.

How Is the Study Useful for Other Situations?

A final standard for the conduct of a qualitative study is its applicability to other situations. This parallels the objectivist concern for generalizability in quantitative research. Strict, probabilistic generalizing, however, can only be done to the population from which a sample was (randomly) drawn. What about other, similar populations? Even in quantitative research, generalizing from one population to another must be done through the reasoning of comparison and contrast rather than through probabilistic logic. Qualitative research, as you recall, is not searching for "abstract universals" but rather "concrete universals" (Erickson, 1986, p. 130), working hypotheses (Cronbach, 1975, p. 125), or working understandings. It does not claim to be generalizable in the statistical sense, but it can still be useful for other settings.

To establish the usefulness of a study, provide rich, thick description of your theoretical and methodological orientation and the process as well as the results. Another useful strategy is to provide as much detail about the context as feasible. Potential users can then determine for themselves if your results will be of use in a new but similar setting. They compare and contrast the specifics of your study with their own setting and judge if they are sufficiently similar for your findings to be insightful. This logic is different from generalizing probabilistically; it is the same, however, as applying findings about one population to another. The reasoning requires careful assessment about the similarities and differences of the instances.

These standards for practice and for judging the integrity and value of qualitative studies—truth value, rigor, and usefulness—are important considerations when designing and conducting a study. Our characters are learning about these as they read and discuss the many writings about the theory and practice of doing qualitative inquiry. Also, they will learn even more as they implement their own studies and experience the complexity of the decision processes involved. They will be mindful of what constitutes good practice. The final, overarching standard of trustworthiness for qualitative research is that it be conducted in an ethical manner, with sensitivity to the complex interpersonal situations and politics that being in the field embraces.

Ethics

Operating as an ethical researcher, however, goes beyond establishing your perspective; rather, you make decisions according to a code of ethics or a standard for conduct that is based on moral principles. Like Kant, we believe these moral principles direct us to act as we would want everyone else to act in any given situation—in ways that treat humanity as an end as well as a means. Put simply, one person should never exploit other people to his or her own advantage. Kant proposes that human beings are born with the ability to discern the difference between right and wrong. This innate practical reason is intelligence that gives us the capacity to make moral choices because all humans have access to a universal moral law. Kant suggests that this law is not bound to any particular situation of moral choice: It applies to all people and all societies at all times. This law guides the qualitative researcher to the ethical stance of not exploiting any person in any circumstances regardless of differences in status, race, gender, language, and other social identity considerations.

Professional groups and social science disciplines have established formal codes of ethics to guide their fields' research activities. So, too, has the United States government. These codes serve as standards for the ethical practice of research and are based on moral principles such as utilitarianism (the greatest good for the greatest number), theories of individual rights (the rights of the individual may supersede the interests of the greatest number), and theories of justice (fairness and equity). Deceptive and downright harmful research conducted earlier in this century led to the development of ethical codes. They are intended to serve as guidelines for practice to ensure that participants in research projects are protected from harm and are not deceived. We argue that each researcher develops his own standards for ethical practice as he encounters situations that demand complex moral reasoning. These personal guidelines, however, cannot be wildly idiosyncratic; they must be cognizant of the formal codes that exist in the discipline or profession and of the writings of qualitative researchers about the ethical dilemmas and issues they have grappled with in their own practice. Some ethical considerations are generic; others are study specific. We discuss three generic ones and give some specific examples.

Keep in mind that ethical dilemmas are not solvable but are reasoned through the moral principle. You must be able to explain your reasoning, although it may not agree with the prevailing dominant principle. For example, undercover investigators for a news network who sought to expose conscious mishandling of food in a supermarket chain lied on their applications for work in the stores. The supermarket chain sued for damages resulting from the exposure of information gathered through the deception. The investigators justified the lie as being for the greater good of society. The courts made the news network pay damages and fines because, they reasoned, lying violated a preeminent principle.

Privacy and Confidentiality

Qualitative research takes place in the field, with real people who live and work in the setting. They are not anonymous to the researcher and, if she is not diligent in protecting their identities, they may not be anonymous to anyone! Thus, assuring confidentiality to the participants is crucial. This challenge has two elements: protecting their privacy (identities, names, and specific roles)[11] and holding in confidence what they share with you (not sharing it with others using their names). We remember studies we conducted as beginners when we unwittingly came close to breaking our promise of confidentiality. Participants sometime ask what others have said to us in their interview. In the spirit of conversational give-and-take, our reflex then was to begin to answer. Fortunately, we realized that the promise of confidentiality was to all participants. Our response was similar to the following: "We said we wouldn't share what you tell us with others, so we can't tell you what anyone has said, either."

Over time and with experience, the response to protect becomes the reflex rather than the reaction to tell. A cautionary note, however: It is also important to remind participants that you will use their words in direct quotes in a written report. Although you will do all you can to protect their identity, an organizational sleuth might be able to figure out who said what. Sharing this conditional aspect of confidentiality is a more ethical (and accurate) stance than pretending that you can be omniscient and powerful and can protect their identities no matter what.

Deception and Consent

Gaining the *informed consent* of participants is crucial for the ethical conduct of research. In fact, university human subject review committees require a sample informed consent form with each dissertation and research proposal. Although often codified in such a standardized form, the idea is that (a) participants are as fully informed as possible about the study's purpose and audience, (b) they understand what their agreement to participate entails, (c) they give that consent willingly, and (d) they understand that they may withdraw from the study at any time without prejudice. This means that the participants are not *deceived* about the study.

All this seems quite clear. On closer examination, however, it gets a bit murky. *Some* deception may be involved in much research: Just how much can we fully tell participants about our conceptual framework (how much do they care)? Do we deceive them when we briefly summarize it? If we take on a role, like Marla does as a volunteer, are we masking our full identities? What if the purpose of the study shifts? Do we inform everyone we have interviewed already? Can participants fully understand what their words will look like in a written report before the report is written? Your task is to be as open and honest *as you possibly can be* as you move through a study and build relationships with members of the setting. The key is that the researcher must take every possible precaution to ensure that no harm will come to the participants as a result of the conduct of the study.

Another aspect of deception needs mention. At times, in some circumstances, the potential benefits of a study may outweigh the demand to be open and forthright. Studies of classroom interaction patterns, for example, have shown the persistent, subtle, and complex ways that otherwise well-intentioned teachers privilege boys and white children (Sadker & Sadker, 1994). Those researchers might not have learned about this inequitable treatment of students in such detail if the teachers studied knew that sexist and racist actions were the focus. Is the deception worth it? Punch (1994) comments on this as follows:

> One need not always be brutally honest, direct, and explicit about one's research purpose, but one should not normally engage in disguise. One should not steal documents. One should not directly lie to people. And, although one may disguise identity to a certain extent, one should not break promises made to people. (p. 91)

He takes a pragmatic position that some "dissimulation is intrinsic to social life, and, therefore, also to fieldwork" (p. 91), but he cautions that care must be exercised so that participants come to no harm. This is a delicate balance.

Trust and Betrayal

Qualitative research involves building and sustaining relationships with people. The long, in-depth interview can be quite intimate and disclosing. Ethnographic fieldwork often entails becoming part of the fabric of the participants' social world, a true albeit unusual member of the community. When the research is over, what happens? The researcher ends the interviews, leaves the field, and writes up the study. One could argue that the very role of researcher involves some deception: You are deeply interested in people's stories, but that interest is conditional and bounded. Siskin (1994) calls this the *seduction and abandonment* inherent in much qualitative research. The image is that you seduce the participants into disclosing their worldviews then abandon them when you have gotten what you want: data. Punch (1994) reasons that this may be particularly painful for those who seek "solidarity in the field" but then must "depart and start writing up their experiences for academic consumption" (p. 94). This "one-night-stand" view of qualitative research is challenged directly by some feminist and postmodern researchers who argue for participatory, shared, and purposeful (other than research purposes) engagement with participants.

Betrayal may come in other guises. Recall the previous quote from Punch (1994) in which he says that you should not break promises made to people. For example, you promise confidentiality to a student but learn, in the course of several in-depth interviews, that the student may be the victim of child abuse. If you are a *mandated reporter* (those with legally defined roles relative to children, i.e., teachers or counselors), you must report this information to appropriate authorities. In so doing, do you put the child at risk for further abuse? Do you violate your promise to protect her from harm and to respect her privacy? In a less dramatic example, suppose you observe unethical or illegal practice. Do you report this to authorities and, in so doing, break your promise of confidentiality to the participants? You will have to reason through the potential consequences to the actors in the setting, yourself, and the profession and the larger social concerns of whatever action you take. Your personal ethical code determines the decisions you reach and the actions you take. Be aware that your personal ethical code may not fully align with a prevailing code. Think of industrial whistle-blowers. Your actions might cause you to lose your job or take you into court.

There are no easy solutions to ethical situations you may encounter in the field. There is no template or a mythical moral calculus to use as you weigh the risks and benefits for the many actors and groups that surround your research. Ethical issues are not solved. We are suspicious of beginning researchers who identify thorny and troublesome ethical situations and tell us they have solved them. Solutions are ephemeral: Someone else might argue for a radically different course of action. Rather, we look for sensitivity to the generic and specific ethics in a study and complex and subtle moral reasoning that identifies a range of risks and benefits for those involved. Such subtle argumentation stands you in good stead for justifying decisions made in the field. Given our increasingly litigious society, knowing your own code of ethics and moral principles becomes especially important should you ever be called on (e.g., in a court of law) to articulate your thinking and justify your actions.

Politics

Politics are ubiquitous in social life; research is no different. By politics, we mean the powers of government, universities, thesis or dissertation committees, and social science disciplines to set research agendas and determine appropriate methodologies. We also include as politics the undercurrents of power that shape organizational life and social interactions. These are often called micropolitics. You will find that you need to consider what constraints surround your study and who has placed them there. Who are the key powerful actors—whether individuals or agencies—and how might they influence your study?

Setting the Research Agenda

The institutions mentioned previously all shape what is considered appropriate to study in both obvious and subtle ways. Funding agents put forth requests for proposals on specific topics, thereby signaling what they consider important. If you want funding from that agency, you will have to conform to its interests. Similarly, university departments, research committees, and individual faculty members (your adviser, perhaps) establish what they consider to be legitimate research questions to pursue. All these shape your project in important ways. As will be discussed in Chapter 3, the postmodern critique challenges this hegemony of the social sciences over inquiry and calls on us to push at the borders of what is considered legitimate work and who deems it so. Doing so has some risks, however, especially for the beginner.

Approving the "Right" Methodology

Just as these institutions and actors shape appropriate research questions, they determine what methodology is "best." Despite a long and respected history in anthropology (see Chapter 3), qualitative researchers struggled long and hard to create legitimacy for their work in applied fields such as urban policy, management, education, nursing, and social work. One still finds departments engaged in the sometimes vicious qualitative-quantitative "paradigm wars" (Gage, 1989). As the postmodern perspective has moved out of literary criticism and into the social sciences, just what constitutes good qualitative research has become contested. These politics are often paramount and have as their victim the student who is trying to learn and understand research methods.

Coping With Micropolitics

Power dynamics operate in all social settings. Some involve the power of personality or position; others involve the politics of race and gender. These are often the most salient and yet difficult for the qualitative researcher. Gatekeepers—those in positions of power in organizations—can support or squash a project (discussed in Chapter 4). Influential actors on the scene can ease access or make it difficult even to schedule interviews. Also, issues of race and gender may play out throughout the entire project. Political dynamics among groups in a setting can torpedo the best intentions of a beginner. Becoming aware of micropolitics in general and those specific to your site will stand you in good stead as you navigate the sometimes turbulent waters of a qualitative project.

USING THE HABITS
OF MIND AND HEART

Fundamental to the qualitative enterprise is the willingness and courage to reflect on the self as learner and knower. This reflection, however, does not occur narcissistically. The reflection embraces the "other" as well as the self *and* the relationship between the two. Marla, Ruth, and Anthony are beginning this reflection process as they face the central challenge of this chapter: understanding how they know what they know and what they accept as evidence for knowledge.

As learners and knowers, they pose questions they want to explore in the studies they will conduct for their introductory qualitative research class. They understand that they have embarked on a process of discovery. Although they are uncomfortable with not knowing exactly where they will end up, they understand that a certain level of ambiguity is inherent in the inquiry process because discovery is iterative and because it involves them deeply in the lives of others. Therefore, sensitivity to interpersonal dynamics and ethics will be highly important to their learning and knowing.

Learning about and knowing the self, the other, and the relationship challenges qualitative researchers to confront and articulate the assumptions they bring to their work: How do I know what I know? How do I think about reality? Do I believe that my actions are predetermined or am I free to choose? Do I believe society is essentially orderly or dynamic? How they answer these questions reveals their orientations to subjectivity, objectivity, and social change. These orientations determine how they will go about doing their research; their decisions are shaped by these personal epistemologies. Their challenge, however, is to articulate these sufficiently to justify actions taken in the field.

In this chapter, we have seen the three students begin to explore their capacities for the sensibilities that will become their habits of mind and heart. They locate themselves on the subjectivity-objectivity continuum. They take a position on social change. They articulate their ethical principles. Through this process of sustained and systematic reflection, they construct their research questions and consider their approaches. This process of acting and reflecting, reflecting and acting, helps them to develop their habits of mind and heart. Knowing themselves and their ways of knowing, Marla, Ruth, and Anthony are ready to design their studies.

NOTES

1. The construct paradigm has been overworked, overused, and trivialized. We acknowledge this. In our teaching, however, the concept has proven useful for orienting students to some deep questions about their work.

2. We draw heavily on their work in this section. To avoid redundancy, we will not reference each point unless we quote directly from their work.

3. In their original work, Burrell and Morgan (1979) do not address this question specifically. The current critique of normal social science, however, introduces this issue.

4. Burrell and Morgan (1979) describe this point as the "sociology of regulation"; we prefer using the term status quo to capture this position.

5. Burrell and Morgan's (1979) terms for the four paradigms were functionalist, interpretivist, radical humanist, and radical structuralist. We have modified three of these terms to positivist, radical subjectivist, and radical objectivist, leaving interpretivist as in the original.

6. Others sort social science paradigms somewhat differently. For example, Popkewicz (1984) presents the positivist, interpretive, and critical paradigms, the latter subsuming Burrell and Morgan's (1979) radical humanist and radical structuralist paradigms. Others, notably

Bredo and Feinberg (1982), follow suit. We believe that breaking the critical paradigm into two—one more subjectivist and the other more objectivist—remains a useful distinction.

7. Burrell and Morgan (1979) would disagree. They assert that "the four paradigms are mutually exclusive. . . . A synthesis is not possible, since in their purest forms they are contradictory" (p. 25). We disagree and note an internal contradiction in their argument. The notion of continuum assumes infinite points; how could we determine the exact point of leaving subjectivist assumptions, for example, and moving into objectivist ones? As they present them, the concepts of paradigm and continuum butt up against one another, leaving some discordance.

8. The postmodern critique calls us to acknowledge that written work is authored by . . . the author! This seems obvious at first glance, but much traditional research is written in an antiseptic, author-free style. Canons of acceptable practice for writing research reports were built around objectivist assumptions; no author should be visible to the reader. The critique demands that we examine and explicate the ways our authorship of text shapes that text. Given this, the notion of representing solely the emic perspective, devoid of our own interpretations (writing), becomes impossible and irrelevant.

9. We draw on the concept of trustworthiness discussed by Yvonna Lincoln and Egon Guba (1985).

10. We have observed that widely used texts on qualitative methods separate out ethics from discussions of reliability and validity. Our position is that these cannot be separated. For a study to be trustworthy, it must be more than reliable and valid; it must be ethical.

11. A current counterargument is that making people anonymous deprives them of agency in the work of the study. Those holding this position argue that the participants themselves should decide if they want to be named in a written report or if the organization or setting should be named. We acknowledge the persuasive politics of this argument but urge caution, particularly for the beginner. The ways that written reports can be used go well beyond the control of either researcher or participants. Through reading and experience, the researcher may well have a more subtle view of potential hazards if an organization or individuals are specifically identified. We urge that the default position should be to mask specific identities unless a compelling reason is put forward not to.

FURTHER READING

Paradigms

Guba, E. G. (Ed.). (1990). *The paradigm dialogue.* Newbury Park, CA: Sage.

Lincoln, Y. S., & Guba, E. G. (1985). *Naturalistic inquiry.* Beverly Hills, CA: Sage. (See Chapters 1-3)

Popkewicz, T. S. (1984). *Paradigm and ideology in educational research: The social functions of the intellectual.* London: Falmer.

Reichardt, C. S., & Rallis, S. F. (Eds.). (1994). The qualitative-quantitative debate: New perspectives. *New Directions for Program Evaluation, 61.* (See entire issue.)

Reflexivity, Subjectivity, and Objectivity

Chase, S. E. (1996). Personal vulnerability and interpretive authority in narrative research. In R. Josselin (Ed.), *Ethics and process in the narrative study of lives* (pp. 45-59). Thousand Oaks, CA: Sage.

Heshuius, L. (1994). Freeing ourselves from objectivity: Managing subjectivity or turning toward a participatory mode of consciousness. *Educational Researcher, 23,* 15-22.

Peshkin, A. (1988). In search of subjectivity—One's own. *Educational Researcher, 17,* 17-21.

Phillips, D. C. (1990). Subjectivity and objectivity: An objective inquiry. In E. W. Eisner & Peshkin, A. (Eds.), *Qualitative inquiry in education: The continuing debate* (pp. 19-37). New York: Teachers College Press.

Ethics

Eisner, E. W. (1991). *The enlightened eye: Qualitative inquiry and the enhancement of educational practice.* New York: Macmillan. (See Chapter 10)

Flinders, D. J. (1992). In search of ethical guidance: Constructing a basis for dialogue. *Qualitative Studies in Education, 5*(2), 101-115.

Punch, M. (1994). Politics and ethics in qualitative research. In N. K. Denzin & Y. S. Lincoln (Eds.), *Handbook of qualitative research* (pp. 83-97). Thousand Oaks, CA: Sage.

Soltis, J. F. (1990). The ethics of qualitative research. In E. W. Eisner & Peshkin, A. (Eds.), *Qualitative inquiry in education: The continuing debate* (pp. 247-257). New York: Teachers College Press.

Trustworthiness

Lincoln, Y. S., & Guba, E. G. (1985). *Naturalistic inquiry.* Beverly Hills, CA: Sage. (See Chapter 11)

CHAPTER THREE

• ◆ •

Planning the Research

⟨━━ ••• ━━⟩

"I actually want to do this study, but I'm not sure that I can do it!" exclaimed Ruth during the break in class. "How can I come up with a reasonable design by next week?"

Marla patted her shoulder and said, "Come on, now. We've read a couple of excerpts from proposals. . . . Remember the one by Fisk? Where she studied all about that chapel? That gives us some idea of what goes into a design."

"Yeah, but that was a big study. I think it was her dissertation. This is just 'small scale!' " grumbled Ruth. "I'm not sure that studying a dissertation helps me at all. What about you, Anthony? What do you think?"

Anthony paused for a moment, then said, "Well, I've been thinking about this. Kent said that we needed to keep these small so they'd be manageable. **Do-able** was the term. We need feedback about whether what we want to do is ok, so I'm going to put something down and see if it flies."

"So, what are you thinking about?"

"I've thought about it some and I'll . . . I'll attend a couple of events at the center, talk to people there, interview the director, and . . . oh, yes, send out some surveys in the community," said Anthony.

"Sounds pretty solid to me, but what do I know! I'm still struggling with how to approach this whole issue of kids with disabilities. I know narrowing it down would help; Kent said to do that. But I'm not sure how to do it. Focus on one kid? On one kind of disability?" Ruth mused.

"Well, think about what grabs you. That's one of the things Kent men-
tioned as being important: that you have to be truly interested in the topic.
That's the **want-to-do-ability**," said Marla. "What do you care about the most?
What matters the most to you about these kids?"

"I'm not sure. It all seems so important," Ruth replied. Ruth seemed
overwhelmed at the prospect of focusing her interests down into a project
that could be completed during the course of the semester. "And I keep
thinking that if I start down one track, I'll miss another important one."

"But wait!" interrupted Anthony. "Kent said that it's important to remember that our projects are . . . What were they called? A 'taste'? Practice? Not
our life's work. Remember the discussion just before the break about having
to let go of some interests? To 'bracket' them? It's not like this is the only
piece of research you'll ever do, right?"

"Well, athletics—sports—are such an important part of my life. I guess I
really want to know—like deep inside their heads—how kids with physical
handicaps think about sports, think about their bodies. I worked with deaf
kids, but I've always wondered about kids who . . . say, are in wheelchairs,"
Ruth responded. "Marla, what are you thinking about?"

"Well, I guess I'm really interested in bodies, too! But for me, it's how
women don't take charge of their own bodies. I remember when I worked
at the clinic two years ago. Women from the barrio would come in for a
prescription—and then we'd never see them again. I often wondered what
happened to them. No . . . I was really worried about what happened to
them," Marla responded.

"But isn't that **their** business?" asked Anthony.

"Sí, it might be, but I heard some of the PAs and social workers talk about
it. So maybe it's worth asking—and looking for answers," Marla replied.

"What are 'PAs'?" asked Anthony.

"Oh, they're physician's assistants—the ones who do just about all the
front-line work in clinics," explained Marla.

"Great!" said Ruth. "You really have something that matters. But I see lots
of ethical stuff there, too, and Kent said to begin thinking about that."

"Ethics. You know I want this work to make a difference. . . . It's a bit scary
to me to think about intervening in women's lives without their participation.
I want to involve the women. I'm really struggling with how to do that,"
answered Marla. "You sound like you have a design, but do you have a
setting?"

"Well, since you asked," chuckled Anthony, "I've decided to take on this
community arts program and how it's working. I'm fascinated by the idea
that it's a grass-roots, community-initiated effort, but I want to know how it's
working . . . **if** it's working. And so do the funders!"

"What do you mean by 'working'?" asked Marla. "Is that the same as what the funders mean?"

"Yeah, I need some idea of what 'working' means. I mean, if I'm going to explore effectiveness, I'll need some idea of what 'effective' means," said Anthony.

"Sure," answered Marla. "You'd have to find out what the goals of the program are, what folks had in mind when they planned it. It matters who had what in mind."

"What do you mean?"

"The community people might have a different idea than the agency that funded it," explained Marla.

*"I know!" Ruth jumped in. "You'd have to find out what the people who proposed it said, and also what they had in their heads as they thought about it. And don't you need to be careful about the politics? What did Kent call it—the **should-do-ability**?"*

"What if I find out that the program directors close doors on me? Or what will you do if the kids won't talk to you?" Anthony wondered. "I see we have to have a plan, but can we change it?"

Professor Kent's assignment to come to the next class with a one- or two-page description of what they hope to do for their small-scale studies puzzles Marla, Anthony, and Ruth. The past few weeks have been enlightening and helpful because they read excerpts from a couple of qualitative studies; they feel somewhat daunted, however, by this new challenge—designing their actual qualitative research studies—no matter how "small scale." Kent underscored how this process is similar to designing a larger, more comprehensive study but on a smaller scale and with certain considerations relaxed.

Our three characters have embarked on the complex process of designing qualitative research projects. It is confusing, exciting, and just plain old hard work. Many considerations go into the preliminary decisions that are represented in a written proposal. Marla, Ruth, and Anthony will consider three: the feasibility of the project—the *do-ability*; their own personal interests—the *want-to-do-ability*; and the significance and ethics of the study—the *should-do-ability* (Marshall & Rossman, 1995). Think of these considerations as points on a triangle. For some studies, feasibility becomes a paramount constraint; for others, it is the ethical issues that may arise. The goal is to find some balance in these considerations so that you can proceed with a manageable project that is sensitive to the ethics and politics of the situation and is sustained by sufficient interest. Interest in the research questions is critical. Even a small-scale project becomes tedious; unless you have a deep concern for the topic, the project will likely flounder. Similarly, designing a project without enough resources to implement it leads to frustration; it, too, may never be completed. Also, the politics or ethical issues you confront may put up barriers. Although you cannot predict all the messy politics or subtle ethical dilemmas that may arise, thinking and talking about them while designing a project can help surface potential thorny issues.

DO-ABILITY

Research projects are implemented in the real world of organizational gatekeepers, participants' schedules, available time (yours and theirs), sufficient resources to buy things such as tape recorders and xeroxing, and your knowledge and skills. Considering all these in designing a study reaps important benefits. Ruth knows children with disabilities from her work at summer camp, but they all attend the School for the Deaf. She will need to find children with physical disabilities. Access is not an issue for Marla, although she will have to think about the officials in the health clinic and their procedures for approving a study, even a small-scale one.[1] Anthony's evaluation project is funded by an outside agency; his worries about do-ability should focus on gaining access to the community members who participate in the arts program. All three have yet to think about details of the costs (time and money) of their projects. As beginners, they have concerns about whether or not they have the knowledge and skills necessary to conduct the research. As they read the methodological literature, practice new skills, and learn as they go along, however, their competence will grow. This competence will serve as a foundation for future projects.

Finally, our characters will have to think carefully about the design for implementing their projects: Elaborate designs (with extensive data gathering efforts) demand heavy allocations of time and, sometimes, money. Their most pressing resource concern will focus on their own time commitments to the projects. As they learn about the time involved in gaining access, scheduling observations and interviews, writing field notes, and analyzing data, they can build realistic designs for projects that are manageable and do-able.

WANT-TO-DO-ABILITY

You need to have a sustaining interest in the topic. Period. All research goes through phases of intense effort and exhilaration coupled with periods of tedium and frustration. Getting through the difficult times requires discipline and commitment. That commitment comes from a deep desire to learn more about the topic and to answer the questions you have posed. Picking a topic just because it seems easy will likely lead to uninspired work. Your interest, often derived from personal experience, is what sustains the work. Our characters already show how they care about their projects: They have experiences and concerns that are reflected in their choices. Ruth is fascinated with how children with physical handicaps deal with sports. Marla's life work focuses on women's health issues. Anthony has developed a strong interest in community involvement in the creative and expressive arts.

Inquiry is shaped by our personal interests and interpreted through our values and politics. When does interest become bias? What about objectivity? All three characters face the challenge of acknowledging their interests and sorting through where their passions for their topics become bias. Ethical and trustworthy researchers, as discussed in Chapter 2, address this issue explicitly. They build in strategies for surfacing potential bias by closely and diligently examining alternative interpretations. They interrogate their emerging findings, asking "What else might explain this?" They try to hold no truths too closely, respecting the notion that all knowledge is conditional and approximate. Also, they are humble in their claims.

SHOULD-DO-ABILITY

Given a feasible design and sufficient interest, ask yourself if the study *should* be conducted. Does it have potential to contribute? Is the topic significant? Could the participants (or you) come to harm? What about the politics in the setting and your own personal politics? Ethics, politics, and importance should be considered at three levels: the personal, the setting and the participants, and social policy.

Marla knows that access to continuous health care is a pressing social problem, especially for women of poverty; therefore, it is a significant social policy issue. Her personal political beliefs, moreover, demand that she conduct a study that focuses on women and that is participatory and involving rather than detached. Her ethical concerns may well focus on the subtle undercurrents of power and prejudice that shape the culture of health care for women. Anthony will have to think about the potential backlash of conducting a mandated evaluation: The politics of the funding agency will have to be balanced against participants' interests. At a personal level, he will have to ask himself if he feels he ought to conduct this project and can do so in an ethical manner. Ruth has a commitment to children with special needs. She is acutely aware of the prejudice and suspicion surrounding physical disabilities. The political and economic issues of access and equity in schools sit high on public policy agendas.

These are the kinds of considerations that need to be addressed in thinking about a research project. One difficulty is that potential "should" issues cannot be forecast with perfect clarity, nor can all the costs associated with a project be predicted. Think about them; talk about them. Consider alternatives. Holding these considerations in mind as you conceptualize and design a study is crucial.

WHAT IS A RESEARCH PROPOSAL?

Think of a proposal as an initial plan to guide your thinking and actions as you conduct the project. The conceptual portion keeps you grounded in specific questions; the design and methodology focus your actions in the field. Keep in mind, however, that qualitative research is uniquely suited to discovery and exploration. If you think of inquiry as a journey, the proposal is your itinerary. You know the general destination, but the precise route you take may change. Retaining flexibility in the proposal and as you conduct the study fosters the responsiveness that is fundamental to qualitative research.

A research proposal consists of two essential elements: **what** the researcher wants to learn more about (the study's conceptual framework) and **how** this will be implemented (its design and methodology).[2] These elements need to be well integrated and congruent in their epistemological assumptions (see Chapter 2). Imagine the conceptual framework as a funnel; the large end describes the general phenomenon—the topic—and articulates the theoretical perspective; the smaller end describes the specific project proposed. The design and methodology section then stipulates how the study will be implemented: where and what you will do, and how you will do it. Proposals for qualitative research typically have the following sections:

Introduction
Conceptual Framework
    Topic and Research Problem
    Purpose
    Significance
    Overview Questions and Subquestions
    Delimitations and Limitations
Design and Methodology
    Overall Approach and Rationale
    Site or Population Selection
    Data Gathering Procedures
    Data Analysis Procedures
    Trustworthiness
    Personal Biography of the Researcher
    Ethical Considerations
Appendixes

The conceptual portion describes the topic and how it is framed, the research problem to be investigated, the general and specific questions, and the potential significance of the study. In this section, you place boundaries around the study (delimitations) and discuss the study's limitations. Throughout, you define important concepts and terms, relying on relevant literature to support points, show gaps in that literature, and establish the importance of the topic. The particular literatures establish the framework that grounds the study.

The proposal's design and methodology section stipulates how you will gather data to address the research questions. This section details the overall approach to the study (also called the design), processes for site and population selection, gaining access, gathering and analyzing data, ensuring trustworthiness, and involving participants, if relevant, along the way. Here you also describe relevant aspects of your personal biography and your stance toward research (your epistemologic assumptions) and the topic. As you should throughout the proposal, here you also retain flexibility because you may alter the specifics of data gathering once the project is under way. Making sound *field decisions* is integral to learning how to do qualitative research; therefore, the proposal stipulates solid, albeit tentative, plans for implementing the study.

Note that a proposal represents *decisions*—or choices—you have made that a particular theoretical framework and design and methodology will help you generate data appropriate for responding to your research questions. These decisions are based on complex reasoning and consideration of a number of research questions, possible frameworks, alternative designs and methodologies, as well as the do-ability, want-to-do-ability, and should-do-ability. Considering all these captures the complex, iterative process of designing a qualitative study: weaving back and forth between possible research questions, frameworks, approaches, methods, and related considerations. As you consider alternative designs and methods (e.g., in-depth interviews and participant observation), the research questions shift. As you refine the research questions, fruitful and appropriate designs become more obvious. All this should be bounded by thinking through issues of feasibility, resources, interest, ethics, and politics. Your job is to decide what will work well, given the unfolding questions to be pursued and the potential constraints. Easy, right?

Building these two sections of a proposal requires that you hold possible choices for both elements in your mind *at the same time.* This early conceptualization and design work is by far the most challenging and rigorous of the entire process of proposal development. It is nonlinear and difficult. It is hard work and will stretch you in important ways. As you consider alternatives, you may find guidance in some of the qualitative research traditions—that is, the approaches and designs that qualitative researchers have established over the years. Although there are many specific traditions, some linked to social science disciplines, we discuss three as the archetypes of qualitative research.

MAJOR QUALITATIVE RESEARCH GENRES

Qualitative approaches to inquiry represent a lively and flourishing community of traditions. They are related, although sometimes the resemblance is hard to detect; they often bicker among themselves, seeking to distinguish one from another along subtle dimensions. We have chosen to discuss three broad approaches or genres, ones that are frequently found in the literature: ethnographies, case studies, and phenomenological studies. Each can be framed by interpretivist or more critical and postmodern assumptions. Recall the discussion in Chapter 2 on assumptions about inquiry and society. What we call **traditional** qualitative research holds interpretivist assumptions: Knowledge is viewed as subjectivist; the researcher should engage directly with participants to understand their worldviews; and society is generally viewed as orderly. **Critical and postmodern** assumptions[3] also view knowledge as subjectivist but, in contrast, view society as essentially conflictual and oppressive. These assumptions critique historic knowledge production (i.e., research) because it privileges social science knowledge rather than practical knowledge. Inquiry is viewed as leading to radical change or emancipation from oppressive social structures. We elaborate this perspective briefly in the following section.

Critical and Postmodern Assumptions

As the 20th century draws to a close, traditional social science has come under increasing scrutiny and attack as those espousing critical and postmodern perspectives challenge objectivist assumptions and traditional norms for the conduct of research. Central to this attack are four interrelated notions: (a) Research fundamentally involves issues of power; (b) the research report is not transparent but rather it is authored by a raced, gendered, classed, and politically oriented individual; (c) race, class, and gender[4] are crucial for understanding experience; and (d) historic, traditional research has silenced members of oppressed and marginalized groups.

One implication of this critique is that we, the community of qualitative researchers, can no longer assume that we write up our research in an antiseptic, distanced way. Reflexivity has become central to the qualitative project, demanding that we examine the complex interplay of our own personal biography, power and status, interactions with participants, and written word. We examined this concept closely in Chapter 2; for now, it is important to remember that the critique assumes that all inquiry is embedded in power relationships and privileged knowledge. The project of the more critical and postmodern perspectives is to interrupt the traditional conduct of research and report writing and to place at the center considerations of how we—the researchers—represent the other—the participants in the inquiry. We argue that these postmodern notions can shape inquiry in any of the three major genres. Although we fear that displaying the genres in a table may appear to oversimplify, we suspect that some graphic representation might help (Table 3.1).

Ethnographies

Ethnographies are the hallmark of qualitative research, derived from the disciplines of cultural anthropology and qualitative sociology. Central to ethnographic work is the concept of culture—a vague and complex term that describes the way things are and prescribes the ways people should act; it thus determines what is good and true (Rossman, Corbett, & Firestone, 1988). Culture captures the beliefs and values shared by members of a group that guide their actions and their understandings of those actions. Ethnographers often focus closely on the face-to-face interactions of members of a cultural group. They are interested in how interactions shape meaning in particular organizational settings and focus on fine-grained interactions, often speech acts.

Ethnographers study cultural groups or communities through ethnography or participant observation (the hallmark methodology). This work entails long-term, sustained participant observation in an intact cultural group. Data gathering techniques are multiple and flexible, typically relying on observations, informal interviews, and the researcher's own experience of events and processes. The ethnographer seeks to understand insiders' views of their lives—the *emic* view—and render an account of that cultural worldview.

TABLE 3.1 Genres of Qualitative Research

Genre	Goal	Mode and Methods	Traditional	Critical or Postmodern
Ethnographies	Seek to understand the culture of people or places	Long-term, sustained engagement; multiple, flexible techniques	How do people's beliefs and values guide their actions and their understanding of those actions?	How do the actions of one group affect the beliefs and actions of other, often oppressed, groups?
Case studies	Seek to understand a larger phenomenon through intensive study of one specific instance	Descriptive, heuristic, and inductive; multiple techniques	What is going on in this case? What are the key actors doing? Why are they doing it?	How do the patterns of action in this case affect power relationships? Do they perpetuate a dominating status quo?
Phenomenological studies	Seek to understand the lived experience of a small number of people	In-depth, exploratory, and prolonged engagement; iterative interviews	What has this person experienced? How does this person understand his or her experiences?	What do the stories people construct about their lives mean? How does their articulation of those stories empower them?

Sociologists also use the ethnographic method with specific emphasis on rules, roles, and relationships within groups, organizations, or social movements. Long-term immersion in the setting is also used as the researcher discovers and interprets the patterned meaning of organizational life. Qualitative sociologists link their work to recurring sociological topics that include political processes and institutions; urban and community studies; stages of life; criminology; organizations and occupations; and medical sociology.

Critical ethnographies take a radical perspective, explicitly examining issues of power and oppression in social settings. They pursue emancipatory uses and the radical change of oppressive social structures. The theoretical framework for critical ethnography is critical theory, drawing on Marxist and neo-Marxist thought, whereas the methodology used is conventional ethnographic research. This perspective assumes a conflict model of society, one in which the powerful groups oppress and dominate those less powerful. Critical ethnographers object to the notion of a value-free science and see a dialectic relationship between inquiry and action or theory and practice.

Although differing strands can be identified, most critical ethnography considers research to be a process of examining the dynamic interplay of culture, knowledge, and action. They link key findings to issues of social power and control. Key concepts are *reproduction* and *resistance:* Institutions and relationships are structured to reproduce the distribution of power based on income, race, and gender; less powerful social actors unwittingly participate in or resist the reproduction of class-, race-, and gender-based hierarchies. The researcher's narrative attempts to be empowering by placing at the center the voices of the less powerful and through advocacy for a particular group. Direct action is not necessarily taken by the researcher. Methodologically, critical ethnographers gather data in ways similar to their less critically oriented colleagues; the lens for analysis, however, is distinctly different.

Our Characters' Choices

Anthony decides to design a mini-ethnographic evaluation (mini because, as you recall, these are to be completed during one semester) that takes an in-depth look at the culture of the community arts program. He will explore the subtle, taken-for-granted values and beliefs about participation, aesthetic standards, and artistic expression. He chooses long-term observation in the center as his primary way of gathering data. He will focus on the culture of the arts program—the patterned ways of determining activities, soliciting community input, and encouraging participation. Anthony could also ally himself with the critical ethnographic approach should he become committed to community activism in the arts and to promoting substantial change in access to artistic expression.

Marla considers ethnography but decides not to focus on cultural beliefs about serving poor women because such a design would be too labor-intensive to accomplish during a single semester, given the complexities of her topic, the context, and her commitment to participation. At this point, she is more interested in the experiences of individual women. She decides to consider some other qualitative genre.

Ruth's interest in children with physical disabilities could be conceptualized and designed as an ethnography. Asking questions about the subtle beliefs and values surrounding disability and children with disabilities would suggest a focus on their culture. In-depth and long-term participant observation in schools or day care centers could result in a rich ethnographic description. As Ruth's interests evolve, however, she finds herself more captured by the stories of the children themselves. Although she considered an ethnography, her interests in the individual children and their lived experiences suggest some other tradition.

Case Studies

Similar to ethnographies, case studies are explorations of a single entity or phenomenon (an event, process, organization, group, or individual) that is "an instance drawn from a class" (Adelman, Jenkins, & Kemmis, 1983, p. 3). They seek to understand a larger phenomenon through close examination of a specific case and therefore focus on the particular. Case studies are descriptive, holistic, heuristic, and inductive. Case studies do not, however, necessarily link to cultural anthropology or qualitative sociology as do ethnographies.[5] Many are organizational studies; others, with psychological roots, focus on individuals.

Case studies are particularly useful for their rich description and heuristic value. Description illustrates the complexities of a situation, depicts how the passage of time has shaped events, provides vivid material, and presents differing perspectives or opinions. By providing detail and complexity, case studies illuminate the reader's understanding of the setting or event, thereby extending comprehension of some complex set of events or circumstances.

Case studies typically rely on a variety of techniques for data gathering and are conducted over a period of time. Although many researchers associate case studies exclusively with qualitative methods, such need not be the case: Case studies may rely on questionnaires, archival records, or psychological testing in addition to interviewing, observing, and analyzing documents. Just as with ethnographies, case studies are methodologically eclectic.

Critical case studies are grounded in a critique of existing social structures and patterns. They assume theoretically that oppression and domination characterize the setting and seek to uncover how patterns of action perpetuate the status quo.

Our Characters' Choices

Marla and her participants choose to design the inquiry as self-reflective case studies of their use of health services. The questions they begin to pose include the following: What are our health needs? How do we seek care? How do we interact with the health care system? How do we view doctors and nurses? Are there other sources of health care we turn to? Do the people in the system understand our rights and responsibilities? The team adopts a critical perspective, specifically a feminist one. This perspective leads them to explore the ways the health care system is structured patriarchically, ways they feel devalued and depersonalized, and how they might participate in sustaining these structures. Marla, as one member of the team, could adopt a class-based perspective, seeking to understand how poverty shapes these women's use of health care.

Ruth could do a case study of a day care center that includes two or three children who use wheelchairs. This is, in fact, where she begins her design thinking: locate a center, identify key actors, gather data, and write about this instance of an inclusive program. Should she have continued with a case study, she would have framed it as an organizational study and defined the parameters of the program; mapped participation, administrative structures, and activities; and surveyed and interviewed a sample of staff, children, and families. Ruth is, however, much more interested in the life stories of the children than she is in the organization or the program, so she frames her work as a phenomenological study.

Phenomenological Studies

A third genre that our characters might consider is a phenomenological study, through which the lived experience of a small number of people is investigated. Extensive and prolonged engagement with individuals typifies this work, often through a series of in-depth, exploratory, intensive interviews. The researcher seeks to understand the deep meaning of individual's experiences and how he or she articulates these experiences.

Phenomenology is a tradition in German philosophy with a focus on the essence of lived experience. Those engaged in phenomenological research focus in-depth on the meaning of a particular aspect of experience, assuming that through dialogue and reflection the quintessential meaning of the experience will be revealed. Language is viewed as the primary symbol system through which meaning is both constructed and conveyed (Holstein & Gubrium, 1994, p. 263). The purposes of phenomenologic inquiry are description, interpretation, and critical self-reflection into the "world as world" (Van Manen, 1990, p. 5). Central are the notions of intentionality and caring: The researcher inquires about the essence of lived experience.

Phenomenologic in-depth interviewing has received increasing attention as a qualitative genre. A deep interest in the substantive topic of inquiry is presumed and is often referred to as a process of *epoche* in which the researcher continuously engages in critical self-reflection about the topic.[6] Seidman (1991) advocates a series of three long, iterative interviews, each with a specific purpose. The first inquires into the interviewee's history and life story. The second orients both the researcher and the interviewee to the specific topic of interest. The third then draws these together in a reflective dialogue about the meaning of the interviewee's experience in light of his or her history.

Although not strictly derived from phenomenology, we include narrative research here because it has become increasingly popular and seeks to describe the meaning of experience for individuals as they construct stories (narratives) about their lives. Narrative research is interdisciplinary in nature and covers a wide range of specific approaches, including life histories, biographies and autobiographies, oral histories, and personal narratives. All hold in common the assumption that storytelling is integral to the understanding of our lives and that it is ubiquitous. This, in and of itself, makes narratives worthy of inquiry.

Narrative research focuses on the structure and content of stories people tell that help them make sense of their lived experiences. Some approaches are technical, searching for the sociolinguistic devices that the narrator uses; others focus on the flow of life events and their meaning, as constructed by the narrator. Methodologically, narrative research entails long, extended interviews with the individual(s) of interest. In the case of life histories and biographies, other sources of data may be introduced into the written report. Some approaches are collaborative, with researcher and narrator coconstructing the final document. In others, the researcher acts traditionally, deriving data from the interview settings and writing the final report. When framed by feminist or critical theory, the purpose may become emancipatory.

Our Characters' Choices

Ruth's choice of a phenomenological study leads her to explore the meaning of bodiedness and participation in sports for children in wheelchairs. She frames her study as evolving over time to capture the lived experience of disability, the meaning sports take on for the children, and how this shapes their understanding of themselves. She will use phenomenological in-depth, iterative interviewing with three children who use wheelchairs.

If Marla were working within the phenomenologic genre, she would have entered the realm of the deeply private experience of being a poor woman trying to access sustained health care. She would have interviewed three or four women over several months following the three-interview format. Her purpose would have been to understand the experience of living in poverty and how each woman's personal history shaped the meaning she brings to that experience. Questions would have focused on the meaning of health, disease, poverty, and interactions with health care professionals.

Our characters' thinking and understanding of qualitative research is growing. They have some notions of the shape of their projects and the genres to which their studies best link. They have considered alternatives and thought about the feasibility, ethics, and politics of their projects. Now, if needed, they could develop full research proposals, although Kent, their professor, does not require this. If, however, they were pursuing funding from an agency or writing theses or dissertations, they would have to elaborate their thinking in a formal proposal. The sections of such a proposal are presented in the following section.

CONCEPTUAL FRAMEWORK

The first major chunk of a research proposal is the conceptual framework.[7] Here, you establish the "what" of the study: what it is about, what literatures it relates to, and what it proposes to study. Throughout, relevant literature is woven into the discussion to provide substantiation for points, clarify logic, define concepts, and justify decisions. What follows are guidelines for sections of the conceptual framework. Keep in mind that you need not label each section; some may be short with only a paragraph or two. We list the sections separately to be sure that you consider each topic, and we call on our characters to provide examples where useful. First, however, we comment on the various uses of related literature in a proposal.

Use of the Literature

Previous research and theoretical writings ground your study in the ongoing conversation about the topic. They also establish the particular framework that guides your understanding of the topic. In discussing the literature, you share with the reader the results of previous studies that are related to yours. Also, you show gaps in that literature to which your study can contribute. Where do you discuss all this? It depends.

Traditionally, reviews of the literature are presented in a separate section of the proposal. Sadly, these reviews are often lifeless and read as dull intellectual exercises. A more lively presentation weaves the literature throughout a proposal, drawing on previous research or theoretical concepts to establish what your study is about and how it is likely to contribute to the ongoing dialogue. Weave this discussion into the sections of the proposal that present the topic, the research problem, or issue, and establish the study's significance. Through this discussion, you build a framework that guides your work.

Some qualitative researchers argue that the literature should not be extensively reviewed at the proposal stage; it might contaminate the inductive, open-ended nature of qualitative inquiry. We hold a different view. Discussing the literature helps you establish your credibility as a researcher, indicating that you are familiar with the conversation in your topic area. Although extensive reviews are not necessary, some discussion is crucial for framing the study. Try for creative, inductive use of previous research and theory to build a case for your study. Use that literature throughout the conceptual portion of the proposal.

Introduction

The introduction to a qualitative research proposal does just that: It introduces the study to the reader and the reader to the study. This section discusses the larger topic that the study relates to and the problem or issue that it will attempt to address. It describes the focus of the proposed research and briefly forecasts the design and methodology. This section also identifies an audience for the document by articulating who might find the study of interest or value. Finally, the introduction provides a transition to the more detailed discussions that follow.

The introduction establishes the credibility of the project and should evoke the reader's interest. Write it with "hooks" that capture the reader's attention. Begin with a sentence that stimulates interest and conveys an issue that is intriguing. For example, Ruth might write: "Children in wheelchairs can jump." Marla could begin with, "Women living in poverty have limited access to sustained health care." Anthony might begin his introduction with, "A community can bring the arts to everyone." Beginning this way provides a succinct statement of the larger topic or issue that the study will address and engages a broad readership.

Some find it easier to write this section last. Sometimes it is difficult to know just where the document will wind up; beginning at the very beginning can be daunting. If you choose to write it early on, be prepared to revise it substantially once the other sections are written.

This is also where you establish your *voice*, or authorial point of view. Different disciplines (audiences) have different norms governing what voice is appropriate for scholarly writing. The choice of voice depends on the focus of action. The first person (I and we) places agency directly with the author. Although we cannot document this empirically, it is our impression that disciplines amenable to qualitative studies encourage the more literary style of the first person. In this case, the writer takes the stand that she is telling the story and has a direct relationship with the action. One danger of writing in the first person is that the author's story might dominate the text. Using the second person—you—engages the reader directly with the text. The third person voice—he, she, and they—is a general construction and shifts attention to the topic of inquiry.[8] Aim for the active rather than passive voice. Use verbs to connote agency and action.[9]

Having offered the reader an overview of the study and established the voice of the text, next describe the general topic and define the research problem or issue that your study will address. This section is the heart of the conceptual framework in which the major theoretical and empirical[10] literatures are identified and discussed and in which important boundaries are placed around the study. Recall that a discussion of the general topic, the issue or problem of the study, research questions, and significance are all interrelated. Although we discuss these in separate sections, you will need to establish the organization in ways that suit your writing style and the development of the overall logic surrounding the study.

The Topic

Topics are what we are interested in. In the case of our characters, these are women's access to health care, children with disabilities, and community arts programs. Topics may come from personal interests or from theory, research, social and political circumstances, and situations of practice. In the beginning, it can be useful simply to name your topic. Ask yourself to describe your interest by filling in the blank in the following sentence: "I want to learn about _____." (adapted from Booth, Colomb, & Williams, 1995, Chapter 3). Next, narrow down the topic by questioning it. Ask the following: What are the component parts of the topic? How do these parts relate to one another? and How does the topic relate to a larger system? Anthony asks about the organizational elements of the arts program, how these interact with one another, how the program operates, and how it fits into the larger community structures.

You might also interrogate the topic by viewing it as something dynamic and changing: What is the history here? What were its beginnings and where is it now? Marla could ask about the history of access to health care in satellite clinics in poor areas: When and where were they first established? Who was involved? What were the early political obstacles?

Further refine the topic by asking about its categories and characteristics: How does it vary? Along what dimensions? How are cases of it different from and similar to one another? Anthony could ask how typical this arts program is, what defines it as unique, and how is it like other community-oriented programs.

With a more complex and elaborated understanding of the topic, you can review the literature to establish what is known, what are the unanswered questions, and what are the recurring issues that research could address. By questioning the topic, you have generated a raft of leads to pursue. Your own interests will narrow these as a guide for reading the literature. This reading establishes a research problem or issue, one that you can address through a qualitative study.

Statement of the Research Problem or Issue

Beginning researchers often confuse a general topic they are interested in with a research problem or issue. Research problems derive from general topics but focus on questions in the literature or recurring issues of practice. This section of the conceptual framework identifies and describes some problem situation or issue that a study can address. Problem or issue statements often focus on what is not yet known or understood well. Embed the problem in the ongoing dialogue in the literature, as previously discussed. This sets your study within a tradition of inquiry and a context of related studies and serves five purposes. First, this discussion establishes the theoretical framework that guides your study. Second, you demonstrate that you are knowledgeable about the topic and the intellectual traditions that surround and support the study. Third, you reveal gaps in that literature that your study can begin to address. Fourth, this discussion leads toward the general research questions that your study will pursue. Finally, you articulate a sound rationale or need to conduct the study.

At this point, you might move to a more precise description of the problem or issue by elaborating the topic question with an indirect question: "I want to learn about women's health care to find out who/what/when/where/whether/why/how _____" (adapted from Booth et al., 1995, Chapter 3). Marla might write several of these statements, giving her a range of questions to pursue. She would read the related literature with these questions in mind to decide which have potential for study and which she is really interested in.

Next, try to put forward a rationale for your study: "I want to learn about women's health care to find out what the perspectives of poor women are in order to understand/contribute to how/why/what _____" (adapted from Booth et al., 1995, Chapter 3). By disciplining yourself to describe what you want to understand more fully and how you want the study to contribute, you are establishing a rationale for its conduct. Marla's sentence reads as follows:

> I want to learn about women's health care to find out what the perspectives of poor women are in order to improve their access to sustained care.

Anthony's reads:

> I want to judge the effectiveness of a community arts program in increasing the participation of community members in the arts in order to inform decision making by program staff and the funding agent.

Ruth's statement is as follows:

> I want to learn about the lived experiences of children with physical disabilities, particularly the essence of their understanding of their bodies in relation to sports, in order to enhance society's understanding and appreciation.

Purpose

A statement of purpose captures, in a sentence or paragraph, the essence of the study. It should describe the intent of the study, ground it in a specific qualitative genre, discuss the central concept or idea, provide a general definition of that concept, and stipulate the unit of analysis

(Creswell, 1994). Traditionally, methodologists have noted four possible purposes for research: *to explore, explain, describe, or predict.* Of these, prediction does not fit the interpretive paradigm; qualitative researchers do not use it. The others, however, are all relevant and useful. To these three, we would add some synonyms such as *to understand, to develop, or to discover.* Notable in its absence, however, is a reference to *empowerment* or emancipation—those purposes consistent with radical assumptions. To stipulate empowerment as the purpose of a study, however, creates some tricky cognitive dissonance. A researcher cannot mandate or stipulate empowerment per se; he or she can, however, discuss the purpose of a study as creating an environment or set of circumstances in which participants may become empowered. The difference in language is subtle but important: An ethical radical paradigm researcher knows the boundaries of empowerment. Although empowerment may be a goal and the ultimate use of the project, its achievement is serendipitous.

A discussion of the study's purpose should convey the emergent nature of qualitative inquiry, thereby preserving the right to make field decisions. The purpose should also capture participants' experiences as the central focus of the study. This strategy reminds the reader that the study is quintessentially qualitative and seeks to explore (explain, describe, and understand) the emic perspective. Here, too, mention what is called the *unit of analysis*—this is the level of action you have decided to focus on. Ask yourself what you want to be able to talk about at the end of the study—for example, individuals, a group, a process, or an organization. This focus stipulates where the data gathering efforts will go.

Creswell (1994) offers the following useful "script" to help you develop a purpose statement:

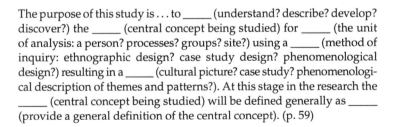

The purpose of this study is . . . to _____ (understand? describe? develop? discover?) the _____ (central concept being studied) for _____ (the unit of analysis: a person? processes? groups? site?) using a _____ (method of inquiry: ethnographic design? case study design? phenomenological design?) resulting in a _____ (cultural picture? case study? phenomenological description of themes and patterns?). At this stage in the research the _____ (central concept being studied) will be defined generally as _____ (provide a general definition of the central concept). (p. 59)

Although we might critique this long and unwieldy sentence on literary grounds, practice using it to get clear about the purpose of your study, its central concept, and overall approach. Marla develops a purpose statement as follows:

> The purpose of this study is to describe the perspectives on access to sustained health care for women of poverty using an action research case study design. The study will result in mini descriptive case studies of the five women collaborators. At this stage in the research, sustained health care is defined as continuous preventive health maintenance; access is defined as regular appointments at a clinic.

Through this exercise, Marla stipulates that she is focusing on individual women and that the purpose of her study is to explore and describe their experiences with health care.

Ruth's purpose statement becomes the following:

> The purpose of this study is to uncover the deep inner meaning of bodiedness for children with physical handicaps using a phenomenological design. The study will result in rich cultural description through stories of these children's relationships with sports. The central concept of bodiedness will be explicated through the children's words.

Anthony's statement is as follows:

> The purpose of this study is to describe and evaluate the effectiveness of bringing arts to members of the community using a mini-ethnographic design. The study will result in an evaluation report to inform decision makers and funders. Bringing arts to the community means providing actual, usable opportunities for people who live in the neighborhood to both appreciate and create various forms of art.

Significance

In discussing the topic, research problem or issue, and the purpose of the study, you are implicitly or explicitly stating why doing this particular study is important and how it may contribute. The topic discussion establishes that this is a worthy area for investigation, as does the problem statement. Formal proposals, however, typically include a section in which the potential significance of the study is more fully detailed.

Reasoning that the study is significant and should be conducted entails building an argument that your work will contribute to one or more of the following domains: scholarly research and literature, recurring social policy issues, concerns of practice, and interests of the participants. Your challenge is to situate your study as addressing a particular, important problem. How you define the research topic and problem shape the study's significance.

The conceptual discussion emphasizes the contributions to the relevant domains. For example, a study of the integration of children with disabilities into the regular classroom could be significant for both policy and practice. Framing the study as a policy study requires that the problem be situated in national and state education policy on special education. Alternatively, framing the study as most significant for practice would necessitate a problem definition focused on restructuring schools to be more inclusive or on classroom practice to support more diverse students in the regular classroom. Either frame is legitimate and defensible; the researcher identifies where the study is likely to contribute the most.

If you are preparing a proposal for a funding agency, you should be sure that statements about the project's significance match the needs and priorities of the agency. The foundation that takes pride in funding action projects will want to see how the proposed research will directly help people or change a problematic situation. If you are seeking funds from an agency with goals of expanding knowledge and theory (e.g., the National Science Foundation), however, you would want to emphasize undeveloped or unsolved theoretical puzzles to demonstrate the significance of the research.

In summary, the significance section responds to the following questions: Who has an interest in this domain of inquiry? How will this new research add to theory, policy, and practice in this area? and How might it be of benefit to the participants and therefore of significance to them?

Overview Questions and Subquestions

Research questions are critically important for guiding your work. Recall that the entire conceptual framework keeps you grounded as you gather data. Stipulating general overview—grand tour—questions and related subquestions is especially useful for delimiting the study. The process of doing qualitative research often raises more questions than it answers; the road you take has many intersections, each more intriguing with possibility than the last. Pursuing the inviting backroad (exploring the unknown) is what qualitative research is all about, but taking each and every turn can paralyze the project. Reminding yourself of the questions driving the study helps keep you on track.

Frame the study as responding to one or two general questions with a reasonable number (e.g., four or five) subquestions to refine the general ones. Questions should be nondirectional; they should not imply cause and effect or suggest measurement. Often, when first posing research questions, beginners ask quantitative questions masquerading as qualitative ones. Beware the question that asks about influence, impact, or amount (e.g., how, or how much, does whole language instruction influence student reading achievement?). Also expect that your questions will evolve as the project unfolds. Because qualitative research refines and redefines as it emerges, you should expect change. Keep the questions open-ended to foster exploration and discovery. Table 3.2 provides some preliminary questions to stimulate your thinking.

As Marla and the women in her study work on the conceptual framework, their general question becomes, "How do we feel about using health services?" They refine this with three subquestions: "What are the dynamics of the clinic?" "How do we feel we are treated as patients?" and "What alternative sources of health care do we rely on?" These subquestions capture Marla's interests in the organization and delivery of health care to poor women, the women's personal perspectives on health care providers, and sources of alternative medicine that these women may (or may not) rely on to ensure their own health. They will most likely refine these questions as the project unfolds and as staff and community members become more involved, but these questions serve as a beginning.

Anthony's overview question is "How effective is this program in bringing arts to people living in the neighborhood?" His subquestions are "Who attends events at the arts center?" "How do they respond to the various activities?" "Who participates in the creative workshops?" and "What are outcomes of the workshops?"

Ruth's general question is "What deep meaning do children in wheelchairs make of their bodiedness and of athleticism?" Because Ruth's

TABLE 3.2 Generating Research Questions by Genre and Strategy

| | Genre | | |
Strategy	Ethnography	Phenomenological Study	Case Study
Evaluation or policy study	What is the culture of the program? How do participants or stakeholders define success or effectiveness? Are these definitions congruent with effective or exemplary programs?	What meaning do participants in the program make of their experiences? How do these contribute to the functioning of the program?	What are the different components of the program? How do they contribute to its effectiveness? What is this program an instance of?
Descriptive cultural study	What do participants believe? What are their values? What is tacit in the setting? How do these beliefs and values shape their understandings and actions?	What is the lived experience of the individual or group? What is the essence of that experience?	What are the different meaning-perspectives of participants in the program? How do these interact with one another? What values and beliefs are apparent in actions and interactions?
Action research	What deeply held values and beliefs guide actions, interactions, and activities? What difference does changing actions, activities, or interactions make to the group or the individual?	What is the meaning of actions, activities, or interactions for the group or the individual? What does changing actions and activities mean?	What are the recurring actions of the individual or group? Does changing them make a difference?

83

study is so closely linked to what she learns, she is reluctant to specify subquestions before talking with the children. Her reliance on the grand tour question is greater than that of her colleagues.

Limitations and Delimitations

Limitations and delimitations of the study place some boundaries around it and set some conditions. These are the reservations and qualifications inherent in any research. You have delimited the study throughout the conceptual discussion by describing what the study is and how it is framed; this implies what the study is not. Limitations, however, derive from the design and methods and help contextualize the study. They stipulate the weaknesses of this study, thereby encouraging the reader to judge it with these limitations in mind. Limitations arise from, among others, small sample size, use of one technique for gathering data, and selection procedures. We urge you not to elaborate these in too much detail. Rather, this discussion serves to remind you, as well as the reader, that no studies are perfect, that findings are tentative and conditional, that knowledge is elusive and approximate, and that our claims should be humble, given the extraordinary complexity of the social world we want to learn more about.

DESIGN AND METHODOLOGY

The design and methodology section of the proposal serves three major purposes. First, it presents a plan—the road map—for the conduct of the study. Second, it demonstrates to the reader that you are capable of conducting the study. Third, it preserves the design flexibility that is a hallmark of qualitative methods. Achieving this latter purpose is often the most challenging.

Typically, seven topics comprise this section: the overall approach and rationale, site and population selection, data collection procedures, data analysis strategy, trustworthiness, personal biography of the researcher, and ethical considerations. Woven into discussion of these topics are the twin challenges of needing to present a clear, do-able plan balanced by the necessity of maintaining flexibility. Several of these topics we have discussed already; others will be detailed in subsequent chapters. Three were discussed in Chapter 2: trustworthiness, personal biography of the researcher, and ethical considerations. Data collection is described in detail in Chapters 4, 5, and 6, and data analysis is described in Chapter 7. In the remainder of this chapter, we discuss overall approach and site or population selection. We also briefly discuss data management and analysis.

Overall Strategy and Rationale

Although general acceptance of qualitative inquiry is currently widespread, you will usually find it necessary to provide a rationale for the specific genre guiding your study. The most compelling argument is to stress the unique strengths of interpretive research in general and the specific approach to which your study links. This is especially important for studies that are exploratory or descriptive, that assume the value of context and setting, that search for a deeper understanding of the participants' lived experiences, or all three. Explicating the logical and compelling connections—the epistemological integrity—between the research questions, the genre, and the methods can be quite convincing. Although the range of possible qualitative genres is quite large, we have focused on three. As our characters depicted, linking your study to one of these approaches depends on the focus for the research, the problem or issue to be addressed, the research questions, and considerations of do-ability. Remember to explicitly reserve the right to modify aspects of the research design as the study unfolds.

Site or Population Selection

Once the overall approach and a supporting rationale have been presented, the proposal outlines the setting or population of interest and plans for more specific selection of people, places, and events. Here you provide the reader with a sense of the scope of your study and whether the intensity and amount of data you can generate will help you fully respond to the research questions.

You cannot gather data intensively and in-depth about all possible participants, events, or places. You make choices. The first and most global decision—choosing the setting, population, or phenomenon of interest—is fundamental to the entire study. This early, significant decision shapes all your subsequent ones and should be described and justified clearly.

Some research is site specific. Anthony's decision to focus on a specific setting (e.g., the community-based arts program in Portland, Oregon) is a fairly constrained choice; the study is defined by and intimately linked to that place. If he chose to study a particular population (participants in community-based arts programs), the study is somewhat less constrained: It could be conducted in more places than Portland. A decision to study the phenomenon of community involvement in the arts is even less constrained by either place or population. If your study is of a specific program, organization, place, or region, your reader needs some detail regarding the setting. Also, you should provide a rationale that outlines why this specific setting is more appropriate than others.

The ideal site is where (a) entry is possible; (b) there is a rich mix of the processes, people, programs, interactions, structures of interest, or all of these; (c) you are likely to be able to build strong relations with the participants; and (d) ethical and political considerations are not overwhelming, at least initially. Although this ideal is seldom attained, your proposal should describe what makes the selection of this particular site especially sound. A site may be well suited for its representativeness, interest, and the range of examples of the phenomena under study, but if you cannot get beyond the front desk, your study will be thin. Similarly, if you feel very uncomfortable or endangered in a site, or if you believe the participants may be particularly uncomfortable or come to harm, reconsider doing the study.

When the focus of the study is on a particular population, as in Marla's case with poor women and the health care system and Ruth's on children with disabilities, you should present a strategy for selecting representatives of that population. For example, in a dissertation study of forced terminations of psychotherapy, Kahn's (1992) strategy was to post notices in local communities asking for participants. Her dissertation committee had lively discussions at her proposal hearing about the feasibility of this strategy. When we were given assurances that this had worked in the past as a way of soliciting participants, we agreed; the strategy was ultimately successful.

Data Gathering Procedures

Once you have made the initial decision to focus on a specific site, population, or phenomenon, waves of subsequent decisions cascade. The proposal describes the plan that will guide decisions in the field. Decisions about selecting people (to interview) or events (to observe) develop concurrently with decisions about the specific data collection methods you will use. You should think these through in advance. These plans, however, are often changed, given the realities of field research, but at the proposal stage they demonstrate that you have thought through some of the complexities of the setting and have made some initial judgments about how to deploy your time. Such plans also indicate that you have considered the resource demands of specific decisions as well as the ethical and political considerations in the setting.

As Chapters 4 and 5 will detail, the primary ways of gathering qualitative data are through interviewing, observing, and reviewing material culture (documents, artifacts, records, decorations, and so on). Ethnographies and case studies rely on multiple ways of gathering data, whereas phenomenological studies typically use a series of in-depth interviews. Your decisions about what techniques to use and with how many people, from what role groups, for how long, and how many times are crucial design and resource decisions.

Consider Anthony's study. The elements of a community-based program are many and complex. Because Anthony interrogated his topic and problem, as described previously, he decided to focus on specific elements of the program: participation at center events, staff and participant attitudes toward the activities, and views of nonparticipating community members about the program. He will document participation through observation and logs kept by staff members. Attitudes toward the program will be obtained through two techniques: in-depth interviews and a survey. Anthony now needs to decide how many participants and nonparticipants to interview and survey. He decides, given the resources available, to survey participants as they attend activities and to invite active participants to be interviewed. He further decides that interviewing 10 to 15 "actives" will give him an in-depth portrait of their involvement and views about the program.

Interviewing and surveying nonparticipating community members will be more difficult. He decides to survey households within five blocks of the arts center. To do so, he will walk the neighborhood on Saturday mornings, leaving surveys and, when possible, inviting household members to sit for a brief interview. He is not sure how many of these nonparticipating member interviews he will be able to do, but he will stop after he has approximately 20.

Data Management and Analysis Procedures

Analyzing qualitative data is time-consuming. It can be tedious but also exhilarating. The specific strategy you adopt depends on the genre of your qualitative study. At the proposal stage, you will need to provide some preliminary guidelines for managing and analyzing the data. These are elaborated in Chapter 7.

For now, consider that the interpretive act remains mysterious in both qualitative and quantitative data analysis. It is a process of bringing meaning to what you have learned (your data) that is necessary whether you speak of means and standard deviations or offer rich descriptions of everyday events. The interpretive act brings meaning to your data and presents that meaning to the reader through the report. We discuss the processes of interpretation more fully in Chapter 7 and writing the report in Chapter 8.

The remaining sections of the proposal—trustworthiness, personal biography, and ethical considerations—draw on those ideas presented in Chapter 2. Here, your task is to outline how you will try to ensure the strength and sensitivity of your study.

USING THE HABITS
OF MIND AND HEART

Our characters have encountered the multiple decisions involved in designing a qualitative research project. The central tension here is to be planful while being flexible and open to change. They have explored the complex assumptions of particular genres of qualitative research, focusing their research questions and placing boundaries around what they will explore in detail. They begin to realize that there are no prescriptions for how to proceed—no templates they can implement magically. As they actively design their studies, the concept of ambiguity takes on more grounded meaning. As they see the possibilities for multiple avenues to "truths," they have to consider alternatives and make decisions; they must be able to explain and justify these decisions. Again, they employ their developing habits of mind and heart. As Anthony realizes, plans are necessary, but his plans may well have to change once he is in the field.

This chapter has discussed the complex thinking and decision making that goes into developing a research proposal. Our characters do not have to elaborate their work in such detail; they do, however, have to consider each element as they move from design to implementation, the topic of the next two chapters.

NOTES

1. Agencies that provide health services often have complex procedures for approving research projects. One of our students spent the better part of a semester working through the various committees in a hospital before she could proceed with her project.

2. The strict definition of methodology is "the study of methods." In common usage, however, it refers to "the process of doing research." We adopt this more common usage.

3. We recognize that, by lumping together two quite different worldviews, we are oversimplifying both. Postmodern ideas actually call into question many of the assumptions held by critical theorists. When viewed through Burrell and Morgan's (1979) paradigms, however, they both fall into the upper two quadrants.

4. These are the canonical triumvirate to which we would add sexual orientation, able-bodiness, and first language, among others. The list could go on.

5. Ethnographies can be argued as special instances of case studies. Their roots in anthropology, a defining characteristic of ethnographies, make them more specialized.

6. Patton (1990) argues that this reflection should cleanse the researcher's biases from the inquiry. Others (notably, Van Manen, 1990) reason that the researcher's experience is vital to an understanding of others' experiences.

7. Much of this section summarizes the more detailed explications of proposal development found in Marshall and Rossman (1995). For further guidance on proposal design, we refer you to this book.

8. The third person can also be distancing, as when the terms "the researcher" or "the investigator" are used. When talking about yourself and your actions, we suggest using "I."

9. We use all three voices throughout this text for specific purposes. When writing about ourselves (our work and our position), we use "we." When directly addressing the reader, we use "you," either implied or expressed. When discussing researchers more generally or our characters, we use the third person.

10. The term empirical has come to be associated with quantitative research when, in fact, it means "based on, guided by, or employing observation" and "derived from or verifiable by experience" (Brown, 1993, p. 809).

FURTHER READING

Proposal and Design

Creswell, J. W. (1994). *Research design: Qualitative and quantitative approaches.* Thousand Oaks, CA: Sage.

Marshall, C., & Rossman, G. B. (1995). *Designing qualitative research* (2nd ed.). Thousand Oaks, CA: Sage.

Strauss, A. L., & Corbin, J. (1990). *Basics of qualitative research: Grounded theory procedures and techniques.* Newbury Park, CA: Sage. (See Part I, Chapters 1-4)

Critical and Postmodern Assumptions

Rosenau, P. M. (1992). *Post-modernism and the social sciences: Insights, inroads, and intrusions.* Princeton, NJ: Princeton University Press.

Ethnographies

Hammersley, M., & Atkinson, P. (1983). *Ethnography: Principles in practice.* London: Routledge.

Van Maanen, J. (Ed.). (1995). *Representation in ethnography.* Thousand Oaks, CA: Sage.

Case Studies

Merriam, S. B. (1988). *Case study research in education.* San Francisco: Jossey-Bass.

Stake, R. E. (1994). Case studies. In N. K. Denzin & Y. S. Lincoln (Eds.), *Handbook of qualitative research* (pp. 236-247). Thousand Oaks, CA: Sage.

Yin, R. K. (1994). *Case study research: Design and methods* (2nd ed.). Thousand Oaks, CA: Sage.

Phenomenological Studies

Holstein, J. A., & Gubrium, J. F. (1994). Phenomenology, ethnomethodology, and interpretive practice. In N. K. Denzin & Y. S. Lincoln (Eds.), *Handbook of qualitative research* (pp. 262-272). Thousand Oaks, CA: Sage.

Seidman, I. E. (1991). *Interviewing as qualitative research: A guide for researchers in education and the social sciences.* New York: Teachers College Press.

CHAPTER FOUR

•◆•

Entering the Field

"Finally, we can get started," said Marla. "At least I didn't have any trouble getting into my setting—the staff at the clinic remembered me from when I worked there before. I've offered to volunteer so I have a reason to be there. I don't just want to sit there and look—I want to be part of the place."

Anthony wasn't so zealous: "Before today, I didn't think 'getting in' would be all that difficult. I saw my setting as the public performances, shows, or workshops sponsored by the community arts center. I would just go. Well, I went . . . and I see that access is much more than simply being there. Just attending events won't tell me how the program has got people involved in the arts."

"At first, I thought Kent was just making access sound like a big deal," Ruth reflected. "I thought, I'll go to a school in Clareville—I know they've got inclusion programs so I figured I could find some kids in wheelchairs there. My family has lived there for years, and schools are public, so what's the problem? Now, I know I need to get permission and stuff. I guess it's not going to be so easy."

"Even after you find the kids—ones in wheelchairs—do you think it's going to be easy to talk to them?" asked Marla. "I'd get someone who knew them pretty well to introduce me to them."

"Hmm. My mom's best friend is the director of an after-school program— she knows me. She might be willing," responded Ruth.

"What if the kids don't really want you around?" asked Marla. "After all, you'll be an outsider. And what if the parents won't let you talk to their kids? I'm not sure I'd let some stranger talk to my child—put her under a microscope."

"You have a point. So what do I tell them?" asked Ruth. "Pretend I've got a brother in a wheelchair?"

"No mentira! Nunca!" exclaimed Marla. "Ay, amigo—just be yourself. Tell them the truth. La verdad."

"I know. Kent even said to be careful around deception. And I don't want to lie or be dishonest," admitted Ruth.

"I certainly don't intend to misrepresent myself," Anthony stated. "After all, I've been hired to make a judgment about their program. I plan to work with them. But that does not mean that next week at the gallery opening I will stand up and identify myself as the evaluator. Doing that would be pretty counterproductive."

"All right," laughed Marla. "I'll admit that not everyone at the clinic is going to know—or care—that I'm doing anything more than volunteering there."

"But, still, it's easy for you to say, Marla, because you're already in your setting," said Ruth. "And even if they're willing to talk to me, how do I know I'm getting at their real feelings?"

"I worry about that, too," said Anthony. "If I tell the staff I'm 'evaluating' their program, won't they get worried?"

"Wait a minute—I thought the purpose of evaluation was to generate information that the program people can use to improve the program. So wouldn't they want you there?"

"Maybe not, since I've been contracted by their funders. One of the readings talked about reciprocity. I guess I'll have to help them see how an evaluation can have some benefit for them. I'll have to show them I am evaluating the program, not them," Anthony replied.

"I guess I'm lucky," said Marla. "I already feel like I'm part of the clinic. My work will start when I look for women in the community to do the study with me. I'll have to be careful that they are not just going along with me because I'm from the university so they think they have to," said Marla.

"I don't want to be a participant. I don't want to be distracted by having to follow someone else's agenda," Anthony protested. "But, at the same time, I don't want them to limit what I can see or whom I can talk to. I hope the staff lets me talk freely to folks at the center."

"You think you've got a problem," Ruth exclaimed. "Kent said I'll need full written permissions from the parents of the kids I want to interview. He *said that takes time. And I feel like I'm walking a tightrope—I need to follow all the procedures, but I don't want to scare the participants off."*

"Well, good luck," offered Anthony. "I'm off to meet with the program director. I thought I'd start by telling her about my cousin because what he does is a kind of community art. As a hobby, he's a puppeteer. He goes around to libraries putting on shows. He lives pretty far away, so she may never have heard of him, but talking about him may be an 'ice breaker'."

"Next week, you can tell us what happens. Vaya con Diós, amigos," said Marla.

Marla, Ruth, and Anthony have designed their studies and made some preliminary decisions about their settings and participants. They are ready to begin collecting data, but first they must get into the sites or connect with the individuals they will interview. Access is more than physical entry or obtaining official permission to collect data. As you can see, they are facing the following crucial questions:

- How do they introduce themselves to the participants?
- Who in the setting needs to know what information?
- What position or role will each play in the sites?
- What relationships will be established? What promises will be made?

As qualitative researchers enter a setting, their objectives are to ensure freedom and integrity—for both the researchers and the participants in their studies. This relationship will vary depending on how collaborative the research is intended to be. Schatzman and Strauss (1973) express a traditional perspective:

> For the researcher, this means his own relative freedom to move about, to look and listen—also, to think in his own terms, and to communicate his thoughts to his own intellectual community. For the host, it means freedom for him and his group to pursue their own work unencumbered and unafraid. (p. 29)

The ethical researcher—that is, one whose conduct is guided by a set of moral principles—achieves this balance of freedom and integrity with the participants through a process of presenting her purpose and negotiating acceptance. The entrance process may appear to happen quickly in some instances or may seem to take forever in others, but access is a continuous process of building relationships in the setting and taking care not to disturb the "delicate interaction rituals" (Hammersley & Atkinson, 1983, p. 56) of the field.

Qualitative researchers develop a repertoire of strategies to gain access to sites. They draw on all their interpersonal resources and skills as well as their theoretical understanding of social relationships and organizations. Ball (1990) likens the process to going on a blind date; the researcher "must charm the respondents into cooperation" (p. 157). Their choice of particular entry strategies may be idiosyncratic, but the objective is the same as their colleagues: to gain acceptance. Like Anthony, who is sponsored by the program funder, you may find that even with official or formal permission to enter, participants still decide how much and in what ways they will share information. One of our students, for example, wanted to study the superintendent's council in a large urban district.[1] The superintendent agreed and invited him to attend council meetings. The student soon noticed that although he could observe the meetings, the principals and department chair who made up the council never spoke to him and were reluctant to answer his questions. He realized that they were limiting his access to the council. Complete access to more intimate meanings and operations of the council would require building the relationships with the key actors. This chapter details the delicate and subtle processes of preparing for and making initial contact with participants at the site.

PREPARATION

Preparation facilitates access. Preparation entails reading, choosing an approach, meeting the gatekeepers, identifying potential obstacles, and negotiating some reciprocity (Jorgensen, 1989, p. 71)—mutual benefit for all parties. Most important, the researcher tries to allow time for the entry process. He seeks an opening or door through which he can discover the players and the operations of the world within. Once the researcher has established initial entry, he can build on the relationship, using his skills to renegotiate arrangements as necessary.

A clearly articulated conceptual framework is essential for entry. The framework helps clarify focus and purpose and provides a rationale for research decisions. The researcher is likely to alter this framework over the course of the fieldwork, but he starts with the questions that emerge from this initial picture. For example, Marla knows she will clarify her questions as she spends time in the clinic, but she begins with a framework of poor women's health issues. Anthony's reading has offered him images of "state-of-the-art" community arts programs; he will need to refine and delineate those characteristics that are relevant to his setting. Drawing from her understanding of sports psychology and human development, Ruth brings a conceptualization of "bodiedness" and athleticism. This conceptualization changes as she learns from the children.

The conceptual framework defines your purpose and strategy. Are you evaluating a program or service? Will program administrators use your results to inform their decisions? Will funders use your findings to continue or withdraw support? Will policymakers or legislators use the information to shape policies? Do you intend to contribute to theory from your discoveries? Will your descriptions change the way people see their world and encourage them to act differently? Your strategy—whether it is to evaluate or inform policy, to describe a culture, or to change practice—shapes your purposes and thereby your actions.

Articulating strategy and purpose is especially important for entry because it affects the participants and influences the way they will perceive the researcher. Qualitative researchers notice that folks in field sites receive them differently depending on what the participants see as the research purpose: Evaluators may be given red carpet treatment but doors often remain closed; university researchers are either ignored or collared by those who have a particular interest in the topic; and action researchers are expected to move in and "go native." Just as in all social interaction, qualitative researchers learn to use their interpersonal skills—within their ethical codes—to shape the way participants see them and their purposes.

As a qualitative researcher, you try to know a great deal about the site before attempting entry. Read and talk to informed people about the setting. Maybe spend some time hanging out at the site. Have a pretty clear idea of why you are entering this particular setting. Then draw on your accumulated knowledge to approach and present yourself to the participants.

INTENDED INVOLVEMENT

In every study you do, you will find that your roles and interactions with the participants differ. Sometimes you get to know the people really well and spend a long time with them. Sometimes you become a part of the setting. Sometimes you feel that you have "taken the data and run." The context of your setting, the strategy, and genre of research all shape your role. In a preliminary way, however, you can think about two aspects of your involvement: how involved you will be in the setting or with the participants and how you will portray this involvement to them.

Will you participate in the activities of the setting being studied, or will you simply be a spectator? If you will participate, do you plan to immerse yourself fully in the setting or to join selectively in activities? Do you intend your involvement to be coparticipation—you and members of the setting will share fully in the responsibility of designing and conducting the study? Whatever your involvement, how will others see your role? Given our acceptance of reflexivity, we believe all researchers are, to varying extents, participants in their settings. Thus, we do not spend time considering whether to be a participant observer or a nonparticipant observer. Instead, we consider the level and type of our participation and how that participation is portrayed to members of the setting.

Degree of Involvement

Participation can be seen as a continuum that ranges from coparticipation[2] to immersion as a participant to isolation as an onlooker. The latter is not overtly involved in the processes of the setting.

coparticipation ◄—— immersion ——— limited participation——► spectator

Still, we believe that even the spectator is active and fully engaged in experiencing what is happening around him or her. The difference is that between the football player on the field and the avid spectator in the stands. The researcher's position on the continuum can change over the course of the study. Marla, Ruth, and Anthony again provide examples of different degrees of participation, including Marla's choice to coparticipate in the inquiry into women's health care services and Anthony's choice to be a spectator at some of the arts events.

The degree of a researcher's participation is usually shaped by design decisions and by what is possible or appropriate (ethically, politically, or just plain naturally) in the setting (remember the discussions in Chapters 2 and 3). Different degrees of participation can either facilitate or hinder data collection. An observer can sometimes learn the most by playing the game, joining in the discussion, or making and serving the soup. Other times, such involvement would be awkward or would actually prevent data collection: Recording children's responses in a reading group is difficult if you are responsible for leading the lesson or awkward if you are pretending to be one of the children.

Immersion and coparticipation enable the researcher to learn the "language" and norms of the setting and are more likely to yield a deep emic understanding than simply standing around and watching people. Full participation in the activities of the culture, however, is often limited by how similar to members of that culture the researcher appears in background, race, and ethnic identification as much as by the nature of the researcher's actions. The more the researcher stands out, the harder she has to work to become a member of the group. Sometimes a researcher may sacrifice possible data she could be collecting while engaged in complicated, eccentric, and often unnecessary entry efforts.

Design also shapes involvement by the amount of time that has been allocated to spend in the field. More involvement requires more time. Time may range from a single observation or interview of a limited duration (such as 1 hour) to long-term and multiple observations and interviews over months or even years. Coparticipation, in particular, is extraordinarily time-intensive. The more time spent in the field and the more involved a researcher is able to be in day-to-day activities at a site, the less likely it is that members of the setting will react to his presence and will change their behavior as a result. The less the researcher is a curiosity, the less people take notice. Usually, the more familiar the participants are with the researcher, the more they trust him and are willing to share their feelings and knowledge. In rare instances, however, the opposite happens; people become suspicious over time. Thus, each researcher makes decisions about participation and duration according to the special circumstances of his study.

The experience of a graduate student (see Demerath, 1996) who conducted a study in Manus, Papua New Guinea (the site of Margaret Mead's research), provides an interesting and unexpected example of acceptance in a foreign culture. He and his wife had little difficulty gaining full acceptance because the role of "anthropologist" has been given an accepted and legitimate place in that community. In fact, the persons with whom they stayed are known as "those who take care of the anthropologists." In this case, the researcher's participation in the community was already defined by the community based on its previous history with researchers (this may be the most extreme illustration of reflexivity we can imagine!).

Portrayal of Involvement

The qualitative researcher also decides how she will present herself to the setting participants. Will the researcher make her presence as a researcher known and be explicit about her purposes? Will the researcher quietly blend into the setting, hiding her purposes and persona as a researcher? Will the researcher simply be "truthful but vague" (Taylor & Bogdan, 1984, p. 25) about her role as a researcher? Even a coparticipator, such as Marla, will portray herself in a particular way. Again, how a researcher chooses to portray her role and purpose to the participants in the study settings is best illustrated by continua (Figures 4.1 and 4.2).

In most studies we have conducted, our participation was overt; people knew who we were and why we were there. Sometimes they formed a vague idea of our purposes and cared to know no more; other times, they questioned us and talked with us about what we were doing. Sometimes they were integral to data collection and analysis. Whether the setting was a classroom, a community meeting, or a cardiopulmonary resuscitation (CPR) training session, we came with a defined role. Our involvement in the activities was negotiated. Ruth portrays herself fully and openly to the children and their parents. Anthony's portrayal

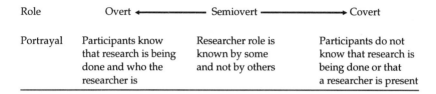

Figure 4.1. How Researchers Portray Themselves to Participants (Adapted From Patton, 1990, p. 217)

is clear and overt to some (staff and some community members) and more ambiguous to others. He may find no need to explain himself to the people who come to the gallery opening or the modern dance exhibition. Marla will be explicit and overt about her role and her purposes as she and the participants in the action research define and implement the study collaboratively.

Research activities can be piggy-backed onto other activities. For example, Marla will facilitate the study at the same time she is serving as a volunteer in the clinic. Although most people at the clinic see her primary role as a volunteer, she does not intend to hide from her coworkers that she is a student facilitating action research. Quite likely, many of the workers will forget about her project, whereas others, including workers and clients, may never be aware of her dual roles. Of course, the women working with her in the action research will see her dual roles.

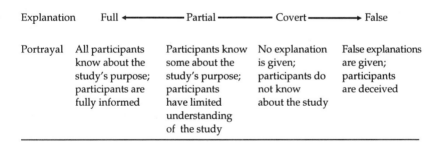

Figure 4.2. How Researchers Portray the Purpose of the Study to Participants (Adapted From Patton, 1990, p. 217)

At times, we have collected data while performing other jobs. Such research is overt because we inform participants of our intent to collect the corollary data; we negotiate informed consent at that time. For example, we collected data on the progress of our students during an action research seminar we led for teams of school teachers.[3] We were teaching them how to conduct action research studies, but we also documented, with their permission, their learning and activities to study the impact of action research on teacher practice.

We have also collected data that we then used for another, unanticipated purpose. We used such data in writing *Dynamic Teachers* (Rallis & Rossman, 1995). We had reams of notes from years of observations of teachers in various school settings from our roles as director and evaluator of a professional development and school improvement initiative; we used the actual data and knowledge gained in conceptualizing and describing dynamic teachers. Another illustration is the chapter that Kaye and Rallis (1989) wrote on advanced cardiac life support (ACLS) training, which was based on their extensive observations of ACLS training during various studies about this type of training. In both cases, the original data collection was overt, but the participants in these instances could not have known about the future uses because we did not know about them ourselves.

The qualitative researcher may choose not to disclose fully his specific focus when he believes that awareness of the details might make participants particularly self-conscious. For example, we have supported students who describe their studies as focusing on classroom interactions in general without revealing their interest in gender or race. In such cases, the researchers felt that, if participants were aware of the specific focus, they might monitor and alter their actions. As another example, if Marla were using a traditional approach to study clinic services for poor women, she might fear that revealing her specific focus on poor women would draw unusual attention to them. Thus, she might say simply that she is studying sustained health services at the clinic.

If Marla told no one in the clinic setting that she was collecting data for a study, however, she would be violating our code of ethics. Covert research is not acceptable. Similarly, if Anthony were to tell the program director only that he was interested in community arts without revealing his role as evaluator, his research would be covert and unethical.

APPROACH AND NEGOTIATIONS

Negotiating entry is a process; it seldom happens quickly and smoothly. The process is one of allocating time for negotiating the terms of the introduction or invitation and for securing written permission.

Time

Qualitative researchers learn to anticipate the time involved in gaining access. In fact, the process of negotiating entry can be as insightful about the people or setting as subsequent observations and interviews themselves. Researchers tend to be wary of any entry that seems to progress flawlessly. Key personnel change jobs, programs move their locations, and weather and other natural events can interfere with scheduling. Most often, the contact people with whom they make the arrangements are pleasant and cooperative, but the researcher's site visit is seldom high on their priority list. The researcher, therefore, must adapt to the schedules and routines of the site and participants.

We recall an entry negotiation that became an odyssey. The study was on high school change (Rossman, Corbett, & Firestone, 1988), and we had selected three schools in different districts. We obtained the superintendents' approval in each district without a hitch. Each superintendent referred us to the respective high school principal. At one high school, we began with letters and a phone call to set up an initial meeting with the principal. One month passed before that first meeting. The principal supported the study but said we needed to meet with his vice principal before any official fieldwork could begin. The vice principal suggested that we meet with the teachers' union, so we scheduled yet another meeting. The union representatives asked us to meet with the department heads to explain the study. The department heads were impressed, so we returned to the principal for official sanction. At this point, however, the principal decided that he wanted the entire faculty to vote their approval or disapproval. At a full faculty meeting, the teachers voted and approved our entry. Finally, we were in.

Each step served as a legitimate screening device for the organization, but 5 months time had elapsed since the original inquiry. Symbolically, we had been negotiating with the organization rather than with an individual. Having passed the organization's protective mechanisms, we were allowed to enter. Because the entire organization had been involved in the decision to let us in, we found we had access to many levels, and we believe that most members were forthcoming. The results were worth the time.

Introduction and Invitation

Unless the site is an entirely open and public place, you generally need to obtain an "invitation" before entering the field. Whether visiting a classroom, a therapy session, a community activist gathering, or a performance, you need permission for or an acceptance of your presence. Even if observing in a public setting as did Whyte in *Street Corner Society* (1943/1981), you need the acceptance of the inhabitants or "regulars" to "see" anything. Getting permission or an invitation is not usually as difficult as it is time-consuming.[4]

Initial contact may be made by phone, letter, in person, or through an introduction. Having more than one method of introduction eases the process. For example, if we do not know people in the setting and have no one to introduce us, we write before calling. "Cold calls" can take the recipient off guard. If we are seen as strangers, the recipient can be leery of our intent. Often, the person we need to contact for entry is busy and important and would be unlikely to accept an unexpected call from someone he or she did not know. A letter allows that person time to prepare a response (or toss it away).

Usually, we try to have someone familiar with our project make an introduction, or we use existing relationships to establish contact. For example, when looking for sites to study teacher-researchers,[5] we sought the support of the director of the National Center for Innovation of a national teachers' association. She helped us choose the schools and placed calls to the principals as an introduction. When we were conducting our evaluation of a district's inclusion initiative, we knew that support of the principals would be important. We asked the superintendent to call a meeting of the principals at which we could introduce ourselves and describe our study. In both cases, we first considered how the principals would react to the individuals we were asking to introduce us. Do they respect the person? Might they resent an apparent power play? Might the person misrepresent us? Because the answers satisfied us, we proceeded with the introductions.

If you are seeking people to interview rather than a setting, you might need to try some additional strategies to make contact. We had one student who posted flyers in a laundromat. A woman religious who was our doctoral student wanted to interview women in other religious orders about their definitions of social justice, so she attended functions at a nearby Center for Equity and Justice to meet women who fit her criteria. Another student found his interviewees by following up respondents to a questionnaire relevant to his topic that a public agency had distributed. Yet another student told her physician about her dissertation topic. The doctor remarked that she had some other patients who might be interested in the topic and offered to pass on her number if they would be willing to be interviewed.

Making initial contact in person is useful if the setting is relatively public or if you know little about the setting. Approaching a site in person with no introduction is also a good idea if you suspect that a formal introduction by someone highly placed in the organization might prejudice participants against you. In these settings, you may simply want to go and "hang around," getting your feet wet to find out what you want to focus on, who are important contacts, and how you might get accepted. For example, if you wanted to observe sports programs at private schools but had no contacts, you might begin by attending games to discover who are the players and what informal rules govern interactions off the field. Similarly, Anthony might initially simply hang around the arts center.

Written Permission

Part of the entry negotiations is obtaining permission—sometimes written and sometimes oral (as discussed in Chapter 2)—from participants. Some people are willing to give permission under certain conditions and not others. For example, some will not allow their interviews to be audiotaped, but they will allow you to take notes. You should try to accommodate your interview partner whenever possible. In some instances, written permission is covered by the formal permission you received in getting access to the institution, as long as you confine your interview questions to topics you agreed on. For example, we did not need permissions from every person in the schools when we did the inclusion study because we had been contracted by the district office and our questions fell within the purview of the participants' work. Still, we recommend that you err on the conservative side by getting written permissions whenever in doubt. Be aware, however, that sometimes the mere mention of informed consent changes the tone of the conversation. This can feel quite awkward. As noted in Chapter 2, however, standards for ethical practice require informed consent.

Whenever the research is piggy-backed on other work, such as using data that were collected for one purpose for another unanticipated purpose, the researcher must ensure that (a) the data originally were collected systematically and ethically, (b) the data do not qualitatively change when analyzed for purposes other than the original, and (c) no one in the original setting objects to or no rights are violated by the new use of the data.

EXPECTATIONS AND RELATIONSHIPS

Unlike in the blind date situation to which the entry process has been compared, the parties in a research study are not likely to "hit it off" or "strike out" with the first encounter. Negotiations are ongoing. The terms or conditions set during entry establish what will be expected of all parties in a preliminary way. Although these expectations can—and likely will be—adjusted as the fieldwork progresses, they set the tone for the relationship that develops. Ultimately, this relationship has implications for how trustworthy the data are considered. Johnson (1975) noted,

> The conditions under which an initial entree is negotiated may have important consequences for how the research is socially defined by the members of that setting. These social definitions will have a bearing on the extent to which the members trust a social researcher. (p. 51)

Trusting relations between a researcher and the members of a setting are likely to yield a trustworthy report, "one which retains the integrity of the actor's perspective and its social context" (Johnson, 1975, p. 51).

Entry requires time because usually more than one group of participants needs to negotiate agreement on terms and conditions. An experienced qualitative researcher recognizes that several parties may be interested in or affected by the research. The several parties were obvious when we performed a court-ordered evaluation in a school system. The court identified "interested parties" as the plaintiff (i.e., the advocacy group representing the parents who had brought the suit), the school system, the parents' advisory group, and the court monitor. We discovered that additional parties fell within the boundaries of the school system: the principals, teachers, and department heads, as well as the central office. Even these groups could be broken down by special interests, such as itinerant teachers. Despite the legitimate interests of many groups, we saw that the logistics of including everyone in the negotiations would be impossible. We singled out the key parties to agree on the terms of the evaluation before we proceeded.

Expectations to be discussed include permissions, how data will be recorded, the roles of various actors, materials and documents the participants will need to find and collate, the amount of time the researcher will spend at the site, what areas are open or closed to the researcher, where the researcher can set up a work space if necessary, and the amount of time or other resources the participants will devote. Negotiations must also cover the more political or symbolic issues, such as reciprocity and gatekeeping.

Reciprocity

Reciprocity recognizes the need for mutual benefit in human interaction. Norms of reciprocity operate in all social life; fieldwork is no exception. Research is a two-way street. The researcher wants something: to enter the site freely and to collect data unhindered. The site participants also want something: not to be seriously disturbed in their work or lives and to gain from participating in the study. At times, they participate to take action on some aspect of their lives through a collaborative inquiry process. They expect some change for the better in their lives. Sometimes participants are satisfied with an intellectual gain; other times, they want more. The qualitative researcher needs to establish expectations for reciprocity at the start to avoid misunderstanding and resentments later—and to ensure that all participants (including the researcher) are treated fairly.

Clarifying the relationship, difficult as it may be, is especially important because research is quite unlike any other social interaction and is often misunderstood. As depicted in the modern university, research is presented as a Western, masculine, and joyless enterprise that many cultures and people find alien and off-putting. Unequal power relationships between the *researcher* and the *researched* give the *researcher* all the authority; she defines the boundaries and the disposition of outcomes. The *researched* is made to feel ignorant, impotent, and easy to forget. In addition, the qualitative research process has the potential to seduce the researched with promises and desert her when the study is over (Siskin, 1994).

Teachers in schools near large research universities often feel seduced and abandoned. These schools serve as research sites, and teachers and students are labeled "subjects." We have heard discussions in which teachers said they felt they had been "raped" by the university people who vaguely or implicitly promised pleasure and intimacy, greatness, and new understanding but seldom even returned to share their results. This inequity between the researcher and researched need not be the norm and is becoming increasingly unacceptable ethically. A mutually beneficial relation is preferable.

Under norms of reciprocity, the researcher obtains data while the participants "find something that makes their cooperation worthwhile, whether that something is a feeling of importance from being [studied], pleasure from interactions with the [researcher], or assistance in some task" (Patton, 1990, p. 253), or actual changes in life circumstances from action research. Again, truthfulness—on both sides—is the byword for establishing reciprocity. The researcher states what she wants and what she intends to do: to move about the setting, to watch, to ask questions, to take notes, and to read documents and other written materials. The site participants also clarify any limitations they deem necessary: A reasonable exclusion may be certain private personnel meetings.

In addition to setting boundaries, participants also make requests and express expectations they have; these may include reassurances of confidentiality and anonymity and may also involve questions about what will be done with the results. Unless the project is collaborative, most participants are not interested in the details of the study; they do, however, want to know any findings that deal with their work or activities. The principals of the schools in our inclusion study asked that we personally share our findings about their school with them; we decided to create school feedback sheets for each principal about his or her school. Some of the school-specific information on these feedback sheets never appeared in the final report because it was important only to the principal.

Usually, people in the settings we have studied had no trouble identifying benefits they could gain from the research. A physician whom we interviewed numerous times during a yearlong study on in-hospital training and organizational change termed us his "administrative yentas"; he viewed interview sessions as therapeutic! The director of a intervention program we were studying disseminated our analyses in a monthly newsletter; she reported that the public relations value was extraordinary. We were pleased that she found such a use for our work. The teachers and principals in the proposed teacher-researcher sites view the study as holding potential for communication between the schools. They have asked that we help them seek funds for Internet connections and technology training so that they could use computers to collaborate on projects they will propose together.

Not all participants are as sophisticated or savvy as those we just described. What if participants, quite legitimately, find Western notions of research anathema and hence know little about the process and its possibilities for invasion or benefit? What if participants are unaware of their rights to privacy? For example, the women Marla tries to involve in her action research may have no experience to comprehend what she is asking of them. They may feel they have little authority to ask questions and seek answers as she proposes they do, nor will they assume the authority to disagree with her. Marla's challenge is to facilitate their empowerment to generate questions and methods that are practical for them rather than for herself as the researcher. As all other qualitative researchers, she will have to be especially sensitive to imbalances of power and authority and to try to surface benefits to the participants.

Reciprocity discussions might also include the question of who owns the data and who can review and edit a written report. Some key players in the setting may want to see the results before they are made public. Some may insist that they read all the field notes and interpretations, and some may even demand editing rights or veto power. Some want coauthorship. We believe that each case must be decided individually. For example, in collaborative action research, participants are appropriately coauthors because they are involved in data collection, analysis, and interpretation. A descriptive cultural study such as Anthony's does not warrant participants' veto or coauthorship because the researcher is presenting his view—his interpretation of the subject. The researcher's obligation is to make explicit that it is his voice that is being presented and not necessarily the voices of the participants. Lightfoot (1983) describes how she shared her portraits of good high schools with their principals. She relates how she decided to hold to her interpretations even when they differed from what the principals saw. Issues such as these should be considered during entry negotiations to avoid misunderstandings that could ultimately limit what use is made of the data. A cautionary note: All these issues cannot be finalized; they often surface unexpectedly. Be aware and remember that negotiations are continuous.

The following painful example illustrates the importance of raising issues of benefit and ownership before the research begins and keeping the discussion open as the research unfolds. We knew a doctoral student who spent a year interviewing and shadowing a handful of successful women leaders for her dissertation. The women were willing to share their thoughts and lives with her because, in part, they felt that their stories were important. They were gratified with the deeper understanding of their own lives they gained from their conversations with the student. When, however, she published the results substituting pseudonyms for their real names, they were furious. "Those are not her stories! They are ours! How dare she steal them to make money?" said one of the women, articulating the anger of the group. Because the doctoral student did not negotiate this particular aspect of the study, she may have hurt the credibility of researchers in general. If Marla chooses to write up and publish the stories of the women in her collaborative study, she and these women may decide to coauthor the piece.

Organizational Gatekeepers

In the beginning of this chapter, it was shown that Marla hopes that, because she is volunteering in the clinic, she will not be excluded from routines that will yield valuable information. Anthony is concerned that awareness of his sponsorship by the foundation to do an evaluation might cause program folk to give him an artificial welcome or to close doors precipitously. Ruth knows she must make contacts that will bring her close to children in wheelchairs. All three realize that no matter how righteous their questions, how sound their methodologies, or how prepared they are, it is the people in the setting who will help them or hinder them and who will open up or block off paths to information. Sponsors, gatekeepers, and key sources of information[6] determine, in part, the quality and quantity of data.

Most bureaucracies have policies or regulations defining who can or cannot have access to what. The individuals who implement or enforce these regulations or policies are typically called *gatekeepers*, the people in settings who control "avenues of opportunity" (Hammersley & Atkinson, 1983, p. 38). Some gatekeepers hold formal positions with legitimate authority to grant or withhold permission. Others possess informal authority and may not be obvious initially. They use their positions to reveal or protect what an outsider may see of themselves, their colleagues, and their organizations. Often, those who hold the keys to revealing information are those who appear unlikely; they may be the nonprofessionals, the backup crew, or the quiet ones. In schools, for example, we have found that custodians or bus drivers will know more about a particular event than the principal or teacher simply because they can see and hear more sides of the stories.

Anyone in an organization can act as a gatekeeper. What makes one person more or less important is the degree to which he or she can lead you to valuable information, send you off in an irrelevant direction, or block your inquiry at the start. As you enter the setting, you ask yourself who holds what information and what routines or strategies these people are likely to use in disseminating their knowledge. Secretaries, for example, are often the first and best gatekeepers. They hold the keys to their employers and often to the entire organization. When we make initial contact with a director or administrator, we have learned to ask the secretary for her name, and we make sure she knows ours; this way, in future contacts we can ask for her personally and build on our previous conversations. This simple personal attention makes us familiar; thus, the secretary-as-gatekeeper is more willing to facilitate our access to relevant information and people. Otherwise, secretaries can put up formidable barriers.

Sponsors can be gatekeepers, and gatekeepers can choose to become key sources of information. The line between the roles is not a clear one. In our inclusion study, our "sponsor" was our central office contact, a highly placed administrator. Technically, her role was to ease our access to the schools. On one level, she filled that role by providing necessary print material and demographics to help us choose sites and by writing official letters of introduction to the principals of the chosen sites. She became a gatekeeper, however, because she was inordinately slow in posting the letters of introduction and failed to obtain some of the legal permissions we needed (eventually, we called the district's general counsel ourselves).

As she developed respect for us as researchers, however, she became a key source of information. She offered suggestions as to which schools she considered appropriate and told us details about what she felt were effective programs in each site. The challenge is to turn a resistant gatekeeper into an active, possibly even collaborating, source of information. A technique that can facilitate this transformation is establishing what is termed *comembership*: The researcher finds some common bond on which to build a sense of shared understanding. For example, Marla, whose primary language is Spanish, will have little trouble establishing kinship with the Spanish-speaking women in the clinic.

We use comembership regularly in our research. Our histories as principal and teacher ease our entry into schools. One tense situation occurred when an angry principal sat us down to tell "what is *really* happening here." For 15 minutes, she shouted about lack of resources to meet the children's extreme needs. Finally, we asked her a question we could only have known to ask from direct experience in a similar situation. From that point on, the interview became a valuable and mutual conversation; subsequently, she cleared the way for further meaningful observation and conversation throughout the school. Our ability to demonstrate that we shared "membership" with her made the difference.

Qualitative researchers may build this bond through some minor or seemingly irrelevant similarity, as long as they are honest and the correspondence is true. For example, Anthony may refer to his cousin the puppeteer to indicate that he has some familiarity with the work of and challenges facing these kinds of artists. A female student of ours who chose to study adolescents at a private boys' school found that if she mentioned her teenaged brother early in her interviews with the boys, they became less nervous and reticent. In the CPR studies, we drew on personal affinities with the training director: Each of us had protested the Vietnam War and each of us likes classical music. The grounds for comembership are less important than that they are genuine.

USING THE HABITS OF MIND AND HEART

Qualitative researchers make scores of decisions in the course of a project; many concern entry to the setting. The challenge here is negotiating a relationship that is ethical, sensitive, and as natural as possible, given its temporary and artificial nature. As we stated earlier, the research process is a heuristic, a discovering experience. The heuristic is highly salient during entry. Each setting—even those with which the researcher believes he is familiar—exists to be discovered, and each researcher has his unique way of discovering. As they make contact and negotiate entry, Marla's, Ruth's, and Anthony's habits of mind and heart facilitate their discoveries.

The challenge of balancing their needs as researchers with those of the people they will be observing and interviewing is both daunting and exciting. Ruth wants to protect the privacy of the children and families she interviews; she also hopes they will feel free to disclose very private experiences and feelings. Marla wants the women with whom she will collaborate to look closely at possible injustices they may experience, but she cannot promise them that the study will yield improvements. Anthony wants to surface areas in which the community arts program can improve, but he does not want the foundation to use the program's weaknesses as reason to withdraw funding.

Because Anthony, Ruth, and Marla are dealing with fellow human beings, they learn to recognize that every entry will be unique and most likely unpredictable. As they build relationships with participants, they will try to be exquisitely sensitive to the feelings, worldviews, and interests of their participants. They work with their subjectivist assumptions (see Chapter 2) to build relationships that enact reciprocity, they present the studies and benefits as they see them, and they are careful that they only make promises they are sure they can keep. They create conversations and engage in dialogue more than they expect neat, tidy answers. Above all, they try to be honest and truthful in their relations with folks in the field. They realize that their entries are fluid, changing processes. As they negotiate—and renegotiate—their entries, they practice their habits of mind and heart. Now, they have access to their sites; they have entered the field. In Chapter 5, we join them as they begin to collect data.

NOTES

1. This is another instance in which we feel it would be inappropriate to cite the individual and the study. Throughout this chapter, we cite only where we feel revealing identities would not be unethical or there is no potential for embarrassment or both.

2. We have not seen this term used before in the literature on involvement. We believe it captures the radical stance of participatory action researchers.

3. This workshop was held at The Capitol Regional Education Center, Hartford, Connecticut, in July 1995.

4. Throughout most of this chapter, we appear to be discussing access to settings, organizations, events, or groups. Some studies are concerned with individuals, however. For example, Ruth is interested in children and their experiences. Most of the suggestions or principles we offer are intended to apply to both settings and individuals.

5. This example is from a current proposal to the Johann Jacobs Foundation for a study of action research and student outcomes.

6. Traditionally, this role has been termed *informant*. We are not comfortable with the sinister connotations of that word. Clearly, we do not see key sources of information as spies or turncoats. We invite suggestions for new terms for this role.

FURTHER READING

Delamont, S. (1992). *Fieldwork in educational settings: Methods, pitfalls, and perspectives.* London: Falmer.

Krieger, S. (1985). Beyond "subjectivity": The use of the self in social science. *Qualitative Sociology, 8,* 309-324.

Patton, M. Q. (1990). *Qualitative evaluation and research methods* (2nd ed.). Newbury Park, CA: Sage. (See Chapter 6)

Thorne, B. (1983). Political activist as political observer: Conflicts of commitment in a study of the draft resistance movement in the 1960s. In R. Emerson (Ed.), *Contemporary field research: A collection of readings* (pp. 216-234). Prospect Heights, IL: Waveland.

Wolcott, H. F. (1995). *The art of fieldwork.* Walnut Creek, CA: AltaMira.

CHAPTER FIVE

Gathering Data in the Field

"Guess I'm in the field all right! I spent an evening observing at the community arts center, and I interviewed the director. I even talked to the secretary about what households I'll survey. Whew! I'm exhausted. Kent didn't tell us how strenuous a day in the field can be," Anthony told his colleagues over their weekly coffee after class.

"Claro, but I love being in the field. I'm talking to folks, watching how things are done, reading memos and stuff. Being so involved in the clinic is getting me some really great data," Marla was almost bouncing. *"With the help of a few PAs, my action research group is forming. Tomorrow I'm meeting with three women who used the clinic several times. I'll explain my idea to them."*

"There you go again, always active and involved. To me, observation is just that. I sat through a whole afternoon in the after-school program, but I just watched and listened. I'm not sure I'm ready to gather data," responded Ruth.

Anthony laughed. *"I did more than sit and look. I was pretty busy watching for what people were doing, looking for what rules are used. I'm experimenting with checklists to help me keep track of who comes into the center and when."*

"I like that idea of just 'hanging out' and talking to the kids and their parents to get a sense of the setting. I'm pretty confused about what I'm looking at. I'm certainly not intending to use any instruments. I may rely on interviews alone," said Ruth. *"Marla, because you'll be working in the clinic, it won't be too easy for you to use any instruments, will it?"*

"But you have to record what you see," protested Anthony. *"And what if someone asks to see your protocols? I don't think you can be so cavalier."*

"Seguro—entonces, I will have to work more before and after each observation session," Marla answered. *"I mean . . . I may decide to develop a protocol, but I'll have to be so familiar with it that I can carry it in my head. Then I'll have to be sure to write up my notes right after I leave the clinic. But that's only for this stage. My action research group may use some protocols or guides, but we'll design them together."*

"Remember what the guest speaker said last week—that her best evaluations are ones where she has a long drive after a site visit. She uses the ride to talk her notes into a recorder, and she even analyzes them as she does it! I think that's the way I want to do it," laughed Anthony.

"You two are too structured. The idea of protocols and recording everything bothers me," Ruth said, concerned. *"I know Kent says we need to record so that we can take a careful look at what we see and hear. I understand that . . . but how do I take notes when moms are walking in and out, and the kids are getting ready to go home. Would that be invading their privacy? A tape recorder would be worse. And what's the difference between ordinary watching and listening and watching and listening to gather data? Marla, if you say you're getting great data while you're working at the clinic, what does that mean? Do you have 'data' from when you worked there before? I mean, what are data?"*

"I think that's what I'm asking too. I think to gather data we've got to get it all down. Be disciplined enough to write as much as we can so that we have something concrete to reflect on and work with," suggested Anthony.

"What you're saying is that we need more than our thoughts to rehash—to analyze and make meaning of, as Kent would say. We need records, notes, charts, maps, maybe even things—that capture moments in time, stuff we can look at again and again," Marla joined in.

"That makes sense. We might want other people to look at some of the data. We've got to be able to talk about where our interpretations come from. I can't do that if it's all in my head," added Anthony.

"As I interview children, I think it'll be important to check out whether they think I've heard them right. I'll still be an outsider, so I may misinterpret what they say," said Ruth.

"That's that emic-etic—insider-outsider—stuff, isn't it? I'm still a bit uncertain about that. If I'm hired as an evaluator, isn't my outsider perspective what they want?" asked Anthony.

"That's why I'm glad I'm doing an action research project. I'm really looking forward to the collaborative part. Then the insider-outsider issues won't be such a big deal," Marla responded. *"The data I'm gathering now are preliminary—my perceptions of which women come back for follow-up care and why. The group of women in the community who want to work with me is just forming—they'll help me set the agenda and ask the questions."*

"In my case, I'm clearly an outsider. When I visit the after-school center, won't my being there change what the kids do? Will they be more inhibited because I'm there?" wondered Ruth.

"Your being there might even make them comfortable—you might provide another body to help out with getting the kids' coats on. After all, they can't do all that stuff for themselves, can they?" asked Anthony.

"Because yours is an open community program, you should have no trouble," said Marla to Anthony. *"Anyway, you can get information because your evaluation has been contracted by the foundation that sponsored the program."*

"There's all the more reason why I may not get the truth!" exclaimed Anthony. *"They may want to look good. Or they may tell me only what they want me to hear. It's that insider-outsider issue again. And am I getting all the different perspectives: of those who put on the program? of those who go to concerts? of those who don't?"*

"You're right about that last group. Aren't the nonparticipants sometimes just as important? In my study, they are. As action researchers we'll have to find a way to see those who don't use the clinic as well as those who do," Marla considered.

"Don't forget artifacts and documents. I'm already wondering about the displays and minutes of the meetings. These things are pretty important for making sense of the entire program," added Anthony.

"At first, I thought observation and interviewing was just a matter of being there. Then I figured it was analogous to being a camera or tape recorder. Just push a button and you've got it. I'm afraid it's a tad more complicated," sighed Ruth. *"Good thing for me that I'm also intrigued by the whole process. But how will I recognize—and capture—data when they're all in front of me?"*

Gathering data is a discovery process. Ruth, Marla, and Anthony talk with people, observe actions and interactions, and pay attention to physical surroundings to learn about aspects of the social world they want to understand better. Interviewing, observing, and studying material culture[1] are the primary ways to discover and learn in the field and are often referred to as methods or techniques. We prefer the term *technique* because it captures the notion of "artistic expression or performance in relation to . . . formal details" and "skill or ability in this area" (Brown, 1993, p. 3235). When used to describe the work of artists and craftspeople, technique implies knowledge and skills that can be learned; the expression of the technique, however, is unique to each artist. Dancers trained in classical ballet master formal aspects of the dance: They learn and practice similar movements. A weaver learns the techniques of warping a loom and throwing the shuttle with skill and grace. When performing, however, a dancer brings his or her unique artistic understanding and expression to the act; each weaver creates a unique piece of fabric. Just as with dance or weaving, qualitative researchers engage in common actions—formal details of the work—but the specific way one qualitative researcher goes about doing that work—performing it—is unique to that individual and his or her project.

The techniques of qualitative research provide ways of viewing and interpreting aspects of reality; they are the formal ways of gathering information. Through the techniques of observing, interviewing, and documenting material culture, qualitative researchers capture and represent the richness, texture, and depth of what they study. Data gathering is accomplished (performed) by practicing the techniques; although composed of elements, it is a seamless enterprise. The techniques provide structure; the resulting complex tapestry—the final report—is a unique expression woven by the researcher.

Textbooks on qualitative research typically treat the skills of observing, interviewing, and studying material culture separately (but see Bogdan & Biklen, 1992, Chapters 3 and 4), but such a separation is a bit artificial. They are integrated facets of a qualitative study, and skill in one relates to skill in another. Our experience has proven that a good interviewer is also a good observer, just as a good observer tends to be a good interviewer. Conducting a rich, informative interview requires strong questioning and listening skills as well as finely honed observation skills. Marla, Ruth, and Anthony are observing while they drive to interviews,

enter offices, and wait for appointments. They notice the body movements and dress of their participants during interviews.[2] These observations signal participants' emotions, attention and interest, authenticity,
and fatigue, for example. These cues also suggest avenues to explore and
when to redirect their questions. In short, observations lead researchers
to other interviews, suggest questions they had not anticipated, and
yield topics they might want to explore. Ideas exchanged during interviews suggest other places to observe and potential sources of material
culture. Aspects of material culture, in turn, may well provide impressions to pursue through observing and interviewing. Findings from one
technique may confirm hunches or suggest new directions. While in the
field, Anthony, Ruth, and Marla find they are continuously observing,
interviewing, and studying material culture, although at any given point
their energies focus more on one particular technique.

Observation, interviewing, and studying material culture are not
passive states, and the researcher is much more than a sponge that simply
absorbs data. A qualitative researcher's mind is trained to be alert and
to work actively. Qualitative researchers develop extraordinarily sensitive antennae to pick up relevant data from numerous sources. Their
techniques vary as they react to incoming data; they analyze and interpret data as they gather them. Whatever is happening in the field, they
discover something new—about the setting, the participants, and themselves. Discovery and learning are integral to gathering data. This chapter describes how qualitative researchers discover and learn through
observing, asking questions of participants and themselves, and exploring aspects of the material world.

DECISIONS ABOUT GATHERING DATA

Although initially appearing simple, the processes of gathering data
entail complex and intertwined decisions and actions. A researcher's
choice of technique at any point in the project depends on the strategy
adopted (Chapter 1), views on epistemology and the social world (Chapter 2), the specific qualitative genre to which the work links (Chapter 3),
and how these preliminary choices interact with participants in the
setting. Is the project an evaluation, action research, or a descriptive
cultural study? What are the researcher's assumptions about reality and

knowledge claims? Is the work an ethnography, a phenomenologic study, or a case study? How do actions and reactions of participants shape what is possible, desirable, and ethical? Decisions in these areas may be forecast in the research design but, because flexibility and responsiveness are integral to qualitative research, the researcher repeatedly revisits those initial decisions and modifies them in light of the unfolding project. Thus, what the researcher does at any given moment is influenced as much by what he encounters and what evolves in the field as by what he anticipated in the project design.

Given choices about strategy, epistemology, and genre, there are three major areas for decision making about data gathering techniques: how deeply or broadly they will be applied, how prefigured or open-ended their focus will be, and what the ebb and flow among techniques will be. Think of these decision arenas as continua, just as in Chapter 2. You can stipulate a position along the continua in designing your project, but be willing to move.

Depth or Breadth

Qualitative researchers decide how deeply or broadly to employ data gathering techniques. Where you position yourself along this continuum involves trade-offs. Given the triangle of do-ability, want-to-do-ability, and should-do-ability considerations, you will be unable to gather data both broadly and in-depth. You must make choices. Gathering data from a large number of participants yields information from many perspectives; this gives the study *breadth*. Focusing on a few participants, in contrast, encourages an *in-depth* understanding not possible with a larger sample.

Ruth gathers data from a few participants, consistent with her strategy of a descriptive cultural study and the phenomenologic genre framing her methodology. Her study is essentially in-depth. Marla and her action research team decide that they want to gather data from the community served by the health clinic: They observe in the clinic for a few weeks, gathering data broadly about the setting. They then decide to interview women and seek a balance between breadth and depth by interviewing 15 to 20 women once and then focusing on 3 women whose stories are particularly compelling. Because Marla is working with a team, they are able to capture both broader perspectives and in-depth portraits of the women's lives. Given the demands of Anthony's evaluation, he must gather data broadly to satisfy decision makers' needs. He begins by observing a variety of events; he supplements this with surveys and short interviews. To elaborate these broad findings, he decides to conduct in-depth interviews with a few users and nonusers. He, too, seeks a balance between breadth and depth.

Prefigured or Open-Ended

Planning interviews or observations entails thinking about how tightly you want to control questions or topics. *Prefigured techniques* carefully specify interview questions or tightly structure observations. Anthony prefigures most of the techniques he uses. He relies on checklists in observing arts activities. He has developed forms with categories for noting actions and interactions and for judging audience reactions to events. He has determined what are the important focuses for his attention based on his reading of the literature about arts programs and his own experiences with the arts. His interviews, similarly, consist of a set of questions that he asks of users and nonusers. He modifies the questions as he moves through his project, but they remain essentially as he anticipated early on.

Open-ended techniques, in contrast, are designed to encourage the important observation or interviewing categories to emerge as the project unfolds. Ruth's decision to approach her study in an open-ended way, consistent with the phenomenologic genre, means that her observations and interviews are more holistic and exploratory than Anthony's. She chooses to do some preliminary observation in the after-school center: She goes there several days in a row, letting impressions—sights, sounds, and scents—shape her judgments about what is important. Her subsequent interviews with children and their families are guided by a small number of topics that she wishes to explore. Moreover, she is careful to listen for what matters to the children; she has developed the topics from her readings but assumes that she will learn considerably more as the project evolves. Marla and her research team identify four or five broad, open-ended questions they will use to start their conversations with the women they interview.

Our characters' stances relative to this continuum are shaped by the specific qualitative strategies they employ and the genres to which their studies link. Evaluations and policy studies are focused and instrumental; although all qualitative research is open-ended, this strategy is more tightly controlled by the researcher from the outset. Descriptive cultural studies, however, are designed to be more emergent than evaluations. Of the three strategies, action research is the most open-ended; participants and researcher collectively determine what is important to inquire about and how tightly they will structure their techniques.

Ebb and Flow

A final arena for making decisions is about the mix of techniques. This mix, too, is forecast in the study's design and may change over the course of the research. In some projects, observing takes the lead and is complemented by interviews and analyses of material culture. In others, interviews and observations proceed hand-in-hand. For still others, interviews may be the primary technique used, supplemented by limited observations.

As noted previously, Marla decides to do some preliminary holistic observing in the clinic to get a sense of interactions and issues. As her action research team gels, they decide to do some broad, focused interviewing of 15 to 20 women. They then complement these structured interviews with in-depth, more phenomenologic interviews with 3 women. Their design emerges as they work together to determine what to focus on and how to gather data. Anthony designs his evaluation to include observing, interviewing, and a survey of community members, both users and nonusers. He implements all three techniques at the outset of the project. Although what he learns through one technique informs his use of another, they proceed as parallel streams. Ruth begins with holistic observing; as she builds relations with children who use wheelchairs and their parents, she relies exclusively on iterative, in-depth interviews.

SYSTEMATIC INQUIRY

The skills involved in gathering data—asking questions, listening, looking, and reading—are skills used in everyday life. Human beings use all three in daily life to establish, maintain, negotiate, verify, and participate in everyday events (Blumer, 1969). These activities are "part of the psychology of perception, and, as such, [they are] a tacit part of the everyday functioning of individuals as they negotiate the events of daily life" (Evertson & Green, 1986, pp. 208-209). People observe, ask questions, listen, and read more deliberately, systematically, and instrumentally when learning something new. A child learning a new game may observe until she discerns the rules, or she may read a book that covers the rules. The child might ask questions of players to discover the nuances of the game. On the surface, the skills used in data gathering are everyday actions that are sometimes consciously used and other times unconsciously used.

Observing, interviewing, and studying material culture as data gathering for research, however, are different from simply watching actions or events, talking to people, or reading about a topic. When employed in a research project, these sense-making activities are used more diligently and systematically. As inquiry techniques, they are differentiated from their everyday cousins by purpose and discipline. Qualitative researchers use these techniques to capture actions, words, and artifacts—data—so that they may scrutinize these data to produce new knowledge about social phenomena.

Data About the Research

As researchers, Marla, Ruth, and Anthony learn to discipline themselves to record data systematically so that they and others may examine and reflect on them. Data are more than just ideas or images floating around in the observer's, questioner's, or reader's head; they are images and ideas documented as completely and accurately as possible to form a record of what the researcher has learned. Once recorded, data take on a tangible reality: They can be examined and reflected on. This reflection transforms the data into information that can be used to build knowledge.

During data gathering, the researcher's challenge is to build a foundation for whatever findings or conclusions are drawn. Recall the discussion in Chapter 2 about knowledge claims. If you claim to know something as a result of your research, data must exist to support those claims. Vague, impressionistic assertions will not do. Observation notes—field notes—describe settings, activities, people, and their interactions.

Interview records may be either direct transcripts of tape-recorded conversations or detailed, hand-written notes of the dialogue. Records about material culture might include photographs, descriptions of objects, or documents. Notes added to interview transcripts and field notes include your comments about methodology choices, difficulties or surprises encountered, impressions, and analytic and interpretive possibilities. All these records constitute the corpus of data from which your assertions should logically flow.

Data About the Process and Yourself

Just as you gather and record observation, interview, and material culture data, you record data about your own research activities and their development. What do you observe and why? What questions do you ask and why? What changes in the preliminary design do you make and why? What preconceptions and prejudices are shaping your project? What problems do you encounter? How does your membership in particular social groups (race, gender, primary language, and age) shape the research? (see, for example, Reissman, 1991). As noted previously, err on the side of telling more details about the "natural history" of the project than too few.

Because qualitative inquiry happens in a natural environment, the discipline to document findings and procedures systematically and thoroughly is even more essential than in a laboratory or experiment in which conditions are controlled. Natural occurrences in the setting—people's moods and health, weather, crises and accidents, political events, and births and deaths—all affect data gathering. For example, Marla and her team find people in the clinic preoccupied with the upcoming vote for statehood in their native Puerto Rico. Conversations swirl around this controversial issue. Marla finds she has to reschedule interviews originally planned for the day of the vote.

Anthony develops prefigured, standardized instruments (observation protocols, interview guides, and questionnaires) aiming to control his biases and to capture participant responses so they can be easily compared. He finds that these instruments limit what people say and how he records what people do. He learns that he cannot always use the same instruments in the same way; he finds this too constraining for the complexity of the arts program and participants' views. Using the same instruments at every art event, every time he observes at the center, or with every person he interviews, moreover, does not yield standardized data. Part of his craft knowledge is knowing when to modify the design and instruments; his skill is how completely he records what he sees, hears, and reads as data. His system includes documenting how, where, and under what conditions he gathered these data.

Data gathering is a deliberate, conscious, systematic process that details both the products—the data—and the processes of the research activities so that others may understand how the study was performed and can judge its adequacy, strength, and ethics. Recording what is learned takes persistence and effort, but a researcher submits to this discipline so that she may analyze her data—and so that others may decide if they agree with the processes and the conclusions. The data are not unexamined impressions; they are strong, complete, detailed documentation that includes the interpretive material of the researcher's perspectives and values. Data gathering entails diligently recording and reflecting, recording those reflections, and reflecting on those recordings.

Practicing systematic qualitative inquiry is both simple and complex—at least as simple and complex as the world you study. Your decisions are driven by your goal: to describe sensitively and accurately the focus of your study. The techniques you use help you do that. Blumer (1969) notes,

> Methods are mere instruments designed to identify and analyze the obdurate character of the empirical world, and as such, their value exists only in their suitability in enabling this task to be done. [The choices made] in each part of the act of scientific inquiry should and must be assessed in terms of whether they respect the nature of the empirical world under study. (pp. 27-28)

As qualitative researchers gather data, they strive to make decisions that respect the specific empirical worlds they study. Unfortunately, no social world is simple, so decisions are not simple either. In the next sections, we describe the three primary ways of gathering data using examples from our characters and our own work.

GENERIC IN-DEPTH INTERVIEWING[3]

In-depth interviewing is the hallmark of qualitative research. "Talk" is essential for understanding how participants view their worlds. Often, deeper understandings are developed through the dialogue of long, in-depth interviews, as interviewer and participant "coconstruct" meaning. Interviewing takes you into participants' worlds, at least as far as they can (or choose to) verbally relate what is in their minds. The skillful interviewer asks for elaboration and concrete examples; these can elicit the detailed narratives that make qualitative inquiry rich. This section details processes and considerations in generic in-depth interviewing; the following section discusses specialized forms of interviewing.

Types of Interviews

Described as "a conversation with a purpose" (Kahn & Cannell, 1957, p. 149), in-depth interviewing may be an overall approach to a study (as Ruth's becomes) or one of several techniques (as with Anthony's and Marla's studies). Interviewing varies in how prefigured it is, how broadly applied, and when it takes center stage in a study. Patton (1990, pp. 280-290) categorizes interviews into three types: informal conversational interviews, the interview guide approach, and standardized open-ended interviews. To these, we add the dialogic interview. *Informal interviews* are serendipitous, occurring while you "hang around" a setting or as you are entering a home to conduct a more formal interview. These are casual conversations, incidental to social interactions; beginners often wonder if these are "real" data. These informal conversations are recorded in field notes as part of the ongoing flow of social life.

The *interview guide approach* is typically used in qualitative studies. The purpose of guided interviews is to elicit the participant's worldview. The researcher develops categories or topics to explore but remains open to pursuing topics that the participant brings up. The researcher identifies a few broad topics (perhaps framed as questions) to help uncover the participant's meaning or perspective but otherwise respects how the participant frames and structures responses. The balance of talk, then, is in favor of the participant: The researcher poses open-ended questions followed by requests for elaboration; the participant responds with long narratives. This approach to interviewing exemplifies an assumption of qualitative research: The participant's perspective on the phenomenon of interest should unfold as the participant views it and not as the researcher views it. The researcher's role is to capture that unfolding.

Standardized open-ended interviews are tightly prefigured, having fixed questions that are asked of all participants in a particular order. Because of the nature of the questions, however, participants respond freely. A degree of standardization in questions may be necessary in, for example, a multisite case study or when many participants are interviewed. The most important aspect of the interviewer's approach concerns conveying an attitude of acceptance and respect—that the participant's views are valuable and useful.

Dialogic interviews are true conversations in which researcher and participant together develop a more complex understanding of the topic. There is authentic give-and-take in these interviews—mutual sharing of perspectives and understandings—and "talk time" is more balanced between researcher and participant than in the interview guide approach. There are several specialized forms of dialogic interviews that we discuss in the following section. Qualitative researchers commonly rely on the interview guide approach and dialogic interviews.

Interviewing is the way to get rich, detailed data about how people view their worlds. The technique, however, has limitations. Interviews involve personal interaction: Cooperation by the participant and interpersonal skills of the interviewer are essential. Interviewees may be unwilling or uncomfortable sharing all that the interviewer hopes to explore. They may also be unaware of recurring patterns in their lives. Sometimes the interviewer may not be able to ask questions that evoke rich responses—either because of limited expertise in or familiarity with the local language or because of lack of skill. By the same token, responses to questions or elements of the conversation may not be interpreted by the interviewer as the participant intended. At times, participants may have good reason for not being truthful (see Douglas, 1976, for a discussion).

Strong interviewers are superb listeners and deeply interested in other people. They are skilled in personal interaction, question framing, and gentle probing for elaboration. An interviewer may obtain volumes of data, but the data are time-consuming to analyze. The choice of interviews as the sole technique should be consistent with the epistemology, strategy, and genre of the study, as in Ruth's case. She argues that the subjective view is what matters; observing would not generate the kind of data she is seeking. Studies looking for a broader view triangulate interview data with data gathered through other techniques.

Whether formal or informal, the interview can be considered a conversation with a purpose. As in any meaningful conversation, both parties have a genuine, although perhaps temporary, interest in the subject. You ask questions for which you truly want answers, and you listen responsively to those answers. A flow develops between question, responses, and the next question, all guided by the topic. Although we often start an interview with an opener such as, "Tell me about your work with the single mothers," we attempt to keep the conversation related to that work. A completely unbounded and unorganized conversation usually ends up telling no story at all.

Seen as conversation, the interview yields a narrative. Although you may enter an interview with a structure and sequence of questions, the negotiated flow and organization depend on the subtle interactions between you and the participant. Narratives can be organized in many forms—for example, around time, chronologically or episodically; around place or space; or around themes or messages to be conveyed. The interview may follow inductive lines, starting with details and then elaborating the big picture, or it may proceed deductively, moving from the gestalt to specifics. Differences in values, beliefs, or purposes between the interviewer and the participant can either foster understanding or create barriers. Membership in social groups as well as personal style influence the patterns and power relationships that develop when interviewing. Because social group identities affect interpersonal relationships so deeply, we briefly discuss that issue next.

Social Group Identities

Doing qualitative research takes you into participants' worlds. In interviews, the dynamics that evolve are shaped by a whole raft of nuanced beliefs, expectations, and stereotypes—both yours and the participants'. Both parties' social group identities either ease conversation or make it tricky. Interview relationships are "fraught with issues of power" (Seidman, 1991, p. 76), many of which reflect the power issues in the larger society. Race, gender, class, primary language, age, sexual orientation, and able-bodiedness all play out in the interview context.

How you negotiate these subtle undercurrents of the special relationship called interviewing depends on how sensitive you are to these issues in your own life and those of the participants.

Does this mean that a white interviewer should not interview an African American, that only gay men should interview other gay men, or that a middle-aged interviewer will be less effective interviewing adolescents than someone in her twenties? It depends. Sometimes the answer is "yes," and sometimes it is "no." The circumstances of the interview, the topic, and the personal styles of both interviewer and participant all help to accomplish the interview; how social group identities play out in creating an open, equitable flow is complex. A middle-aged interviewer may elicit detailed responses from an adolescent because the younger person sees the interviewer as a parental figure—someone easy to talk with who will not judge her (unlike her peers). If the adolescent has had difficult parental relationships, however, a different scenario might ensue. A gay man interviewing his peers may assume much. The interview might unfold with a great deal of tacit sharing: When the participant responds with, "Oh, you know what I mean," the interviewer says, "Sure," assuming that he understands just exactly what the participant means. Such tacit understanding, although reflective of comembership in a social group, precludes eliciting and recording rich, detailed data. A straight person might probe for more elaboration because he does not fully share an understanding of the experience. The comfort people feel with others they think are like them, however, can be powerful in setting a tone for open communication. The task is to be acutely sensitive to these issues, reflect on them, and assess how they play out in the interview experience.

Racial and language differences played out in interviews that an Anglo student conducted in a Hispanic community in the southwestern United States. The researcher's questions sought to establish a chronology for events in the participants' lives. She asked, "After you came to this country, then what happened?," expecting the narrative to follow a then-to-now sequence based on her Western, Anglo worldview. The participants, however, understood their lives episodically, linked by feelings, rather than as a linear progression. The interview stalled because the researcher asked for elaboration about sequence rather than episode. The participants' responses did not make sense to her because of this deep cultural difference in how they understood time.

We recall long conversations with an African American colleague who studied institutional racism at a predominantly white university. She was intrigued with African American students' experiences of racism. We talked and argued about whether a white researcher could do the study as successfully as she. Would black students feel comfortable talking with a white researcher? What about tacit understandings? Could a white researcher elicit detailed narratives? Could a white researcher even get students to participate in the study? The answers were not absolute: A white researcher would bring some unique and important perspectives to the study; our African American colleague brought others. Whomever the interviewer, he needs to be sensitive to ways that various social group identities affect the interaction while being open to alternative worldviews.

These issues are tricky and subtle. Given interpersonal sensitivities and skill in eliciting narratives—the ultimate purpose in interviews—we argue that sharing social group identity can be powerful. For example, as women, we are particularly sensitive to the history of research about women done by men and how impoverished is that research. It is crucial, however, that the researcher be skilled interpersonally and sensitive to subtle cultural cues. No level of comembership will overcome a thoughtless, rude, and ungracious interviewing style.[4] When you interview, try to be aware of and work with issues of social group identity and the particular way the participant organizes her experience, but because you have an agenda—to gather data—you cannot ignore your research needs in structuring the interview. Seek an equitable balance between your needs and theirs that fits your questions and participants' responses, listening for the questions implicit in their answers.

Follow-Up Questions

Interview questions elicit elaborations and clarifications from the participant. You ask for more detail, hoping to discover the deeper meanings or more concrete examples. Inviting the participant to elaborate indicates that you are truly interested in more than superficial accounts; you are interested in learning what the participant experiences: what he or she felt, saw, smelled, and thought about. Skill in asking good follow-up questions comes from "knowing what to look for in the interview, listening carefully to what is said and what is not said, and being sensitive to the feedback needs of the person being interviewed" (Patton, 1990, p. 327). Use both verbal and nonverbal cues. Nodding the head, facial gestures, saying "uh huh," and even silence can signal to the participant that you understand or that you would like more detail. We are not implying that the participant is holding information back; she may not yet have explored the idea. Asking for further detail invites the participant to understand the experience more fully and provides you with the detail you seek.

Consider the following excerpt from an interview conducted early in Ruth's study. This interview is with a 11-year-old boy who is one of only three or four students who use wheelchairs in a middle school. In this example, there are several places where Ruth could have asked the student to elaborate; we indicate these in italicized, bracketed comments.

Researcher: How do you feel about how you're treated by others in the school?

Student: Terrible. I've told my parents I want to get out of there. I don't like it.

["*Tell me about what was so terrible. Do you remember specific things?*"]

Researcher: If you decide you really want to get out, what might keep you there?

Student: It doesn't matter because my parents won't let me get out anyway. They like it too much . . . because it's close to the house.

["*Is that a big source of conflict with them?*" or "*Tell me about the talks you've had with them about this.*"]

Researcher: Do you think this makes you work less hard in the classroom?

Student: Not really. I know that wherever I am, I'm still going to get good grades . . .

["*Tell me what grades mean to you. What makes you want to get good grades?*"]

Student: But it makes it a real drag that my parents won't let me go to East Overbrook. But it doesn't mean I'm going to try to flunk out.

[*"What's so attractive about East Overbrook? Why would you rather be there?" "Trying to flunk out would be pretty drastic. Have you ever thought about it?" or "It seems that it's been pretty difficult for you. What specifically has been so tough?"*]

The student's responses about what made school "terrible" could lead to important insights into how he felt different and marginalized. They could lead Ruth to understand that another school could be more supportive of and thoughtful about students with all sorts of disabilities. We suspect that she could have uncovered much more data on the student's values and beliefs as well as on his specific experiences including his successes at school. His responses throughout this excerpt needed immediate, thoughtful follow-up questions. As Ruth becomes more skilled in asking follow-up questions, her interviews will improve. Beginning researchers often struggle with follow-up questions because they are not *actively listening* to participants; instead, they are thinking about their next question. With practice, the interview becomes more like a conversation; follow-up questions become part of the natural flow. Table 5.1 provides examples of requests for more detail and elaboration.

Generally, we find that if we are sincerely interested in the topic, participants appreciate requests for elaboration because they facilitate reflection and self-discovery. In one case, a program director thanked us for the opportunity to articulate reasons why he felt especially pleased with some aspects of his program but not others. He told us that, because of participating in the interview, he felt he understood better his management style and future options. Asking for elaboration is not usually difficult if both parties are genuinely interested in the topic.

Some of our most challenging interviews, however, have been with believers in or advocates for a particular topic—those with a true passion. These people often articulate their positions and are unwilling to consider that their ideas or projects might have any negative aspects. Digging beneath the surface without appearing rude to these conversational partners is not easy. We take care not to intrude or violate their

TABLE 5.1 Follow-Up Questions

Question	*Purpose*
Open-ended elaborations	
Would you tell me more about that?	More detail
That's helpful. I'd appreciate it if you'd give me more detail.	More detail
I'm intrigued by what you're telling me, but I'm not sure I get the whole picture yet.	More detail
Open-ended clarifications	
I want to be sure I understand. Could you go over that again?	Rephrasing
I think I see what you mean, but I'm not sure I understand fully.	Implying that more detail will help
Detailed elaborations	
Who else was there?	Others present
When did all this happen?	Timing of events
How were you involved? What was your role?	Interactions and roles
Describe the room.	Physical environment
Where did this happen?	Location

senses of privacy, but we do want elaboration. We once interviewed a leader of a school reform program. His program was philosophically sound, but we had heard that implementation was not proceeding smoothly. When we asked about what was actually going on with the program, his response was a predictable description of how many schools were in the network, generalities about what teachers were doing, and how excited they were. We pushed for specific evidence of schools' activities but got nowhere. We had to take a different tack, so we asked, "What if a school in the program is not meeting the first goal after two years?" This hypothetical question enabled him to launch into several examples of problems that schools were encountering.

Your interview conversations can take many forms, depending on the decisions you have made about questions, strategy, epistemology, and genre. In addition to generic in-depth interviewing, there are specialized forms including ethnographic, phenomenological, elite, and focus group interviewing. Each is described briefly in the next section.

SPECIALIZED FORMS OF
IN-DEPTH INTERVIEWING

Each of the qualitative research genres claims to use specialized interview forms. Ethnographic researchers interview participants about culture, phenomenologic researchers search to define lived experiences through dialogic interviews, and case study researchers seek a balance between the emic and etic perspectives. Two other specialized forms that might be used in any strategy or genre are elite and focus group interviewing. With any of these, children may be the participants. Although we do not view children as requiring a special form of interviewing, they do require extra consideration; we address this last.

Ethnographic Interviewing

Deriving from the discipline of cognitive anthropology, ethnographic interviewing elicits the cognitive structures guiding participants' worldviews. Described as "a particular kind of speech event" (Spradley, 1979, p. 18), ethnographic questions are used to gather cultural data. Spradley (1979) identifies three main types of questions: descriptive, structural, and contrast. Descriptive questions allow the researcher to gather examples of the participants' language. Structural questions discover the basic units in that cultural knowledge, whereas contrast questions elaborate the meaning of various terms that participants use. As the researcher's knowledge of salient cultural domains grows, card sorts may be used to develop taxonomies of those domains. In these, the researcher asks the participant to place cards with cultural terms on them in semantic relation to one another—for example, "x is a kind of y" or "x causes y." These sorts then help the researcher better understand the relationships embedded in cognitive structures. The success of this technique, as in all interviewing, is highly dependent on the skills of the researcher.

Anthony might use ethnographic interviewing to uncover the domains of understanding about the arts and ways of participating in arts events. He could structure interviews to understand the terms people use to describe the arts program and then engage a few participants in card sorts in which they depict ways of participating—for example, "dancing in the streets is a way of participating in the arts."

Phenomenological Interviewing

This form of interviewing is a specific type of in-depth interviewing grounded in the theoretical genre of phenomenology. As noted in Chapter 3, phenomenology is the study of participants' lived experiences and worldviews. Phenomenology assumes that there is a "structure and essence" to shared experiences that can be determined (Patton, 1990, p. 70). Interviewing elicits people's stories about their lives.

Seidman (1991) calls for three iterative interviews for the phenomenologic date gathering process. The first asks the participant to narrate his or her personal life history relative to the topic; the focus is on past experiences up to the present. The second brings the narrative into the present, with a focus on specific details of participants' experiences of the topic. The third asks participants to reflect on the meaning of their experiences—"the intellectual and emotional connections between the participants' work and life" (Seidman, 1991, p. 12). Questions in the third interview ask the participant to integrate the two previous interviews. For example, the researcher might ask, "Given what you have said about your life before you became a *mentor teacher* [italics added] and given what you have said about your work now, how do you understand *mentoring* [italics added] in your life?" (Seidman, 1991, p. 12).

During the process, the researcher tries to bracket the presuppositions she brings to the study to identify the phenomenon in its "pure form, uncontaminated by extraneous intrusions" (Patton 1990, p. 408). The data are clustered around themes that are portrayed in the interview text. The final product articulates the "bones" of the lived experience of the phenomenon, describing its deep meaning for the participant. A variant of this type of interviewing is "voice-centered interviewing" (Brown & Gilligan, 1990), which seeks to uncover the enmeshed, contrapuntal voices that speak through a dialogic interview text.[5]

Ruth relies on phenomenologic interviewing as her primary technique. She identifies a small number of children who use wheelchairs and their families and invites them to participate in three iterative interviews about the lived experience of using a wheelchair. Her focus is on the experience of this phenomenon, how the children and their families understand it, and what it means for their everyday lives. The previous excerpt was from Ruth's second interview with the very first student in her study in which she was trying to understand his current experiences of *using a wheelchair.*

Interviewing "Elites" or "Experts"

A specialized case of interviewing focuses on a particular type of interviewee. Elite or expert individuals are those considered influential, prominent, well-informed, or all three in an organization or community and are selected on the basis of their expertise in areas relevant to the research. Valuable information can be gained from these participants because of their positions in social, political, financial, or administrative realms. Access to elite individuals, however, is often difficult because they are usually busy people operating under demanding time constraints. The researcher may have to adapt the planned-for flow of the interview based on the wishes and predilections of the person interviewed. Although this is true with all in-depth interviewing, the elite individual is typically quite savvy and may resent the restrictions of narrow or ill-phrased questions. He or she may want an active interplay with the interviewer. Elites respond well to inquiries about broad topics and to intelligent, provocative, open-ended questions that allow them the freedom to use their knowledge and imagination. In working with elites, great demands are placed on the ability of the interviewer, who must establish competence by displaying a thorough knowledge of the topic or, lacking such knowledge, by projecting an accurate conceptualization of the problem through shrewd questioning.

Anthony interviews elite individuals as part of his evaluation: the program director and community leaders. These individuals are quite skilled in "managing" interviews because they are often called by newspaper reporters to comment on local events. His challenges, then, are to find time to meet with these people and then to ask crisp, focused questions that provoke thought and reflection but do not take too much of the participants' time.

Focus Group Interviewing

The technique of interviewing participants in focus groups comes largely from marketing research. Groups are generally composed of 7 to 10 people (although they can be as small as 4 and as large as 12) who are not well-known to one another and have been selected because they share certain characteristics. The interviewer creates an open environment, asking questions that focus closely on one topic (hence its name), to encourage discussion and the expression of differing opinions and points of view. The interaction among the participants is the critical characteristic of this type of interviewing. This technique assumes that an individual's attitudes and beliefs do not form in a vacuum: People often need to listen to others' opinions and understandings to clarify their own. Often, the questions in a focus group setting are deceptively simple; the trick is to promote participants' talk through the creation of a permissive environment. Anthony's focus group brings together nonusers of the arts center on one Saturday morning. Seven people discuss how they spend their free time and react to the possibilities that are available at the center.

Interviewing Children

Whatever the form of interviewing, children may be your participants. Interviewing children is fun and frustrating. Young children are often lively and active; it is unrealistic to expect them to sit face-to-face and engage in a long dialogue with a researcher. Talks can occur, however, during other activities. For example, join them at lunch or snack time, invite them to work on a puzzle with you, or sit with them as they play with blocks or Tinkertoys. Fascinating perspectives often emerge during these activities. We have interviewed young children—8-year-olds—in a focus group. At snack time, we invited them to join us around a large, round table. Six of them came. Much talk ensued about the tape recorder; they played with it, recording their own voices, and playing those segments back, accompanied by shrieks and laughter. Then we settled down to business—snacks! As we munched, we talked with them about Katie, a classmate with multiple sclerosis. What was it like having her in their class? What did they have to do differently? One particularly articulate girl described how she knew Katie better than the others because they had been in class together last year too. She elaborated about Katie's needs for extra time and how she spilled her crayon box all the time, but that was OK because "that's just how Katie is. No big deal." The data gathered were eloquent in depicting a truly inclusive classroom in which Katie's needs were part and parcel of everyday life.

Interviewing young adults is also fascinating. Some adolescents prefer the intimacy of a one-on-one interview, whereas others find a focus group setting more conducive to talking about their lives. In a study of early graduation from high school, the researcher found that students preferred talking with her privately. So much anguish colored their decisions to leave high school early that the students felt uncomfortable talking about it with other people around. The researcher was trained as a counselor; she was skilled in asking probing questions with delicacy and tact. In another study, we found that talking with high school students about the curriculum and graduation requirements worked well in small groups. Ideas flowed and "popped" as one student shared his experiences, triggering recollections and insights in the others. Given this variability, it makes sense to vary your interviewing strategies when working with young adults or to be prepared to modify the strategy if it is not working well.

Ruth interviews children who use wheelchairs. With the younger ones, she engages them in play activities through which they can talk about the child's life—joys and challenges in navigating a world designed for people who can walk. She joins them for lunch or recess to defuse the focus on straight face-to-face talk. With older students, she tries one-on-one interviewing; with some, it works; others appear to feel too shy or reticent for much talk to ensue.

Another primary way of gathering data is through observation. Observation generates field notes as the running record of what you notice in a setting. Like other data gathering techniques, it may focus broadly or in-depth, and it may be open-ended or particularistic.

OBSERVING PEOPLE, ACTIONS, AND EVENTS

As noted at the beginning of the chapter, observation is fundamental to all qualitative inquiry. Even in in-depth interview studies, observation plays an important role as the researcher notes body language and affect in addition to the participant's words. Observation takes you inside the setting; it helps you discover complexity in social settings by being there. It entails systematic noting and recording of events, actions, and interactions. The challenge is to identify the "big picture" while noting huge amounts of detail in multiple and complex actions.

For studies relying exclusively on observation, the researcher makes no special effort to have a particular role; to be tolerated as an unobtrusive observer is often enough. Classroom observational studies are one example often found in education. Through observation, the researcher learns about actions and infers the meanings those actions have for participants. This technique assumes that actions are purposeful and expressive of deeper values and beliefs. Observation can be tightly prefigured, using structured, detailed notations of behavior guided by checklists, or it may be a more holistic description of events and activities.

In the early stages of a study, qualitative researchers often enter the setting with broad areas of interest but without predetermined categories or strict observational checklists, as do Ruth and Marla. The researcher is thus able to discover the recurring patterns of events and relationships. After such patterns are identified and described through early analysis of field notes, checklists or protocols become more appropriate and context sensitive. Focused observation may then be used at later stages of the study.

Taking Field Notes

You need to turn what you see and hear (or, perhaps, smell and taste) into data. You do this by writing field notes—the written record of your perceptions in the field. Field notes have two major components: the descriptive data of what you observe and your comments on those data or on the project itself. The former are called the *running record*, and they are exactly that: You capture as much detail as possible about the physical environment and the activities and interactions among the people in that environment. The second component is your commentary on that running record and is typically referred to as *observer comments*. These may include your emotional reactions to events, analytic insights, questions about meaning, and thoughts for modifying your design. The running record is the data about the research; the observer comments are the data about the process and yourself. Such observational field notes are also added to interview transcripts to augment and interpret the exact words of the interview. The particular form that raw field notes take is idiosyncratic. You need to find what works for you; what is crucial is having as much detail as possible. Raw field notes are typically taken by hand in the setting. In some settings, you might be able to use a laptop computer, but be careful that the technology is not distracting or obtrusive. In rare instances when taking notes would be totally inappropriate, you need to find a way to remove yourself to a quiet place to write notes that you will elaborate later. The bathroom can be used for this purpose!

Making Raw Field Notes Usable

As soon as possible after fieldwork, it is critical to write up the raw notes. Writing up involves transcribing hand-written notes into the computer, elaborating skimpy data, and adding commentary. Try to organize the notes while doing so, thus doing some preliminary analysis. Ideally, these write-ups occur the same day or the day after. This is a good time to catch vague statements and clarify unfounded assumptions that appear in the data. For example, if our notes say, "All students were expected to have partially filled out a similar chart from the day before," "She looked nervous," or "The cases at the clinic this week were more difficult than last," we try to add why we knew what was expected of the students, what actions led us to believe the woman was nervous, or what cases we observed this week and why we saw them as more difficult than the previous week's. Usually, if the fieldwork was done quite recently, what we have said in our notes sparks our memories for details; if our memories are blank, we recognize a hole and try to seek further information later.

This is the stage when you write "thick descriptions" (Geertz, 1973). Thick descriptions present details, emotions, and textures of social relationships. Denzin (1994, p. 505) notes that "[A]n event or process can be neither interpreted nor understood until it has been well described." Thick descriptions are necessary for "thick interpretation" (Denzin, 1989, p. 83). In an early attempt at field notes, Anthony writes, "Fifty people from the neighborhood attended the dance exhibition. Several ethnic groups and both genders were there. Everyone enjoyed themselves." Later, he writes:

> Eaves-dropping on a cluster (three women, one man; black, white, Hispanic) near the sculpture of "City Girl," I heard conversation about

how the artist has done the girl's hair. One asked, "How could she get the corn-rows so realistic?" Another begins to describe the method she heard about in her ceramics workshop. Conversations turns to how (can?) artists make a living. One leaves to refill her glass; she returns with a tray of finger-foods.

From time to time, you may need an assist to remind you of your focus in writing field notes. Creating or adapting existing instruments can be helpful in recording data. Tables, checklists, diagrams, blueprints, and sketches that chart spatial relationships, classify or quantify interactions or verbal content, map work flow or work stations, or illustrate social relationships serve to make data out of what you see and hear. Because your task is to record what you see and hear, for it to become data, use whatever instruments will facilitate that process.

EXAMPLES OF FIELD NOTES
AND INTERVIEW TRANSCRIPTS

We are often told that until a student sees examples of field notes or interview transcripts, he has difficulty imagining them. We understand that situation because no clear and constant rules exist for creating them. Each researcher develops her own style for taking field notes and formatting interview transcripts; some are more useful than others, but as long as the records produce data—that is, if they capture what the researcher sees and hears so that she and others may scrutinize and reflect on the data—nearly any style is acceptable. In this section, we offer examples of field notes that Anthony, Ruth, and Marla have taken. All the examples have been word-processed and "cleaned up." The observer comments are in **bold** and bracketed. (See Appendix C for actual formatting of Anthony's field notes.)

Anthony's Field Notes

10/2. 4-6:15 p.m. Watercolor class.
The class is a watercolor workshop. The 12 students (5 males; 7 females) have been together for 3 weeks (this is their 4th lesson). The instructor (Barney) signaled it was time to begin class by turning on a slide that showed an impressionist painting.

[I'm not sure who it was. Maybe a Seurat.]

He explained that they were going to learn a new technique, but he wanted to talk about impressionist painting first.

He asked the class to give their "impressions" of the painting. I could hardly hear him, even though the room is not large. Class members responded: "old-fashioned"; "shadows"; "soft"; "bright colors"; "people look like they are going to move."

[Not sure the class knew what he wanted. They were enthusiastic but seemed mildly confused.]

B: "Yes, that's all true. He accomplished that effect by using quick, short brushstrokes—almost like little dots." Barney spoke a few sentences about the brushstrokes and colors the painter used. He stood at the front of the room with his arms immobile at his side, stiff and dull.

[Can this guy paint, let alone teach painting?]

S: "Yeah, I heard Monet did that. But this doesn't look like Monet."

[I think it would have been better if he had used a large print of the original or a poster. Anything but a slide. I can't tell what he's trying to demonstrate. I wonder if this is part of a curriculum and he is just using it because he thinks he is supposed to. He doesn't seem to have a handle on the point he's trying to get across.]

B: "OK, let's get to work. Today, you'll need the fat brushes, sponges, and a cup of water next to your colors." Suddenly Barney loosened up and became an artist.

[He was almost dancing!]

He began to demonstrate a technique with sponges and water. He didn't talk a lot, but his hands flew across the paper and between the paper and the materials. The class gathered around. Almost as quickly as he began, he turned away from the easel and told them to try it.

[He didn't even ask the group if anyone had questions about what he just did, but he wandered among them, pointing out things, making suggestions, and answering individual questions.]

People worked at their easels. The room was quiet. Not much talking except with Barney. People seemed absorbed in their painting.

[The behavior norms must be established already. Everyone knows what they are supposed to do, where the materials are, and how to interact with each other and Barney. The atmosphere is very ordered but comfortable. Industrious is the word.]

After sitting at the side of the room, I wandered around looking at the painting. Finally, I whispered a few questions about how they learned to do certain procedures, if this was their first watercolor class, and how many paintings they had worked on in this class. With one exception, this was everyone's first class. They practice different techniques, but they are each working to complete one full watercolor.

[I felt as if I'd seen two different people in Barney. What was that attempt to teach about impressionism at the beginning of the class?]

Ruth's Field Notes

9/24. Field Notes at Culverton After Care Center. Mid-afternoon.

Culverton After Care Center is housed in an old reconverted elementary school building. The entrance looks like the entry to almost any old school you know: linoleum tiles underfoot; yellowish lighting; coats hanging on wall hooks; boots and shoes strewn across the floor; backpacks dropped in piles. I enter soon after the children so their noise and chaos linger. Patsy, one of the aides, makes a futile attempt to push the droppings toward the walls so the pathway is clear. I can see hand smudges on the cream-green walls. Already, I feel the familiar warmth and moderate grime of a place where children are moving too fast to be orderly and too busy to wash.

I enter the large room to the left where snacks are spread out on a table. I estimate about 25-30 kids from about second grade to middle school age. One group has already gobbled up their snacks and are heading to the closets that held the gym equipment. I see one boy squirt a juice box all over the wall and floor in the corner. Nobody but me catches his act. He giggles and sprints away. [I wondered how much juice—and other foodstuff coated these walls!] *Actually, only half of them are going to the gym. The other half are going to the art room. A few are carrying books. Later I found out that they probably went to the "quiet room" to read. There is also a game room.*

I look for the kids in wheelchairs. I know there are eight in all. Three (Amanda, Mark, and Jill) are with the group going to the gym. Another (Winnie) is in the art room. Sammy usually goes to the reading place so he's probably there. I can't see [and didn't find out] *where the other three are. So far, the ones I see seem to be part of the crowd of kids. I can pick them out, but they don't stand out. I decide to follow the kids going to the gym.*

[Already I'm thinking about how I can get to talk to the girls and boys in wheelchairs. I don't want to be too formal, at least not at first. Right now, I'm just standing there.] *A boy throws a ball at me, nearly hitting me* in the nose. He calls to me, "We need another person on our side. Wanna play?" So I drop my notebook and join in. I see that Amanda is on the other team. She's in the middle of their players. Jill is off to the side: She doesn't go onto the court. She looks like she's going to cheer. I see that Mark is on our team. I start to watch Amanda play, but the ball comes to me, and I get into the game. I do notice that she makes two baskets.

After the game, I get talking to the kids. They ask me who I am. I tell them I'm a student at the university, and I want to see what they do at the center. They ask a dozen questions [most I can even answer!]. Then I ask them to introduce themselves [their identities are on the attached sheet]. We talk about playing basketball, and they tell me about the league they belong to. One laughs about how it's the only league where kids do wheelies on the floor. [I'm surprised that Amanda is their captain. I want to find out about that. And I wonder how she learned to play.] The talk is moving fast so I can't get it all. Then we play some more.

When it's time for parents to come, I walk to the entrance with Amanda. She is kidding me about my team losing. I hand her her coat from its hook, and she wheels out.

[I really had fun today. I don't know what data these notes are, but I'm getting a sense of the center and the kids.]

Marla's Interview Transcript

10/22. Interview with Teresa, woman who used clinic but didn't come back. Done in Spanish and translated. Open-ended questions. M means me; T means Teresa; MC means my comments added while transcribing.

M: You've heard about the group of women I am with? We're talking with women like you who've lived in the neighborhood for a year or more. We want to know about what kind of services are important to you. Especially health services. Tell me a little bit about yourself. Do you like living here?

T: It's not so bad. I mean, I have a job. There's food. And the kids. There's lots for them to do. You know, they aren't always hanging around.

M: So . . . life's maybe a little better here . . . for you?

T: Oh yeah, it's better. Not the weather, but you know, we have more. I never had a wash machine before.

M: Is having clean clothes important to you?

T: Yes, I even iron the girls' dresses.

[MC: I want to get to health, but I'd rather she brought it up.]

M: What else do you have here that is important, that maybe you did not have before?

T: Oh . . . things . . . you know . . . like . . . um . . . oh! Supermarkets! So many choices. You don't have to get just what is at the little market. I don't know if that's so good (laugh) . . . The kids, you know, eat not so good: lots of potato chips and stuff.

[MC: Ah, here's my chance!]

M: Do you ever worry about their health? Or yours?

T: Yeah, but what can I do? I take them to the clinic when I have to. You know, I have to for the school, with all those shots. And the dentist clinic.

M: What about you? Your health?

T: Oh, I don't get sick.

[MC: I know she used the clinic once. Doesn't she remember that? Maybe she doesn't consider that to be sick?]

M: So you're pretty tough?

T: (smiles) Maybe so! I don't get so sick.

M: If you did, what would you do?

T: I guess I'd call my cousin. She lives the block over. She'd come help me with the children.

[MC: I wonder if she just doesn't see the clinic and doctors as an option.]

M: Do you think you'd ever need a doctor? Would you ever use one?

T: Oh, I don't know about doctors. I just don't know.

[MC: I wait here for a few seconds. I'm hoping she will tell me what she means.]

T: I think the kids need them for the shots. But I just don't know about doctors.

[MC: Maybe she means she really doesn't know about doctors . . . what they are for?]

M: Do you know anything a doctor could do for you? How to use one?

T: Umm . . . no.

M: But you used the clinic yourself once. Did a doctor help you then?

T: The clinic . . . yes. But I didn't see a doctor. I mean you don't see a doctor at the clinic. Do you?

M: Do you remember who treated you? What they said? What they did?

T: I remember. I had red spots on my skin. A nice woman looked at it. She gave me cream. It went away.

M: Did you ever go back? Did they tell you to come back?

T: Maybe. But I had the cream. The red came back once, so I used what was left. Why should I go back?

M: Did the woman who treated you seem to know what she was doing? Did she explain everything to you?

[MC: I should not have asked her both of these questions at once, but I want her to talk in general about the experience at the clinic.]

T: I guess so. She told me how to use the cream. I didn't ask her anything else.

M: Can you think back to the whole visit to the clinic . . . and tell me why you came, what you were thinking about as you were there, as you waited, how you explained your problem, how you were treated? Just kind of tell me the whole story.

T: I didn't have to wait too long. And it was pretty comfortable. I was kinda scared, 'cause I didn't know what the place was like. I came because my boss noticed the red. He told me to come. I didn't know. They were real nice, but they acted like I should of known what to do. I didn't know how to fill out the papers they gave me.

[MC: I realize how much she does not know, does not know, does not know. I guess we need to let people know!]

T: Yolanda, she's my oldest daughter, she was with me. She helped me. I got called into a room. Everything was real clean. The woman in the blue blouse came in. Asked me so many questions. She was real smart. I don't think she was a doctor. She said her name was Sara, not doctor somebody. I didn't understand all that she said. But I liked her. And the cream worked.

[MC: Ah, she talking. It sounds as if the clinic is not an integral part of the community. She would not have come if her boss had not told her to. Now I have specific questions. Let's see if she would go back.]

STUDYING MATERIAL CULTURE

Qualitative researchers often supplement observing and interviewing with studying aspects of material culture produced in the course of everyday events. These might include objects, such as children's school-work or photographs from a staff picnic, but are typically documents—the written record of a person's life or an organization's functioning. Journals, diaries, minutes of meetings, policy statements, letters, and announcements are all examples of material culture that researchers gather and analyze to better understand the social worlds they study. Gathering documents and other aspects of material culture is relatively unobtrusive and potentially rich in portraying the values and beliefs of participants in the setting.

Archival data are another example of material culture. These are the routinely gathered records of a society, community, or organization—for example, attendance records, test scores, and birth and death records. Marital patterns among a group of native Mexicans, discovered through fieldwork in a community, could be tested through marriage records found in the offices of the county seat or state capitol. Descriptions of articulated funding priorities by policymakers could be corroborated (or not) through an analysis of budgetary allocations.

The analysis of documents often entails a specialized approach called *content analysis*. Best thought of as an overall approach, a method, and an analytic strategy, content analysis entails the systematic examination of forms of communication to objectively document patterns. A more objectivist approach than other qualitative methods, traditional content analysis allows the researcher to obtain an "objective and quantitative description" (Berelson, 1952, p. 18) of the content of various forms of communications. The raw material of content analysis may be any form of communication, usually written materials (textbooks, novels, newspapers, and electronic mail); other forms of communication, however—such as music, pictures, or political speeches—may also be included.

A postmodern or critical approach to material culture might construe all products of a society as text: movies, plays, or advertisements, for example, could form the basis for such analyses. The strategy here is to critically analyze what is portrayed and symbolized in such textual representations and what is absent or silenced. Anthony, for example, could examine the "text" of an arts event from a socioeconomic perspective, searching for evidence of middle-class values and oppression of working-class ones.

Further examples may help. When we are in an office of a principal who tells us, "all children in *my* school learn," we look for evidence of children's work. One principal described how she assisted teachers to implement inquiry-based, student-centered learning by revising their lesson plans to meet state requirements. She was pleased to open her files and illustrate the before-and-after plans. Seeing these materials clarified for us her efforts as well as her purposes. In another case, in which we were also looking at a student-centered, inquiry-based classroom, neither interviews with the teacher nor observations in the classroom were as powerful as the booklets and newsletters the class had produced or the videotape a parent had made of the class during the entire year.

Material culture can offer data that contradict words and sights. A counselor may declare his or her deep interest in every one of his adolescent clients, but a daily schedule jam-packed with an impressive numbers of clients in short sessions with no time for reflection may lead us to doubt his or her sincerity. Letters to the editor of the local newspaper complaining of the glaring graffiti on the walls of and the debris around the community center can belie the director's contention that his or her board and the neighborhood are having success in cleaning up the area. The zoo's program director promises new hands-on activities for members; the glossy brochures advertise "new ways to see the animals." The schedule, however, lists traditional sit and watch the animals perform events. All these schedules, booklets, advertisements, plans, and letters are objects that may become data and can enrich understanding of the phenomena studied.

USING THE HABITS
OF MIND AND HEART

The challenge that Ruth raises in the vignette that begins this chapter is how to develop the skills to recognize what can become relevant data and render these sights, sounds, words, images, and artifacts into data. Like Ruth, the beginning qualitative researcher can be overwhelmed by the plethora of potential data. Other beginners wonder where the data are; they say, "nothing's happening." Again, the habits of mind and heart are crucial: They open your eyes and ears to what is going on and sensitize you to what is important, and they provide the structure for creating interesting, useful, and accurate data. It is in this creative process—constructing field notes, interview transcriptions, and memos—that diligence and perseverance pay off. As our characters gather data in the field, questions arise. We turn to these in Chapter 6, relying on our own work and that of our students for answers.

NOTES

1. We use material culture to describe artifacts and written material that may be available in or about the setting or about individuals. These may include documents, minutes of meetings, newspaper articles, clothing, diaries, personal objects, and decorations—anything relevant that may reveal information about the person, setting, or event.

2. Well over half of people's perceptions derive from nonverbal cues (Mehrabian & Ferris, 1967, p. 248).

3. This section draws, in part, from Marshall and Rossman (1995).

4. These qualities, of course, are culturally defined.

5. Voice-centered analysis is addressed in Chapter 7.

FURTHER READING

Bogdan, R. C., & Biklen, S. K. (1992). *Qualitative research in education: An introduction to theory and methods* (2nd ed.). Boston: Allyn & Bacon.

Delamont, S. (1992). *Fieldwork in educational settings: Methods, pitfalls, and perspectives.* London: Falmer.

Gilligan, C., Brown, L. M., & Rogers, A. (1990). Psyche embedded: A place for body, relationships, and culture in personality theory. In A. Rabin, R. Zucker, R. Emmons, & S. Frank (Eds.), *Studying persons and lives.* New York: Springer.

Hertz, R., & Imber, J. B. (1995). *Studying elites using qualitative methods.* Thousand Oaks, CA: Sage.

Hodder, I. (1994). The interpretation of documents and material culture. In N. K. Denzin & Y. S. Lincoln (Eds.), *Handbook of qualitative research* (pp. 393-402). Thousand Oaks, CA: Sage.

Patton, M. Q. (1990). *Qualitative evaluation and research methods.* Newbury Park, CA: Sage. (See Chapters 6 and 7)

Rubin, H. J., & Rubin, I. S. (1995). *Qualitative interviewing: The art of hearing data.* Thousand Oaks, CA: Sage.

Seidman, I. E. (1991). *Interviewing as qualitative research: A guide for researchers in education and the social sciences.* New York: Teachers College Press.

Wolcott, H. F. (1995). *The art of fieldwork.* Walnut Creek, CA: AltaMira.

CHAPTER SIX

•◆•

Issues That Arise
in the Field

࿄⋯•⋯ࣷ

"Did I blow it yesterday!" Anthony groaned to his friends. *"I was taking notes during one of the watercolor workshops and a woman stopped painting and started yelling at me to stop writing. She said I had no right to comment on her painting. She said she knew I was 'The Evaluator'—made me sound dangerous. I tried to tell her I wasn't evaluating her work."*

"That must have been terrible. What did you do?"

"I stopped writing, of course. But then I missed a bunch of notes. How do you take notes if it makes the participants nervous?" asked Anthony.

"I've run into that with some of the women we're talking to," Marla agreed. *"It feels awkward to be writing all the time while they're talking to you—and I want to respond to them. So I write down key words and, as soon as I leave them, I write it up. If they don't mind, I use a tape recorder."*

"Do you find that a lot of them mind the tape recorder?" asked Ruth. *"I'm so afraid that it will scare the kids I'm interviewing that I haven't used one. Maybe I should ask them?"*

"I would. Sometimes, the women like talking into it. They feel I'm hearing them extra!" Marla told her. *"And it does free me to pay attention to them. I still write down key words and make notes afterwards."*

"Now that I think about it, I should be asking them if it's OK. I can't assume they're all alike," Ruth said. *"I've read so much on kids' self-esteem—*

it's really helped me understand what these kids say. So I'll use what I know to help me in the interviews."

"It's hard to remember everything, no?" sympathized Marla. "It's good for me that I used to work in the clinic or else I'd be lost!"

"Tell me about it!" agreed Anthony. "I was having a rough time putting everything together—so many activities going on. It really helped when the director took me on a grand tour of the center . . . and of her mind!"

"What do you mean?" asked Ruth.

"First, she took me around to what she could show me: studios, galleries, classrooms. Then we sat in her office, and she talked me through what she calls a typical week at the center. Also, about what some of her hopes are. She really introduced me to the place," responded Anthony.

"So, how did the watercolor woman know you were 'The Evaluator'?" asked Marla.

"Yeah, there must be some kind of underground! You won't believe what happened to me," interrupted Ruth. "A parent who was picking her kid up one afternoon came up to me. Asked me when I was going to talk to her son. I thought she belonged to one of the kids in a wheelchair. I figured she was going to chew me out. I had permissions and all, but just the same. . . . But her son wasn't even one of mine. She said that a lot of the kids want to talk to me—that they think I really listen to them. How did that happen?"

"It's pretty easy to see that you're really interested in kids," said Anthony. "The word gets around."

"That 'word' can get in the way, too," cautioned Marla. "At first, some of the women in the barrio thought we were coming to check up on them. That's when we had to get more women involved in the planning."

"I know it's OK to change our plans, but how much change is too much?" wondered Ruth. "Sometimes I feel like I'm doing a different study."

Anthony joined her concern. "I'm worried about that, too. I keep asking myself, what am I looking for? There's so much going on. What's important? What isn't? What if I miss something? Sometimes I'm not sure what to record. The other day, when I was eating lunch, a man came up and started to tell me all the things wrong with the center. I'm never sure if I should listen to that stuff."

"Todas las decisiones! My mind feels like it's exploding," moaned Marla. "A lot of things I notice aren't even what I expected to be data. One of the PAs brings her old magazines in to put on the table in the waiting room. I noticed that the issues of Quick and Healthy Cooking get torn up or taken. I mean, women seem to be tearing out recipes or just taking the whole magazine home. I asked Amalia if that bothered her. She said she was just glad they were used. Somehow, I think I've got some valuable data there, but I'm not exactly sure what. And what do I do with it?"

"Since we're all griping, I've got another. I've started thinking about when I finish. How do I say goodbye? Those kids have grown on me," said Ruth. "And how will I know when I have enough data?"

"I think I'll know," answered Anthony. "It'll be when the programs start to get clear. When I have enough to stack them up against what they hoped for—what they can be."

"I expect my teammates will tell me. Or they'll just get tired and stop. Really, we'll know when we can use what we find to change things," said Marla. "Anyway, we're friends now, I think. I probably won't feel like I'm leaving."

"Meanwhile, every day in the field is like a whole new story," said Anthony as they parted. "I never know what I'll run into. Things that can't be taught in class because they are all new and different. Things we have to decide on the spot. I always wonder afterwards, am I making the right decisions?"

Working in the field raises questions. These concerns or worries typically focus on preparing to gather data, getting comfortable in the setting, identifying and creating the data, doing fieldwork in another language, modifying the design as the project unfolds, systematically reflecting on the process, and deciding when to end the study. This chapter addresses these worries through posing nine questions that you may encounter while doing qualitative fieldwork. These questions are listed in Table 6.1 with some suggestions for addressing them.

"HOW DO I PREPARE TO GATHER DATA?"

Qualitative researchers think about how to get ready to gather their data: As described in Chapter 4, access and entry are not casual or random encounters. Although serendipity does play a part in the success of entry, at that point the researcher has already made decisions that influence the encounters. The conceptual framework (see Chapter 3) is a road map the researcher uses to guide data gathering. Reading, hanging around, and talking informally with people are all ways to build familiarity with the setting or subject and to start filling in the framework. Background and

TABLE 6.1 Questions About Gathering Data

How do I prepare to gather data?	Rely on your conceptual framework Talk informally with people in the field Visit the setting to gain first impressions
How can I get comfortable in the field?	Be yourself; do not try to assume an artificial role Establish what you have in common Ask for a "grand tour" Get involved in ways that seem to fit Pay attention to "the underground"
What are the data?	Pay attention to what is going on Write down your hunches and first impressions Do not focus too quickly Do not try to "get it all"
How do I turn sights, sounds, and objects into data?	Take field notes assiduously Tape interviews or take detailed notes Write, write, and write some more
How can I change my research plan?	Hold onto your conceptual framework Be prepared for the unexpected Consider the unexpected and modify your plan
What do I reflect on?	Pay attention to your intuitive insights Note how people react to you Think about what these reactions mean for the study
How do I leave the field?	Set some boundaries Establish these boundaries with participants Alert people that you will be leaving Revisit the research agreements you have made
I am bilingual. What language do I use?	Use the language most comfortable for participants Plan the time to translate into English

a road map can prepare the researcher for the changes he will most likely make, the roadblocks he will surely encounter, and all the surprises and challenges he will face.

Marla, Ruth, and Anthony have read and reflected on their questions to develop conceptual frameworks that evolve as their work progresses (recall the discussion in Chapter 3). Their reading, reflection, and frameworks give their studies purpose; this, in turn, shapes their understandings and implementation of the various data gathering techniques. Marla is aware of current problems in health care for poor women; she wants to link her findings with action to improve their health care. Because Marla is doing a critical case study, she and her team use multiple methods to examine a few specific cases. She starts with participant observation; her action research design requires that she include participants in the data gathering. From her initial observation and informal interviews, she learns what questions are important to women in the community served by the clinic, and she finds volunteers to form a collaborative research team. Together, they frame the specific questions and determine the data gathering techniques.

For his miniethnography of the community arts program, Anthony also uses multiple techniques, but he focuses on the interactions he sees in the community regarding the arts. Anthony has learned about some exemplary community arts programs in other cities, so he has a sense of what high-quality community arts programs can be. He also gathers demographic data about the local community to inform his evaluation. Anthony knows the director needs information to improve the program, so he plans to gather data on the activities and events offered and on what the community may need and be receptive to in the arts. He narrows his focus as he learns.

Ruth began with a foundation of knowledge from her work in the summer camp. To prepare for fieldwork, she reads extensively on children with disabilities. She hangs around an after-school center that happens to serve all children, including a few who use wheelchairs. Because of her experience as an athlete and her background in psychology, she becomes intrigued with the idea of wheelchair-bound children and physical activity. Therefore, she expands her reading to broaden her understanding of "bodiedness." She chooses a phenomenologic study, relying on interviews. Her focus is words and the meanings they convey.

"HOW CAN I GET
COMFORTABLE IN THE FIELD?"

You have negotiated entry and are finally in the field, ready to gather data. What do you actually do in the setting, however? Although you may feel awkward and self-conscious, try just acting naturally as activities and conversations unfold. What you learn in these first few forays will generate new sources for further interviews and observations. You will find you are able to connect with people, and details will fit together. Sometimes the setting is not familiar to you, so you may have to make a conscious attempt to get comfortable in it. We have found that certain strategies help. Establishing some comembership (described in Chapter 4) is one such strategy. Another is building a genuine interest in the activities of the organization or individual. Observing an activity that is routine to the organization or individual and asking questions about that activity is a common strategy.

You might find a **grand tour** of the setting helpful, whether your focus is an organization or an individual. Sometimes this is quite literally a tour—of the school, the office, or the neighborhood. Other times, it is a "tour" of the participant's understanding of his or her lived experience. The tour introduces you to the participants' worlds; it provides a shared experience—albeit small—that can shape future interviews and observations. The informal questions and answers exchanged are often more intriguing than a formal interview in someone's office.

When we interview principals, for example, we start by asking them to show us around the schools. The principals' commentaries as well as what they choose to highlight tell us much about them and their priorities and leadership. During one grand tour, a principal stopped regularly to pick up discarded candy bar wrappers on the stairs saying, "Someone could slip on this." This same man always addressed students with respect and interest. These early impressions of him as a caring and sensitive person were corroborated by data we continued to gather. Similarly, what we learned on grand tours of inclusive schools guided our interviews and sharpened our observations in individual classrooms. For example, during the grand tour of a high school, we observed unusual camaraderie among students, teachers, and security guards in the lunchroom. Our fascination with this scene pushed us to explore student-adult relationships in other areas of the school.

The grand tour can be especially important when the setting is unfamiliar to you. When studying humane societies and zoos, grand tours helped us establish the particular philosophies of the different groups. One zoo director emphasized the importance of holding all the animals in habitats that are as close to nature as possible. She pointed out undusted cobwebs hanging from doorframes—they were allowed to remain because they were "natural." In another site with a similar stated philosophy, the director squashed spiders in an immaculate cage area. We wondered why spiders were not considered part of nature! These actions suggested avenues for exploring the depth of staff beliefs about nature and apparent contradictions between espoused values and values in practice.

Likewise, grand tours of the training facilities for cardiopulmonary resuscitation (CPR) and advanced cardiac life support studies not only familiarized us with settings that were unfamiliar but also shaped our actions. In hospitals, for example, we learned where and when the procedures of interest were likely to be performed, what equipment was available, who actually performed the procedures, and where we were (and were not) welcome. From these tours, we discovered new questions to ask and identified limitations to the studies. We got a sense of what kinds of protocols or checklists might or might not be possible. For example, witnessing a Code Blue (cardiac arrest) was unlikely; we reasoned that we would have to rely on records made by staff who were present for such dramatic events. Because we saw how busy nurses were during these emergencies, we realized they could not do much data gathering for us. We had to modify our design and data gathering techniques.

Specific actions and stances in a setting are related to the researcher's degree of involvement with participants. Are participants sources of information or active collaborators? The degree of involvement with participants depends on the design of the study, how long you anticipate being in the setting, and the willingness of participants (see Chapter 4). If your only interaction is to be a single interview, act fairly formal and appreciative. If you will be conducting iterative interviews with participants, building a more friendly relationship over time is important. This depends, of course, on the personality of the person being interviewed. For example, a student of ours interviewed a famous ballet master during the course of a year, but their relationship remained respectfully formal. Another student interviewed African American women educators who lived and worked in Africa. With some, she developed strong, intimate relationships; others were distant and formal.

In cases in which participants are directly engaged in gathering data, the relationship is collaborative. When we conducted a long-term, state-funded evaluation of teacher assistance teams, we worked closely with department of education personnel who managed the program. We designed the evaluation together. They felt that it was their study, with us supplying technical assistance. We acted accordingly, consulting with them as each step unfolded. Team leaders filled in the case status records, which were our main sources of data. These forms were delivered to the program directors, who relayed them to us for processing and analysis. When the lengthy printout sheets were ready, we sat together with the program personnel to interpret analyses. Over time, these personnel became our colleagues and friends.

Because the observer is also the observed, the researcher's actions soon become part of what we call the *underground*. Word spreads through the informal channels in a setting about how the researcher behaves and what the study is about. These stories of what the researcher is up to go through several iterations as people add their interpretations in the retelling. Awareness of the underground's messages can be a source of comfort—or discomfort—to the researcher. By the time we called the principal of the third school in our inclusion study, the underground had pegged us as "OK." On the phone, the principal was especially cooperative and told us, "I hear you all are pretty good—that you know schools." The hospital underground repeated for months the story of how one of us successfully filled in for a nurse in a simulated Code Blue (cardiac arrest). In another study, we found out that we were referred to as "the doctors," a pun both on our advanced degrees and on the fact that we were conducting a study.

Negative feedback from the underground can also reveal problems or misunderstandings. We have learned at times that we behaved gratuitously or as if we were saviors from the ivory tower—in the eyes of participants. In one study, accusations by his colleagues that we were playing favorites with a director filtered out to us. Had we not been aware of these negative feelings and made an effort to address them, we would have most certainly gathered limited (or even skewed) data. As it was, we cannot be certain that we still did not have problems, but we were aware of them and they revealed conflicts in the setting.

We have learned to keep our ears tuned in to any hints from the underground. Any organization or individual has secrets and closes doors to a researcher. As we have already made clear, participants in the study have a right to their privacy. Still, many of the "secrets" are more or less transparent in the underground, tacitly hidden from "outsiders" but nonetheless apparent to the astute researcher.

Although an underground is not readily accessible (thus its label), participants often try to communicate messages—both positive and negative—in feedback through the underground. Part of our work in the field, therefore, is to discover and gain access to the underground. Whenever we hear references to us or our work, we dig around to find the details behind the reference. For example, when a participant slipped and called one of us "doc," we probed to find out what he meant and who else used that nickname for us.

As you become comfortable (or try to become comfortable), you are apt to make promises to participants. We have learned to be careful about making promises in the field. Although we adamantly contend that the participants should have access to final reports, we consider carefully to whom we promise raw data or field notes, and we seldom promise editing rights. Collaborative efforts, however, do not require promises, just comfort in working together.

"WHAT ARE THE DATA?"

Beginning researchers often ask what to look for and how to know what are data and what are not. Gathering everything will not help analysis, but how do you know what is relevant and what is important? We believe that to be a good qualitative researcher, you develop sensitive eyes and ears, like an artist's or a detective's. This eye (or ear) detects both the figure and the ground—the detail within the whole. You are able to see patterns where others see only individual items. It is a *both-and* kind of thinking. In the classical field-dependence test, you see the face as easily as you see the vase or the old woman as easily as the young woman.

One way to see the figure and ground equally is to train your eyes to draw a mental boundary around the field and then separate out activities, actors, and places within the field. How do the three spheres relate: Which actors are involved in which activities and in which places? Are all actors active? Is activity occurring in all places? Does one activity, actor, or place stand out at one time and something else at another time?

Where do they intersect? This field dependence-independence exercise can clarify your focus.

Developing a sensitive eye or ear is a mixture of skill and craft. Qualitative researchers are focused but remain open to surprises and serendipity. Most important, they develop comfort with ambiguity because although the data may be concrete, their meaning and, therefore, their appearance, changes. Data do merge and emerge. Try not to settle for the first explanation. You identify themes, but be willing to abandon them to create new ones when the originals no longer serve. Seek relationships but do not force fit anything.

Often, the relevant data are obvious: the size and enthusiasm of a crowd attending an event, the effectiveness of a math teacher whose students are applying the proof he has just demonstrated, and the reasons why people say they attended the famous author's lecture. Equally important, however, data are sometimes unobtrusive: the worn carpet leading to the teacher's desk, the sticky glass covering the museum exhibit, and the soda cans and candy wrappers left outside the computer room door. The sensitive eye picks up less obvious aspects of material culture that might be relevant data.

Less obvious data often reveal another story. For instance, during our CPR study, we noticed that instructors passed and certified nearly everyone who attended the course, even though most of the students failed the test based on Red Cross standards. Although we knew that these students had not mastered the technical skills to save a life, they readily told us about their pride in accomplishment, their confidence in their ability to save a life, and their readiness to perform CPR if necessary. These unanticipated data suggested an alternative outcome from the training: the confidence, rather than the skill, to perform. In another instance, a student told us about an evaluation of a training program for entry-level office workers. Her interviews indicated that the program was having minimal effect but, over the duration of the program, she observed that participants' dress became increasingly formal and business-like. The meanings of these observations are open to varying interpretations, but each proved to be relevant data.

Some students tell us that they do not need to seek out data; that as they spend time in their setting, participants offer unsolicited information. People answer unasked questions, explain unquestioned actions, and point out what they consider important scenes or activities. Usually, these data can be relevant. Still, we caution any researcher to filter these offerings through a critical eye, scrutinizing their centrality and accuracy. We remember an art teacher gushing over a quilt he claimed was designed by a group of students to represent their diverse cultures. He gave us pictures of the finished quilt and insisted that it was a marvelous illustration of the progress this multicultural mix of students had made in accepting each other. We noted that no one else mentioned the quilt, so we began to ask about it. Although everyone remarked on its beauty, few indicated that it symbolized any strides in intercultural communication. Some even intimated that the teacher had designed it and done most of the work. Experiences like this have taught us to question unsolicited information.

"HOW DO I TURN SIGHTS, SOUNDS, AND OBJECTS INTO DATA?"

You create data when you record in field notes or interview transcriptions what you have seen and heard. These sights, sounds, and objects become, in effect, artifacts that you refer to when you analyze, interpret, and write about what you have learned. The sounds and sights on audio- and videotapes are data, just as the words you write in field notes are data. Try to take notes that record as completely as possible what you learn in the field. The notes should contain descriptions of settings, people, activities, dialogue, and emotions. They definitely should include your impressions and commentary (recall the discussion about observer comments in Chapter 5). These records are objects. As objects, they are data that may be labeled, categorized, and organized—that is, they may be analyzed and interpreted. (See appendixes for examples of how Marla, Ruth, and Anthony turn what they see and hear into data.)

We try to document as much as we can while we are in the field, but writing field notes while observing or interviewing can be overwhelming, requiring an ambidextrous researcher who also has two heads. Sometimes, taking notes is awkward, inappropriate, or just plain impossible. Still, we have to be sure we capture what we witness. Whatever the status of our field notes, we make time as soon as possible afterwards to complete them, filling in details we were unable to write down at the moment. Sometimes, we escape to an empty corner or a women's room to complete our notes (recall Chapter 5); at other times, this filling in must wait until we are in our car after an interview or observation. Sometimes, we have no choice but to leave the task until we are alone in the evening. The sooner we can complete the notes, the fresher our memories are and, thus, the richer and more accurate the field notes.

Whenever possible, we try to tape-record sessions in the field. In interviews, tapes are especially useful to capture quotes accurately while we are attending to the conversation. If we are moving around or listening to several activities occurring at once, a tape recorder will clearly be of no use. When we can make recordings, they serve to corroborate our notes. Sometimes, we choose not to fully transcribe the tapes; we listen to them to confirm or fill in what we have written or remembered. Whenever using a tape recorder, the unbreakable rule is to obtain permission for its use. A hidden recorder is never acceptable.

Tape recorders can raise concerns. For whatever reasons, some people fear having their spoken ideas recorded. A doctoral student who was studying professional development and the advancement of women working on assembly teams at a car factory was repeatedly refused interviews if she used a tape recorder. The women, who were more than willing to speak to her without a tape recorder, expressed fear that supervisors would hear their voices as they told their stories and would somehow hurt them. The student respected their wishes and simply took notes. Unexpectedly, her study revealed a company whose supervisors regularly encouraged and supported women to use their training to assume more responsibility and leadership, but the women were still apprehensive that their words would be misunderstood or misused.

In some cases, people in a setting do not allow us to take notes. We remember a dramatic example that taught us to be sensitive to the idiosyncratic needs of the participants. During the grand tour of a school we were standing near the mail boxes in the main office, scribbling away. A teacher entered, shouting that someone had stolen the bag containing her medications from her desk. We continued to take notes. The teacher turned to us and nearly screamed, "You stop writing down what I'm saying. It's none of your God-damned business!" The moral of the story: Do not worry about writing down everything that happens!

We have known people who fear tape recorders because they have difficulty articulating their ideas. For example, upon reading a transcript of an interview, one participant implied that the tape had misinterpreted him: "Sure, I may have said that. But that's not what I meant!" Others report feeling foolish when they read transcripts of their words: "I sound so stupid—I keep repeating myself"; "I didn't realize I use 'um' so much. Um, I must have said 'um' twenty times on this page alone"; or "I don' wan' ya ta use no tape. Make me soun lak I don' know nuttin. I jus neva had nuf learnin lik ya-all has." Rendering speech into writing poses difficult problems.

For these reasons, we negotiate with participants about sharing the transcripts. If we want to use a quote, we make contextual decisions as to whether or how we will edit the words. Some idioms and accents or the presence of numerous "ums," when transcribed, obscure the actual message you are hoping to convey by using the quote. For example, the last person quoted previously was a perceptive and intelligent custodian with valuable insights about the organization we were studying. After hearing his response, we transformed his spoken words into standard English because we felt it was ethical to respect his preferences. Our intent was never to make him appear ignorant. We also feared his accent would reveal his identity and wanted to ensure his privacy. In each case, you must make a considered judgment about the effect of editing a transcript; be diligent to document what decisions you make and why.

"I'M BILINGUAL. WHAT LANGUAGE DO I USE?"

Because we live and write in the United States, we presume that the outcome of your research will be presented primarily in English; the analysis that follows flows from this assumption. There are many complex and fascinating circumstances surrounding interviewing and language. Sometimes the researcher conducts an interview in a language other than her primary language—for example, a student from Uganda or Taiwan interviews in English, or a German graduate student interviews American doctors about socialized health care. Another circumstance is when the researcher interviews in her primary language, which is not English—for example, a Puerto Rican researcher interviews in New York City in Spanish. A third is when both interviewer and participant are fully and fluently bilingual; they slip between the two languages during the interview. You may think of other configurations. Because these researchers work in the United States, they must figure out ways to represent what they have learned in English.

Ideally, the interview is conducted in the language that feels most comfortable for both the participant and the interviewer. If the researcher is fluent in the language the participant prefers, there are fewer issues to deal with than if she is not fluent. Fluency enhances understanding of specific terms as well as deeper knowledge of cultural meanings. The researcher understands subtle and idiomatic uses of phrases and terms. Without such fluency, however, she may not fully comprehend connotations or may not make connections with the assumed knowledge that comes from membership in a cultural or linguistic group. We recommend that the researcher conducting interviews in a language other than her primary one be aware of the potential to miss nuanced meanings. The researcher could engage someone fluent in that language to help with the analysis and interpretation of data.

When a researcher conducts interviews in a language other than English, at some point they must be translated into English if she works in an English-speaking context. In this case, the researcher's workload increases enormously. Depending on the researcher's fluency in English, the task of transcribing a tape in Spanish, for example, and then translating it into English at least doubles the work. We know of no shortcuts to this process except for the fully bilingual person who, when analyzing, can apply English categories to Spanish texts, for example. Moreover, when analyzing and presenting the research, additional considerations arise. If you have translated from another language into English, what constitutes the direct quotes? Can you use translated words as a direct quote? How do you signal that a translation is accurate and captures the subtle meanings of the original language?

Marla and her team conduct several interviews in Spanish; this is Marla's primary language, although she is fluent in oral English. They do not fully translate all the tapes into English; instead, they listen to them several times and then select segments for translation. They decide that, in the final report that Marla must submit for her class, they will provide an appendix that includes examples of interview segments in both Spanish and English, showing the reader how they have translated them.

As our society becomes more multicultural, an increasing number of people are fully bilingual. In a research setting, they may move from one language to another, depending on setting and topic. One principal we interviewed spoke about the children in Spanish, the pedagogical and organizational issues in English, and community politics in Spanish.

"HOW CAN I CHANGE MY RESEARCH PLAN?"

Marla, Ruth, and Anthony find that the data gathering process is not linear, clear, or rigid. As they enter their settings, they get confused. As they spend more time on their projects, they modify their data gathering techniques. Ruth is unsure about what to look for at the beginning; eventually, she decides to use interviews to learn about the life experiences of children in wheelchairs. But, after she meets Katrine, she adds another disability, deafness. After reflecting on her informal interviews with the health care team in the clinic, Marla realizes that her techniques must include the poor women of the community who are affected by the problems she is concerned about. Anthony's early observations and survey returns reveal that people in the community may not understand that the program is available to them, so he holds several focus groups to explore both community interests and ways to "market" the programs.

In another example, our reading, reflection, and conceptual framework for the study of inclusive classrooms helped prepare us to gather data. At the outset, our purpose was to learn how children with disabilities were doing in these settings. We assumed that our observations would focus exclusively on these children. As we read more about inclusive education and as we sat and watched in classrooms, we realized that we needed to look at how all children were learning in inclusive schools, so we broadened our observational focus.

"WHAT DO I REFLECT ON?"

You will directly encounter the phenomenon of reflexivity as you gather data. No matter how unobtrusive you try to be, you cannot help but become a part, however small, of the setting. Marla's presence in her site is obvious and interactive because she is working as a volunteer and collaborating with others for data gathering, but neither Ruth nor Anthony are invisible in their settings. The children get used to Ruth, but her presence adds an external dimension to each interview. At a large public performance, Anthony may not be noticed as an evaluator, but he is, in fact, a member of the audience. You are part of the social world you study; you affect that world. How people in that world respond to you is often as informative as answers to your questions or what you see through observations. Your presence in the field is inseparable to the outcome or product of data gathering. As we have noted many times, including your reactions and impressions as observer or interviewer comments in your field notes is a crucial element of documenting the processes and decisions of your work.

Reflexivity also involves those observed. The families of Ruth's children react to her, too. They may see her as an intrusive student from the ivory tower who could never understand their realities. They might also assume that she is interested because she or someone close to her has a disability. Still, they might even believe she is a "spy" from some conservative coalition that is protesting increased funding for special education. Their hypotheses grow out of their personal backgrounds and beliefs as well as what Ruth looks like and what they see her do. Similarly, Anthony's audiences create ideas and explanations for his presence and questions.

Because they are researchers with specific purposes, and not casual observers, Anthony and Ruth test their reflexive reactions—their emergent hypotheses—as they gather data. They form hypotheses based on initial data and then revise those working understandings in light of additional data. They continue to watch, ask, and listen. They become analytic and reflective during the data gathering processes. Ruth monitors her reactions; she then examines these reactions to determine to what extent her own fears, sophistication, or dislikes shape her impressions. At the same time, she considers how the childrens' values and prejudices might be interacting with hers to influence their acceptance or dismissal of her. Because she tries to be aware of reflexivity, Ruth's observations are multifaceted in that she questions her role, constructs hypotheses, and tests impressions against additional data.

As part of their reflection, Marla, Ruth, and Anthony examine the contexts they are studying. Anthony considers the history of community involvement in this area of the city. How have residents reacted to other activities and events such as the arts program? What are the demographics of the community? Has anything happened recently that might influence the way residents respond to the arts center? Marla also seeks out information she may not know already about the community. She asks what the clinic workers have viewed as problems in the past and if any unique history exists that she should know about. When Ruth observes at the after-school program early in her study, she might ask the following: How long has this group been together? Have children come and gone? Has the group had other observers? How was she introduced? and Are the children predominately of a different gender or ethnic group than Ruth? As researchers, all three recognize that their interviews and observations, as well as the material culture available to them, are embedded in a larger context and place in time. They make this larger context and history a part of their data gathering.

"HOW DO I LEAVE THE FIELD?"

As you gather data, you will notice that, wittingly or not, you are analyzing them. In fact, the early stages of data analysis occur simultaneously with data gathering. You see patterns emerge; you gather more data to check out the possible patterns. You identify a category; you ask questions to elucidate. Finally, this ongoing analysis signals when you have enough data.

In theory, because it is heuristic, field research is never complete; new data are constantly being generated and new discoveries can always be made. In practice, fieldwork is seldom a one-shot event or a single episode. An ethnography calls for long-term immersion. A phenomenological study requires iterative interviews. Case studies might necessitate successive observations and interviews with several persons. For almost all studies, follow-up visits or phone calls are necessary.

At some point, however, you become aware that you can make sense of the people or settings you have been studying—you can tell a coherent story about what you have learned. You realize that the data seem redundant, your major insights are supported and explicated, or you just plain know you have answered your questions. Maybe you have completed the contracted number of visits or funding has run out. The strange has become familiar. Time has come to leave the field.

Leaving the field may simply mean that you do not return to a site or seek another interview. If you have been in the field for only a short while, chances are you have not established deep or intimate relationships that will be ending. If, however, you have built relationships, leaving the field can be a bit like "breaking up," to use a dating metaphor (Ball, 1990). If the parties became close, ending fieldwork can be painful. Jonathan Kozol relates such pain as he says good-bye to his participants in *Amazing Grace: The Lives of Children and the Conscience of a Nation* (1995).

Often, we have continued, on a different level, relationships we have built with participants in our studies. There is no longer a study to bring us together; we are just friends. One such personal friend is the director of a teacher assistance team program we evaluated several years ago (Rallis, 1990). Our partnership (Rossman and Rallis) as friends and coauthors began when one of us was the evaluator of the other's program. We came to know each other as we spent time together in the field of the project. Although that project ended, we continue to spend time together and still work together. Leaving the field, then, does not always mean ending relationships.

Whatever the relationships a qualitative researcher encounters, we have to think about the impact we might have had on participants. It may be more than we suspect. Siskin (1994) tells of a high school student who was deeply moved by the attention the interviewer paid her during a 30-minute interview. The student said she told the interviewer "stuff" she would not reveal to parents, teachers, or social workers. Later, at a crisis in her life, she asked if she could talk to the researcher again. Delamont (1992) argues that the qualitative research experience qualitatively changes both the researcher and the researched; neither will ever be quite the same again.

USING THE HABITS
OF MIND AND HEART

Our characters are facing the challenge of thinking on the run—of making decisions while working in the field. Once again, it is those habits they carry in their minds and hearts that help them answer questions that arise in the field. Because of the ambiguous nature of qualitative research, they can never anticipate all the questions that will arise. As they prepare and become more comfortable in their new role as researchers, they remember that their strong good sense about other people will serve them in good stead. As they figure out what are the data and how to record them diligently, they engage in the systematic inquiry that marks their work as ethical, trustworthy, and credible. Their habits also tell them when and how to leave the field. They discern when they have enough data to tell a coherent and meaningful story. They know that the time to analyze and interpret—to write the story—has come. Analyzing and interpreting is the subject of Chapter 7.

CHAPTER SEVEN

•◆•

Analyzing and Interpreting Data

⟨୨⟩ ⋯ ⟨ୣ⟩

"Boy, do I have a lot of data. The problem now is trying to make sense of all of it," moaned Anthony. "I'm not sure what I'm doing but I heard from a friend who took this course a year ago that this is the hardest part. And we thought designing our projects was work?"

"Me, too. I've got interview transcripts, my field notes, the journals two of the women have kept. . . . I've spent a fair amount of time every two or three days going over stuff and making sure it's all 'clean,' as Kent said. I think I'm in pretty good shape," responded Marla.

"I've had several really long interviews with the kids, but I haven't transcribed them yet. That's going to be a huge task," said Ruth. "Remember what Kent said about devoting five or six hours to each hour of interviewing? Whew!"

"Yo lo sé! I've had to chain myself to the computer to keep up with mine!" said Marla. "Pero, it's been incredibly useful. I've discovered things the women talked about that I'd forgotten. Like, right after the interview, they flew out of my mind! Transcribing their exact words has got me back into it. And then when I share a transcript with one of the women, she has lots more to say. It's like a stimulus to talk more deeply."

"Are you doing it in English or Spanish?" asked Anthony.

"A lot of my interviews are in Spanish," answered Marla. *"I don't bother translating them because so far my coding works across the languages. How are you doing?"*

"I've got all sorts of data," said Anthony. *"Remember, I've got those surveys—they're pretty easy. The responses fit into about five categories. And there's my interviews and the field notes. I've made a couple of starts, but I wish I'd kept up with it more."*

"I'd like to try using one of those software programs Kent talked about," commented Ruth. *"I'll bet it makes it a whole lot easier."*

"Yeah, but remember what the doctoral students said when they made that presentation in class? That using the computer doesn't do the analysis for you; it just helps with some of the organizing," cautioned Anthony.

"But one of the students said that, if you use software, you can sometimes see patterns you might have missed," countered Ruth. *"Just that would be real helpful. Where are you in all this, Marla?"*

"I don't think I'd feel comfortable using something like that. I'd like to keep my hands on all the text I've gotten. . . . I think I'll use magic markers, in lots of different colors," Marla mused. *"I'd like to do some preliminary work, and then get the women involved. One is real interested in helping me analyze the data; the others just don't have time. I wish they all could work on this. I guess trying to do an action research project and make it participatory is tough! I have to respect their boundaries, but I feel a bit uncomfortable doing most of it myself."*

"I hear you," sympathized Ruth. *"It feels like I'm playing God coming up with what matters to these kids. I just care about them a lot! They've been so open and want to talk about what it's like for them. But their stories are all so different. I don't seem to be coming up with themes, like Kent said we should."*

"I'll tell you what I've started doing," offered Anthony. *"When I've entered my field notes into word processing, I format it so I've got big margins on the right-hand side. I've printed out several days of field notes and tried to code them. First, I've read through and put codes down; then I've gone back and entered those into the big margin. I'm only using four so far. I guess others will come up as I go along."*

"Just remember that you may have to redo all those codes, if you learn new stuff or your analysis develops! I'm not sure I would want to do that all over again!" cautioned Ruth. *"Better to wait until the data are all gathered, then just burn on it!"*

"But the coding is only a piece of it. First you have to know what you're coding for!" Marla reminded the other two. *"In some ways this reminds me*

of analyzing literature. Look at the whole and figure out what the author meant."

"That's the point!" said Anthony, ". . . sorting out the meaning of structures, events, of people. Asking how they relate. What rules are operating. Making those taxonomies and typologies. I've started to ask, do a certain number of people have to attend a workshop for it to be a workshop?"

"What was it that Kent said? That coding is . . . what was it? Something about being the formal representation of all that analytic thinking? Was that it?" asked Marla.

"Yeah. The coding's not the thinking; the coding's where we end up. The hard thinking comes first," commented Anthony. "I like the analogy to a wine connoisseur: You have to have tasted a lot of wines and thought about their tastes a lot, before you can pass judgment on any one."

"Either that, or be prepared to go over and over the wine—I mean data—coding it more than once!" said Ruth. "Just thinking about this is making my brain hurt! I need to go back to my little miniproposal and see what I thought I was looking for. That could be a trigger to help me think about more categories."

"But that's one of the things Kent keeps repeating: coding isn't a one-shot process. . . . It can go on and on. Just when you think you've got it, something else comes up!" responded Marla.

"We need to be able to put forward a story line for what we've learned. One that someone else could support. I need to demonstrate what's happening in the program so that people can buy it. There's all that stuff about trustworthiness, remember?" said Anthony.

"I still think it feels weird trying to splice up what the women have talked about and summarizing it down into a paper," Marla worried. "It takes all our work together . . . and makes it seem so—limited—or trivial!"

"That's just part of the process. The work is the whole project; the paper summarizes all that for Kent," reminded Anthony. "I think writing analytic memos will help a lot. Have you two tried that yet?"

"I took a stab at one. About how the women feel ignored when they come into the clinic," responded Marla. "I'm going to work on it more and then share it with them, before I hand it in to Kent next week. It's about four or five pages long."

"I don't know," mused Ruth. "Analytic memos are supposed to help our thinking along, but it seems so formal to write them. I always find it hard to get started writing. I just seem to clam up."

"Not a problem around us, Ruth! Just write!" suggested Anthony. "Sit at the computer and pretend you're writing to a friend. Tell him what you're *doing and what you're learning. Put in some juicy quotes. Then throw it away, if you don't like it!"*

"No, no!" interjected Marla. "Don't ever throw away what you write. Think of it as 'work in progress.' You don't have to share those with anyone; they're for you. Think of writing as part of the analyzing process."

"Well, all I know is, interpretation turns me on," said Anthony. "I've loved figuring out what's really going on at the gallery opening. I mean, are people truly enjoying it or are they just pretending because it's what they think they are supposed to do?"

"I'll admit, it is exciting," agreed Ruth. "I'm just not sure yet whether I should go looking for particular themes or if they will emerge from the data. Which is it?"

Analyzing and interpreting qualitative data is the process of systematically organizing the interview transcripts, field notes, and other materials you have collected; bringing meaning to them so they tell a coherent story; and writing it all up so that others can read what you have learned. It entails organizing these materials into "chunks" (analysis) and bringing meaning to those chunks (interpretation). One way to think about analysis is that it begins at the same time as a study does—at the conceptualization stage. The conceptual framework of the study, the attendant research questions, the strategy for research and design, and the genre to which your study links all provide preliminary foreshadowing of the analysis. Think of analysis as your emerging understanding of what you are learning. At the beginning of a study, this understanding is formalized in the conceptual framework, as we have noted throughout the previous chapters. Decisions made early on shape your study. Moreover, as you gather data, this framework constrains and directs just what data you collect. Decisions made in the field focus your analysis as you discover important but unanticipated ideas and shift emphasis in interviews or observations. All this is part of data analysis and interpretation.

Two metaphors are useful for understanding data analysis. Imagine a closet full of clothes; these are your data. You can organize the clothes by color (blue slacks and sweaters together), by type (all the slacks in one pile), by season for use (heavy winter clothing), or by fabric (cottons all on the same shelf). Each organization (your analysis) is valuable and justifiable, depending on your purpose. As another metaphor, picture a child's playroom filled with toys. Some are dolls, others are trucks and cars, and still others are puzzles and crayons. The child could pull together all the red toys into one pile and the green ones into another. The child could then re-sort the toys into ones that move (trucks and trains), those he or she can build with (Tinkertoys and Leggos), or those she can draw with (pencils, magic markers, and crayons). Data analysis is a similar process of sorting, categorizing, grouping, and regrouping the data into piles or "chunks" that are meaningful. Plan to group and regroup your data several times throughout the analysis process. Each grouping allows you to see different aspects of the data, enriching your understanding and insight into what you have learned.

Throughout a study, you are analyzing and interpreting data, although it may be more focused and instrumental at various times. A particular interview may shape the direction your study takes. Observations yield important insights that you pursue in subsequent observations or interviews. This emergent learning, discussed in Chapter 1 and illustrated in Chapters 5 and 6, is the hallmark of qualitative inquiry: You learn as you go. The way you organize that learning—the categories and themes you chunk what you learn into—is analysis. The meaning you make of these chunks is interpretation.

DECISIONS ABOUT ANALYSIS

The analysis strategy in a qualitative study is based on several decisions: when you formally analyze, how open-ended or prefigured the analysis is, and the genre to which your study links.

Ongoing Analysis Versus Analysis at the End

In terms of when you formally analyze, there are basically two options: ongoing analysis or analysis at the end of data gathering. Ongoing analysts formally reflect about the data, ask analytic questions, and write analytic memos throughout a study. Those who analyze at the end wait until all (or most) of the data are gathered and then begin the task of asking analytic questions. There are advantages and disadvantages to both. Most beginners find it easier to focus on building relations and gathering data, holding off on formal analysis until the end of the study. More experienced field-workers tend to analyze as they go. We recommend that the beginner try to do some analysis as the study unfolds; it makes final analysis easier and less daunting. Keep in mind the following pointers to facilitate analysis, whether ongoing or toward the end:

- Keep your questions in mind. Remember what you are trying to learn about. Stay connected to the qualitative genre framing your study.
- Modify your data gathering based on what you are learning, not chance. Ask analytic questions as you go along.
- Write all the time. Note hunches, thoughts, impressions; write analytic memos. Keep a journal and reread it from time to time; write a letter or email to a friend (be sure you keep a copy).
- Talk your ideas through with people. Develop a critical friend or talk with the participants.
- Read and read and read what others have said about the topic. Use the research literature, movies, novels, poems, and art to gain insight.
- Be creative. Use metaphors, create images, draw pictures, use visual images, and draw concept maps. Think about how you might characterize what you are learning; What is it like? What images does it evoke?

In addition, practice good management skills for keeping the data organized and accessible; these facilitate analysis, whether done concurrently or at the end. Discipline yourself to log the day's activities, noting the date, what you did, names, times, and places. Write down attendance at events, chronologies, descriptions of settings, and maps of settings. Do not rely on your memory, which, several months into a study, will (more than likely) fail you. Build in time in quiet places for note taking. One of our students diligently went to a nearby Dunkin' Donuts shop after each data gathering session to log his activities and write notes about his impressions. Such practices pay off by keeping the data intact, complete, organized, and accessible. They are invaluable for defining categories for data analysis, planning further data collection, and especially for writing the final report. Be diligent in these management tasks!

Structured or Open-Ended Analysis

Another decision to be made is how prefigured or open-ended is the analysis. Prefigured studies are controlled by the researcher: Questions are specific, the study is implemented as planned, and analytic categories have been identified at the conceptualization and design phase. Open-ended studies, in contrast, pose grand tour questions, are open to the unexpected, and let the analytic direction of the study emerge as it progresses. Forecasting or closely stipulating analytic categories does not occur with open-ended studies. In practice, studies fall somewhere along a continuum, as with the assumptions you make about social science and society (discussed in Chapter 3). Most studies are more or less either open-ended or prefigured; few are all one way or the other.

Qualitative studies tend to be designed with at least some open-ended features. Whether you make tight analytic decisions before data collection or begin the process during data collection depends on the genre of your study and its duration. Generating categories of data to collect, or cells in a matrix, early in your study can be an important focusing device. Tightly structured, highly organized data gathering and analyzing schemes, however, often limit flexibility and hide the unusual, the serendipitous—the paradox that can lead to insights. Try to find a balance between efficiency considerations and the flexibility of your design.

Analysis Related to Qualitative Genre

Analysis is also shaped by the genre framing your study. Phenomenologic studies are open-ended, searching for the themes of meaning in participants' lives. Broad categories are sought, with subthemes to elaborate the topography of meaning. Ruth's study focuses on the sports experience of children with physical disabilities. Focusing questions capture the children's feelings of shame or joy in sports activities, how their families support their independence, and the meanings associated with "differentness." These questions provide preliminary categories for Ruth to rely on as she begins to analyze the data. (Ruth's analysis is elaborated in Appendix A.) A feminist phenomenologic study would search for the deep meaning of women's experiences. The conceptual framework would elaborate important categories for data gathering and analysis: women's experiences of patriarchy, how oppression plays out in their lives, specific instances of discrimination because of gender, and what strategies the women use to confront or acquiesce in domination. Just as in Ruth's case, the research questions (as stipulated early on and then modified) provide a starting place for analysis.

Ethnographies usually begin with broad domains for gathering data that then shape analysis; they are balanced between structure and openness. Central to ethnographic studies is the concept of culture. Although vague and ambiguous, the concept focuses attention on widely shared and deeply held beliefs extant in a cultural group. Anthony's study focuses on program staff's and community members' beliefs about the arts, participation in events and activities, and the value to the community of the program. These categories—arts, participation, and value—are guides for his analysis. (See Appendix C for details on Anthony's processes of data analysis.) A critical ethnography would search for the class-, race-, or perhaps gender-based structures of domination that shape participation by community members. The critical ethnographer would search for evidence of hegemony or paternalism in the program, asking whose conception of the arts is expressed in the program and how participation is defined. Analysis would focus on ways community members reproduce or resist possibly elitist and exclusionary ideas inherent in the program.

Case studies are uniquely intended to capture the complexity of a particular event, program, individual, or place. They focus holistically on the organization or individual. The conceptual framework and research questions, however, stipulate this broad focus more closely. A case study of an organization would specify the elements of interest—for example, leadership, decision making, and informal communication. These categories then provide the initial ways for thinking analytically and for a first cut on coding the data. A critical case study assumes that the case exemplifies oppression and domination in specific ways. Marla assumes a feminist and class-based perspective with her interests in poor women's health. As her project unfolds, she and her team focus on the ways that clinic services are structured to perpetuate middle-class values that exclude the poor women's choices in health care. (This collaborative process is detailed in Appendix B.)

Analysis, then, proceeds logically and systematically from decisions made early on; it does not begin de novo at some point in the study. Decisions made about the specific strategy, assumptions about knowledge and truth, and the genre most congruent with these decisions all forecast analysis. Whether you analyze as you go or hold off until the end of a study, whether you have stipulated analytic categories at the conceptualization stage or let them emerge, and whatever the qualitative genre framing the study, the processes of analysis are similar. We next discuss the generic processes of analyzing and interpreting qualitative data and then present specific strategies for analyzing interview data, field notes, and objects of material culture.

GENERIC ANALYSIS

Data analysis is the process of bringing order, structure, and meaning to the mass of collected data. It is time-consuming, creative, and fascinating. Analytic procedures typically fall into the following six phases:

- Organizing the data
- Familiarizing yourself with the data
- Generating categories, themes, and patterns
- Coding the data
- Searching for alternative explanations of the data
- Writing the report

Each phase entails data reduction as the reams of collected data are brought into manageable chunks and interpretation as you bring meaning and insight to the words and actions of the participants. Data analysis and interpretation have parallels with the creative process (Bargar & Duncan, 1982), which entails immersion, incubation, insight, and interpretation. During the processes of organization and familiarization, you immerse yourself in the data, becoming deeply involved in words, impressions, and the flow of events. Then let the data "stew" on the back burner of your mind; this leads to insight about the salient themes and meaning embedded in the data. You then code and recode the data in instrumental ways, developing the interpretations that are written in the final report. Be prepared for the amount of time analysis and interpretation take—generally two or three times the hours gathering the data entailed. Thus, for a 90-minute interview, plan 3 or 4 hours for category generation and coding.

Organizing the Data

As a preliminary step, inventory on note cards the data that you have gathered. You might also perform the minor editing necessary to make field notes retrievable and generally "clean up" what seems overwhelming and unmanageable, if you have not already done so. We cannot emphasize enough how important it is to do this cleaning up and organizing as you go along. It saves time, creates a more complete record, and stimulates analytic thinking. Be sure that you know where and when you took field notes, who was there, and what the event was. Check to be sure that interview transcriptions are dated and you are sure whom you interviewed.[1] Also, be sure that you have written down hunches and analytic ideas throughout the study; this shapes and refines your thinking and provides insights for analysis. At this time, you could also enter the data into one of several software programs for analysis (Richards & Richards, 1994; Tesch, 1990). The data generated by qualitative methods are voluminous. Be prepared for this sheer volume. Find a way to store the data so you know where different pieces are and so they are safe. As analysis proceeds, however, be confident that your organizational scheme will change.

Ruth's preliminary organization is very simple. Because she is relying primarily on interviews, she keeps her transcripts in files identified by the children's names. As she becomes more confident about the salient themes, however, she reorganizes segments of data into those themes. She then creates folders (or files in a software program) for the themes. As she writes the final report, she relies on this thematic organization, which pulls together data from five children and their families. (See Appendix A.)

Anthony initially organizes his data by the various data gathering techniques he uses: He has one folder for interviews and others for the survey returns and observations. As he gets more deeply into analysis, however, he also organizes the data into events based on his reasoning that telling the stories of participation and beliefs about it are best depicted through concrete incidents. His observations at arts events (the opening of the gallery and a dance exhibition) and his interviews with people who attend them are all in one folder (See Appendix C). Marla's strategy is similar to Anthony's. She initially organizes the data by source: her observations, field notes of team meetings, and interviews with prospective team members. She and her team then reorganize the data into salient themes. They also develop files for data about the three women on whom they focus in-depth. These files contain the team's notes, transcriptions of interviews, and the women's journals. (See Appendix B.)

Familiarizing Yourself With the Data

Read, reread, and once more read through the data. This intense and often tedious process enables you to become familiar with what you have learned in intimate ways. What if you have not transcribed all your interviews? How can you read through them? Students often ask if they must transcribe all the interviews they have conducted. We usually temporize, saying "it depends." There is no substitute for transcribing interviews: It familiarizes you with the data, provides leads for further data gathering, provokes insights, and stimulates analytic thinking. Transcribing is not a mere technical exercise. Not all people are visual learners, however; some learn better when they listen. If you are an oral learner, you are probably better served by listening, listening, and listening again to tape-recorded interviews. You might even listen to them in your car as you drive. You can then note passages that you will transcribe selectively (not while driving, please). However you choose to do it, you must become intimately familiar with the data. This takes extraordinary discipline.

Generating Categories, Themes, and Patterns

This phase of data analysis is the most difficult, complex, ambiguous, creative, and fun, but there are few descriptions of this process in the methodologic literature. Thoughtful analysis demands a heightened awareness of the data, a focused attention to those data, and an openness to the subtle, tacit undercurrents of social life.

As you read through field notes or listen to interview tapes, images, words, and emotions sift through your mind. During this immersion process, your task is to identify salient themes, recurring ideas or language, and patterns of belief that help you respond to your research questions. This is an intellectually challenging phase of data analysis; through interrogating the data and reflecting on the conceptual framework, you engage in significant intellectual work. Generating categories is, to some extent, an art; recall the discussion of data gathering techniques as art in Chapter 5. Just as you uniquely implement these techniques, so too analysis and interpretation are an expression of your individual understanding of the phenomenon you study. You may organize your clothing by fabric; someone else might do it by color.

The process of category generation involves identifying patterns in the data: recurring ideas, themes, perspectives, and descriptions that depict the social world you are studying. Recall that early category generation links back to the conceptual framework of the study. In reading related literature, you will have identified what other researchers found salient about the topic; what they wrote about can be a preliminary guide. Do some concept mapping in which you brainstorm what are the important ideas that recur: Put them down on paper, and then draw arrows to show how you think they relate to one another. Look for recurring words that participants use to describe something. Try some analogies. Talk to a critical friend. Set yourself the task of telling that person the three or four important ideas that you are learning from your study. All these strategies help category identification.

Patton (1990, pp. 306, 393-400) describes inductive analysis as a strategy to identify salient categories or themes. You may construct indigenous typologies (classification schemes)—the emic view—or analyst-constructed typologies—the etic view—to describe patterns in the data. Indigenous typologies are expressed by participants and are generated through your analysis of how they use language and what they express. Analyst-constructed typologies are created by the researcher and do not necessarily correspond directly to the categories of meaning used by the participants. This process entails describing patterns, themes, and categories that you see in the data and may well be subject to the "legitimate charge of imposing a world of meaning on the participants that better reflects the observer's world than the world under study" (Patton, 1990, p. 398). Through logical reasoning, you may identify ways of conceptualizing data that then generate new insights or typologies for further exploration. Usually presented as matrices, etic typologies suggest missing elements in your analysis; you may discover areas in which data might be logically found. Patton (1990) cautions you not to allow these matrices to lead your analysis; instead, use them to generate sensitizing concepts to guide further explorations: "It is easy for a matrix to begin to manipulate the data as the analyst is tempted to force the data into categories created by the cross-classification to fill out the matrix and make it work" (p. 412).

Coding

As Marla states in the vignette at the beginning of this chapter, coding is the formal representation of analytic thinking. It is not, however, simply a "bookkeeping" task; it is complex and iterative. Coding entails thinking through what you take as evidence of a category or theme. Categories are concepts—abstractions. In coding the data, you will have to be clear about what words or phrases illustrate and elaborate each of those concepts. What do Marla and her team take as evidence of gender discrimination in the clinic? What does Anthony judge to be a perspective on participating in arts events? How does Ruth decide which stories told by the children show joy? Because abstractions are ephemeral and vague, your task is to make them concrete through snippets and segments of data. These decisions—what constitutes evidence of a category—should be solid and grounded in the data. As noted in Chapter 3 in the discussion of trustworthiness, the grounds for these decisions should be clear to anyone who reads your work; they should not be capricious or insupportable.

Plan to code your data more than once because thinking in terms of evidence stimulates insights, often generating new categories or seeing categories collapse. The first coding should be simple and elegant: Use four or five large categories initially. Then recode the data, refining those categories or adding new ones. These "big-chunk" categories may well become the major sections of the final report—the chapters of the story you want to tell about what you have learned.

The mechanics of coding vary, depending on your style and what works for you. Despite this age of software alternatives, many researchers use hard copy and code the data by hand. Anthony formats his word-processed data with wide margins on the right-hand side. He codes the data by bracketing chunks and writing a word representing a category in the margin. He could use symbols instead of words, but he needs to use a scheme that is simple and clear to him and to others. Marla plans to use colored magic markers to indicate categories. If you should use this option, have plenty of copies of the data handy because blocking over with magic markers gets messy. Both Marla and Anthony then make

TABLE 7.1 Anthony's Data Summary Form

	Interviews	*Field Notes*	*Material Culture*
Category: "strong participation"	ML #1: 14, 17 JB #2: 2, 14, 30 DE #1: 3-4, 6, 11 JC #3: 5, 7-9 JE #1: 2-4, 8, 19 KG #2: 7, 15-17	10/3: 9-11, 15 10/7: 18-22, 24, 27 10/12: 2-3, 5, 18	10/3 Attendance receipts 10/7 Center log 10/9 Meeting minutes
Category: "involvement in decisions"	DE #2: 5 JE #1: 14-15 FR #4: 16-17, 22 JB #2: 2-3, 17	10/1: 1-3, 5, 7 10/9: 6, 8-10 10/22: 3-6, 18, 22	10/9 Meeting minutes

lists on 5 × 8 cards, on which they note particular categories. This process pulls together in one place all the instances of, for example, strong participation in Anthony's case. He lists that evidence of participation is found in an interview, with whom the interview was conducted, and on what page the instance is found. One of his 5 × 8 cards is presented in Table 7.1. He indicates interviewees by their initials (ML), the interview by number (#1), and the pages on which he has found evidence of strong participation. He lists field notes by date and page numbers. Evidence in material culture is listed by date and type.

Searching for Alternative Understandings

As you identify categories and patterns among them, you will have to challenge the very patterns that seem so apparent. You must search for other plausible explanations for the story line you are developing. Alternative understandings always exist; you will need to search for, identify, and describe them and then demonstrate how the interpretation you put forward is sound and grounded in the data. For example, Anthony remarks that high attendance and the party atmosphere at the gallery opening indicate the pleasure and enjoyment people have in seeing the displays. He also questions, however, whether the actions of the participants might not be the result of expectations; they think they are supposed to enjoy themselves. He might also consider that the food and friendship, not the art, are a possible cause.

Recall that you are building an argument or interpretation about what you have learned in the field—an argument that is more compelling than the other alternatives. This argument builds logical relationships among your assertions, documents them with evidence, and presents a summation of your conclusions that relate to what is known in the literature. You are evaluating the plausibility of your interpretations and testing them through the data. This entails a search through the data during which you challenge your interpretations, search for negative instances of the patterns, and incorporate these into your interpretation. That Anthony notes a pattern of participation and pleasure across events supports his first interpretation.

Part of this process is to assess the data for their credibility, usefulness, and centrality to your major points. Although rigorous procedures can be set up to determine if a participant is consistently truthful, a more reasonable stance is to approach the data with humility, noting that the data are what participants said to you in interviews or what you observed, rather than making broad assertions that imply Truth (with a capital T). You also need to consider whether or not the data are useful in illuminating the questions being explored, and whether or not they are central to the story that is unfolding about the social phenomenon. Some data are just more relevant that others; your task is to make decisions diligently about what is significant and what is not. Involving a critical friend can be useful for being sure that you are not excluding data that hint at an intriguing counterexample.

Writing the Report

Writing about qualitative data cannot be separated from the analytic process. In fact, it is central to that process because, in the choice of particular words to summarize and reflect the complexity of the data, the researcher is engaging in the interpretive act, lending shape and form—meaning—to massive amounts of raw data. The interpretive process illuminates the multiple meanings of events, objects, activities, experiences, and words. Writing reveals these discovered meanings to the reader, so writing must include description. Because the writing process is so crucial, we discuss it fully in Chapter 8. For now, we turn to a brief discussion of three specific analysis strategies drawn from cognitive anthropology, phenomenology, and narrative analysis for analyzing interview data.

STRATEGIES FOR ANALYZING INTERVIEW DATA

Three strategies for analyzing interview data offer refinements in the generic process detailed previously. Grounded in different genres of qualitative research, they provide different insights into the analytic process.

Analyzing Ethnographic Interview Data

As mentioned in Chapter 5 in the section on ethnographic interviews, cognitive anthropologists are interested in uncovering the structures by which participants organize their lives: the classification schemes—the mental maps—that guide their understandings of their worlds. These ethnographers search for cultural domains of knowledge—categories of cultural meaning that include smaller categories. They conduct field-work, gathering data through participant observation and interviewing. Through this work, they uncover salient cultural domains, assigning them *cover terms* (the name for the domain), *included terms* (what is in and what is outside the domain), and *semantic relationships* (how the terms relate to one another).

As the researcher builds an understanding of cultural domains, he or she engages participants in structured interviews, often guided by card sorts. The researcher writes included terms—words—on cards and invites interview participants to sort these cards into semantic relationships that depict their mental models. Examples of semantic relationships include the following: "x is a kind of y"; "x is a reason for doing y"; "x is used for y"; or "x is a characteristic of y".[2] Participants then move the cards around to show how terms relate to one another. The purpose is to flesh out a classification scheme or relationship—the cognitive structure—operating in participants' minds. For example, Anthony could write several terms down on cards—for example, free drawing, Impressionism, and charcoal—and ask participants how these terms relate to one another in their experience of art. Participants would sort the terms into important categories and show how they relate to one another.

In writing up what has been learned, the cognitive anthropologist describes major cultural domains with their included elements and relationships among them. This analytic strategy builds a deeper understanding of how participants view aspects of their worlds, enriching the cultural analysis that cognitive anthropologists seek.

Analyzing Phenomenologic Interview Data

Phenomenologic analysis requires that the researcher approach the texts with an open mind, seeking what meaning and structures emerge. The first step in reducing text is to read them and mark the passages that strike you as interesting. You often rely on your intuitive sense of what is "interesting." Use your judgment as a guide for what is significant in the transcript. An essential part of the process is to then examine those passages to discern and identify what prompted your initial interest. You can check with the participant to see if he or she agrees with your assessments of what is important and interesting. Each transcript is unique; the meaning of the experience of interest will emerge from that transcript. You choose what you will focus on; Seidman (1991), for example, mentions conflict, beginnings, middles, endings, and expressed hopes. Assign the identified important passages of interest codes that represent themes. Using these words, generate a profile, a narrative, depicting the meaning of the phenomenon for the individual.

Gilligan (see Brown & Gilligan, 1990) recommends four readings in her voice-centered interview process. Each reading listens for a different voice of the self telling a different story. The first reading establishes the who, what, when, where, and why of the story. In the second reading, the reader listens for the self: Who is the narrator? How does the narrator speak about him- or herself? The third and fourth readings look for relational voices: the care voice and the justice voice. The result is an understanding of the contrapuntal voices describing the lived experience of the self.

Analyzing Narrative Data

Gathering narrative data—the stories people tell about their lives—is an increasingly popular qualitative research genre that we linked to phenomenologic inquiry in Chapter 3 because of its deeply psychological orientation. It is not unlike the voice-centered analysis mentioned previously. We separate it out, however, believing that it merits direct attention. Although there are many different strands of narrative analysis, all proceed on the assumption that people make meaning of their lived experiences by narrating those experiences. Some narratives are organized chronologically; others are structured around episodes; still others are hypothetical narratives. The analysis of narrative data can be highly structured or open-ended. In the former, the researcher looks for structure in the narrative, focusing on the abstract (a summary), orientation (place, time, and participants), complicating action (sequence of events), evaluation (meaning of the action), resolution (what happened), and coda (return to the present).[3] Consider the following excerpt from an interview Marla and her team conducted with one of the women they focus on in-depth:

Researcher: Tell us about the first time you went to the clinic.	Abstract
Woman: Well, I had to walk over from the bus stop and it was raining . . . really pouring. I had two bags of groceries and it felt like they weighed a ton! It was hard . . . so hard. That stupid girl behind the desk—she acted like I wasn't even there. Looked right through me. Just yammered on the phone.	Orientation Complicating action *Being ignored*

In the boxed text, Marla has analyzed the structure of the narrative, indicating where the abstract, orientation, and complicating action occur. She also analyzes the theme apparent in it: being ignored. Both structure and content form the basis for the analysis. In writing up the research, both are included.

A less structured analytic strategy focuses on the thematic content and searches for examples of being ignored in other interviews with this woman as well as interviews with other women. This and other themes become the major organizing scheme for writing up the research.

TABLE 7.2 Anthony's Checklist of Actions

Time	No. around wheel	Interactions	Actions
9:00-9:30 am	/ / / /	Questions: / / Comments: / / /	Touching pots Picking up glazes
9:30-10:00 am			

STRATEGIES FOR ANALYZING
FIELD NOTES FROM OBSERVATIONS

As noted in Chapter 5, observations range along the prefigured/open-ended continuum. Some are tightly structured, relying on checklists to record types of actions or interactions and their frequencies. Others are holistic, recording the flow of events in the setting. Analyses guided by checklists entail counting the distribution of actions and interactions, interpreting these as indicators of a specific theme. Anthony uses checklists to document interactions between potters and community members at an outdoor crafts show. He records the number of times community members go to the potter's wheel and the interactions between potter and community members. His checklist is depicted in Table 7.2. He makes hash marks (/) for each person or interaction as a running tally of presence, interactions, and actions. Anthony will interpret these data based on his judgments about whether these actions and interactions represent interest on the part of community members, how intense that interest is, and how it links to other aspects of the program.

Holistic observation field notes are a running record of events. To supplement his checklist, Anthony wrote down as much as he could about the environment and the ebb and flow of activities. He drew a simple map of the small park where the crafts were displayed, noting the surrounding shopping and residential areas. He included as much detail as he considered relevant. As happens with many beginners, when he first tried to write a running record, he was overwhelmed by the enormity of the task. There are so many sights and so many actions to try to write down! Following the advice of Kent, he let events unfold. Now, his field notes are more focused, depicting actions and interactions between a few community members and the craftspeople. He reads through these notes, writing codes in the margins where there is evidence of intense interest and involvement.

STRATEGIES FOR ANALYZING
MATERIAL CULTURE

Material culture is composed of the unspoken and expressive. It has been called the "mute evidence" (Hodder, 1994, p. 393) of a cultural group. Because it expresses deep beliefs and values through written texts and artifacts, however, it is, in fact, quite eloquent. Analyzing such materials proceeds from the assumption that understanding what people do— what they produce—tells the researcher as much as what people say that they do. For example, worn tiles in front of the chick-hatching exhibit in a museum indicate interest, empty beer cans in the recycling bin suggest alcohol consumption patterns, a coffee urn in the office suggests conviviality, and shortcuts across a lawn show preferred walking paths. Material culture, whether written or actual objects, provides the researcher with insights into actions and their meanings in a setting.

Analyzing such materials, however, involves higher levels of inference and interpretation than with interview data. In interviews, participants tell you their meaning of events; with material culture, you must infer that meaning. It is, therefore, a risky business, but one that can enrich a qualitative study. Remember Marla's question about her observations that copies of *Quick and Healthy Cooking* disappear; she does not know how to interpret this information so she checks with someone in the setting. Inferring meaning entails making judgments about whether the cultural artifacts you have gathered corroborate interpretations based on other data, elaborate on those interpretations, or contradict them (Rossman & Wilson, 1994). For example, as Anthony interviews community members about their involvement in planning the arts events, he learns that participants feel excluded from decision making. He then reviews minutes of the advisory board meetings, looking for evidence of how community members' preferences are included in their deliberations. He discovers that dance events—the most preferred activities— have not been on the agenda for the past three meetings. The artifacts of the program—its records—corroborate participants' views. When he interviews the director of the program, he learns that this individual has a strong commitment to participatory planning. The evidence Anthony collects, however, contradicts this view. In this case, Anthony interprets his data as providing some evidence of a disjuncture between the rhetoric of the program—being participatory—and its reality.

USING THE HABITS
OF MIND AND HEART

Our characters grow in their understandings of the habits of mind and heart as they work through the complex process of analyzing their data. The tension they encounter is finding a balance between the minutiae of daily research experience (data) and the general assertions (theory) that move analysis beyond the specific. They have to find a balance between inductive and deductive reasoning. They begin to see that they could organize the data in many ways: by color, season, or fabric. They learn that each way yields important insights, but the schemes they settle on are uniquely their own. They immerse themselves in the data, searching for story lines that make sense and that represent the data—what they have learned—fully, accurately, and ethically. In this sense, they build grounded theory. At the same time, however, they draw on existing theory to provide analytic insights. Aware that analysis and interpretation are creative acts, they articulate the logic guiding their decisions.

Immersion, incubation, insight, and interpretation are the phases of creative insight involved in analyzing qualitative data. This chapter has depicted the generic processes that qualitative researchers work through, whatever the genre framing their inquiry: organizing, familiarizing, building categories, coding, and searching for alternatives. As they work through these processes, they are mindful of the final product: a written representation of what they have learned. This is the focus of Chapter 8.

NOTES

1. This may seem simplistic and obvious. In a long study, however, you may find that you forgot whom you interviewed or when it took place.

2. A full list of semantic relationships includes the following: strict inclusion, spatial, cause-effect, rationale, location-for-action, function, means-end, sequence, and attribution. See Spradley (1979) for more detail.
3. This discussion is adapted from Reissman (1993).

FURTHER READING

Miles, M. B., & Huberman, A. M. (1994). *Qualitative data analysis: An expanded sourcebook* (2nd ed.). Thousand Oaks, CA: Sage.

Patton, M. Q. (1990). *Qualitative evaluation and research methods* (2nd ed.). Newbury Park, CA: Sage. (See Part III, Chapters 8 and 9, pp. 369-506)

Richards, T. J., & Richards, L. (1994). Using computers in qualitative research. In N. K. Denzin & Y. S. Lincoln (Eds.), *Handbook of qualitative research* (pp. 445-462). Thousand Oaks, CA: Sage.

Silverman, D. (1993). *Interpreting qualitative data: Methods for analyzing talk, text, and interaction.* Newbury Park, CA: Sage.

Strauss, A. L., & Corbin, J. (1990). *Basics of qualitative research: Grounded theory procedures and techniques.* Newbury Park, CA: Sage. (See Part II, Chapters 5-11, pp. 57-194)

Tesch, R. (1990). *Qualitative research: Analysis types and software tools.* New York: Falmer.

CHAPTER EIGHT

•◆•

Presenting the Learnings

♋ ·· ℃

"Now for the big question: How are you two writing up your findings? They're due next week," Ruth asked her friends after the next to last class.

"I need to write a formal evaluation for the director of the community arts center. She has to give something to the program officers at the foundation, so I'm planning on a report that she can use for them. You know, something that tells what's good about the program and what they need to improve. That's what I'll turn in to Kent," answered Anthony.

"But how will you write it? I mean, how will you organize what you found?" probed Ruth.

"I've thought about that a lot. I think I'll do a kind of history of community arts in the neighborhood," said Anthony. "I discovered that folks in the area have been interested in art for a long time. It seems it took this project—with some outside funding—to pull it together. For years there's been a drop-in arts program for kids after school in the building that houses the center. And a lot of other artsy things have been a part of the culture here. So I want to capture all that leading up to what the center is today. Some folks talked about what they want the center to become, so I'll probably finish off with that."

"Wow, that even sounds interesting. Kent was looking for final reports that were not boring—ones people were likely to actually read and use," remarked Ruth.

"I know. And that's the point," responded Anthony. "These community arts programs could really go somewhere. What they're doing now is only a start. So I want them to use my information to know the program better—so the foundation will continue to fund it and so that the staff will make some of the recommended changes."

"Are you making recommendations?" asked Marla.

"No, but I am reporting ideas and suggestions from people I talked to." Anthony turned to Marla, "What are your plans?"

"I don't think I am going to write up a formal report," responded Marla. "We need to present our findings, but Kent said that alternatives were OK."

"I was wondering what that means. What will you do instead?" Ruth asked.

"Well, we found that one of the main reasons women in the neighborhood don't come back to the clinic is that they don't know they're supposed to. Some move away, but they're not the majority. Most just think that the pills they get will do the trick. They don't realize that sometimes their problem is chronic, that they need continuous treatment. We spoke to one woman who has asthma. She thought using the spray once would fix her forever, so she never refilled the prescription. When her breathing still was rough, she just thought the doctors couldn't help her," Marla told her colleagues.

"So . . . what will you do with that information?"

"Well, a formal written report, especially if it's in English, won't do any good for the people. We learned a lot about the kinds of health problems women there have. We've talked to the PAs and doctors about these problems. So we've designed a newsletter that we will leave in the clinic. Each week we'll talk about one health problem and pass on advice we got from the PAs. We'll do them in Spanish and in English. I'm going to turn in the first newsletter to Kent," said Marla.

"I hope it works. I hope the women read it and change their habits. Next time do one for men!" laughed Anthony. "But you found out more didn't you? How will you present all of it?"

"I'm not sure yet. The clinic needs to change as well. We're thinking of ways we can get our findings to the board—the people who make the policy decisions for the clinic. We asked to be on the agenda of their next meeting. I think we'll hand out a one-pager that bullets our findings. Things like needing to staff the clinic with PAs who are bilingual," Marla replied.

"You both have a handle on what you want to do. Me—I'm still clueless!" moaned Ruth.

"That's what you always say—and then you come out ahead in the end. You'll get no sympathy from us. Just tell us what stands out for you most about your kids," directed Anthony.

"I'll never forget one little girl telling me about how she can play basketball. What struck me was how she described that moment when she realized she could play! It turns out that most of my kids have a similar story."

"So maybe you will tell these stories of their lives," suggested Marla.

"I'd love to be able to write something like Jonathan Kozol's stuff. Something that can have that kind of impact because the readers really get to know—and care about—the people he writes about. I guess I'll try to tell the stories of kids in wheelchairs through turning points in their lives."

"That's cool. You know, maybe after I finish this course—this degree—I'll ask the women in my study if they want to write their stories with me. I think other people would want to hear them. Maybe we can get them published," mused Marla.

"When you're rich and famous, remember us! Kent's hooked us on this qualitative research, so we'll probably both still be plugging away 'producing knowledge from our data.' "

"Still, for me the question is how we write—or present—something that is true to our discoveries and, at the same time, appeals to whatever audience we want to use it. I'll be happy if I can figure out how to accomplish that!" concluded Ruth.

Anthony, Marla, and Ruth are at the final step in the research process. They have collected and analyzed their data. They have made their interpretations. They have moved from field texts of notes and documents to research texts of codes, categories, and memos and finally to interpretive texts. They are ready to present what they have learned. Whether for class, for the participants in their studies, or for other audiences, they have options for how to present their findings. They also have a variety of ways to organize the presentation of their material. How they choose to present and organize their findings depends on their purposes, the questions they posed, and to whom they are presenting. As Marla suggests, they may even need to prepare more than one presentation of the findings if they have several audiences.

Like the three students, you are also at the presentation stage. You have turned your data into information that has become knowledge; now you want to share this knowledge with others. Whatever you have learned, chances are that you do not want it to be ignored, relegated to a dusty shelf or forgotten file; you want your work to make a difference, to be used by some audience. You are at the final stage of the heuristic— the discovery process. Once again, you use your habits of mind and heart to consider the prevailing context and to design an engaging and useful presentation of your findings. The format you decide on could be any- thing from a formal written report to a multimedia demonstration, depending on what you have discovered, who your audience is, and the extent of your resources.

Your habits of mind and heart are just as important at the end as they were at the start of the study. To finish your project, you have to know when you have enough data. Your political sensitivity shapes your choice of presentation. Just as you have conducted the entire research project, you complete the final report (whatever form it takes) with deep interpersonal and ethical sensitivity. You are careful that your findings do not deliberately hurt anyone. It is also important that you ensure that your findings are grounded in your data and that you articulate the logic behind any decisions you have made. You are reflexive; you remain acutely conscious of yourself as the author of your presentation.

This chapter explores the possibilities and challenges you will face in this final step in your research. Although we introduce various ways to present your work, we recommend that you always include some form of writing to force you to articulate and clarify your findings. Writing, especially descriptive writing, is essential to the discovery process. We discuss purpose and voice. We suggest several strategies for organizing the material. Finally, we review the uses for research in light of the habits of mind and heart you have adopted as a qualitative researcher.

PRESENTATION

Sharing what you have learned draws from both your systematic and creative sides. You want to engage your audience and, at the same time, convince them that what you are giving them is real. To accomplish the latter, you must demonstrate that your work has been "systematic, analytical, rigorous, disciplined, and critical in perspective" (Patton, 1990, p. 433). To engage your audience, your work must be "exploring, playful, metaphorical, insightful, and creative" (Patton, 1990, p. 433).

Fortunately, today you are seldom limited to producing a traditional written final report in which you convey your findings. You may choose from numerous options—or create your own. Your choice is constrained only by the disposition of the audiences, your purpose, the nature of the findings, and available resources.

Audience and Purpose

As you consider how to present your findings, have an audience in mind. Who cares about what you have learned? Who should know about this? What are they interested in? Different groups have different norms and expectations, so you need to know something about your audience. Academic audiences want a term paper, thesis, or dissertation; they also read scholarly journals and monographs. Sponsors feel they have contracted to get a full report. Popular audiences read various types of books and autobiographies (see Delamont, 1992, pp. 163-182). All these role groups also watch videos, listen to tapes, and interact on the World Wide Web. The type of audience will, in part, determine the format of your presentation. Consider creating more than one product to avoid having to say everything to everyone at the same time (Richardson, 1994).

For our three students, the professor and their classmates provide the first and most obvious audience. Kent, however, has already told them alternative formats are acceptable, depending on other audiences for their work. A second audience for Anthony's evaluation is the decision makers: program staff and funders. He will most likely produce an evaluation report, but he may find that an oral briefing is sufficient for them. Anthony would be wise to offer a brief executive summary or abstract that summarizes the essential findings, his conclusions and recommendations (if any), and outlines his procedures (to establish reasons for confidence in the findings). People are more likely to read the summary than the report, and they will need a written summary if they did not require a full report. If Anthony's clients request an oral briefing, he may consider (depending on his resources) preparing a multimedia presentation drawing on the various arts represented in the center to tell the history of the arts center in the community.

Marla has several very different audiences. She hopes to change the behavior of the barrio women who might need the clinic's services, so these women are an immediate audience. She and her collaborators are planning a series of newsletters using information from their case studies; the newsletters will be readable and will be distributed in places where barrio women will find them and read them. She also hopes to influence clinic practices and procedures so that they make more sense to potential clients; thus, another audience is the clinic staff and board of directors. Marla's team may communicate their findings to the staff through formal and informal conversations. They will orally brief the board and leave with them an executive summary. Beyond the clinic-related audiences, Marla envisions telling the story of poor women's health care so that a greater society can comprehend—and perhaps address—this aspect of poverty and the disenfranchised and disempowered. A book of the case studies sold on the popular market is a possibility for reaching this broad audience.

Ruth's audiences are less easily defined. She wants her story about the turning points in the athletic lives of children with physical disabilities to reach people who work with those children, but she does not want to limit her audience to special educators. She submits her story to a journal for teachers. She knows she would also like to reach parents and maybe the general public, so she considers writing a script for a video that would capture the story visually as well as in words. Her roommate, a student of cinematography, has already explored possibilities for producing a documentary.

Ruth, Anthony, and Marla consider how to present their information so that it will be used. They think about their purposes; do they aim to explain, describe, influence, change behavior, entertain, or advocate? Marla is concerned about action, Anthony's intent is to influence decision making and to improve the program, and Ruth wants to tell a story. Most of their ideas break the paradigm of the traditional, linear, attempting-to-be-objective, written report. They assess the learning styles of intended and potential audiences and design their presentations accordingly, choosing what they hope will be the most effective medium.

Possible Formats

Presenting what you have learned is a form of knowledge dissemination. As recently as 10 years ago, the options for disseminating knowledge were limited to a few media: written material, television, film, and radio. Today, these media are more developed and variegated, and you can now choose from a whole world of technology applications. Use the following list as a stimulus to thinking about ways you could present your findings:

- Paper
- Descriptive essay
- Journal or magazine article
- Analytic memo or report
- Monograph
- Individual conference presentation
- Conference symposium
- Roundtable discussion
- Story
- Novelette
- Biography or autobiography
- Video
- Handbook
- Letter to editor
- CD/laser disc/interactive video
- Teleconference

Examples of the formats, even the more unusual, abound. Pour over articles in journals in your area or on your topic to find potential models or spark your imagination. Attend relevant conferences to observe both the good and the bad. Borrow ideas from other fields, such as film and literature and journalism. We had a doctoral student who presented her findings from a study of first-year teachers in the form of a novel (Chatman, 1990). Bolman and Deal (1993, 1994) and Bolman, Deal, and Rallis (1995) have shared the cumulative findings from years of work in educational organizations in a series of novelettes focusing on a principal, a teacher, and a school board. Another student used findings from a study of student teachers to prepare a handbook that could be used to guide student teacher supervisors. An accomplished photographer who studied the meaning of a chapel in the lives of students and teachers at a boarding school exhibited the photographs that comprised part of her findings; the photographs were also included in her dissertation (Fisk,

1996). Research on teaching, learning, cognition, and technology culminated in the production of the Jasper series[1] of interactive videos to enhance children's problem-solving processes in math and science classes.

Advances in technology suggest multiple new avenues for dissemination. Several students have produced videos that supplement their written work with visual compositions.[2] The World Wide Web is a natural pathway. Graphics packages offer new and alternative ways to display findings. The use of hypertext allows interaction with audiences. Teleconferences enable researchers to disseminate their information and take live questions from remote audiences.

Because so many different possibilities for presentation exist, a cautionary note is in order. Be sure you have a reason for the method you have chosen if you are using an alternative format. In other words, do not use technology just because it is there—or because you think you will be avant garde. Surely you have yawned as "talking heads" on a video screen impart so-called knowledge that would have been more interesting had you read it.

Voice

The voice you choose to tell your story—to relate your discoveries—is as likely to determine the impact you will have on the audience as the findings themselves. Voice engages the reader; it conveys passion and interest—or lack of it. Boring texts and dull presentations are those in which individual voices have been suppressed and homogenized through professional socialization into the "omniscient voice of science" (Richardson, 1994, p. 517). Boring texts are not read; dull presentations are not heard.

Your presentation, written or oral, need not be dull. You have spent time in the field looking, asking, listening, and reading. You have interpreted events, activities, conversations, and objects and constructed your own meaning or understanding of them. You are the learner; the findings are what you have learned. Remember who you are, why you undertook the study, and the decisions that grounded your inquiry (Richardson, 1994). The story is yours to tell, even if the story is about another or others; Denzin (1994, p. 503) states that, "The Other who is presented in the text is always a version of the researcher's self." As storyteller, you choose the voice.

Voice implies subjectivity and not clean, scientific objectivity. Denzin (1994, p. 507) notes, "All texts are biased, reflecting the play of class, gender, race, ethnicity, and culture, suggesting that so-called objective interpretations are impossible." You choose a voice that allows you to reveal yourself and to articulate your biases. Establishing who you are frees you to tell the story of the "Others." Ruth, for example, will blend the first and third persons as she writes about the children she has come to know as follows:

> Amanda is a champion basketball player. She captains her winning team with enthusiasm, joy, humor, and lots of practice. She told me, "I guess anything is possible—as long as we're all patient. I know I'll never walk and chew gum at the same time, but I *can* wheel and dribble at the same time!" Amanda is a 12-year-old who uses a wheelchair. I met Amanda and her teammates as a part of my study of how children in wheelchairs see themselves as athletes.

Choosing a voice is tricky because the voices of the researcher and the participants become enmeshed. Brown and Gilligan (1990) refer to the "polyphony of human discourse" (p. 3) and the self behind the self. As has Jonathan Kozol in his moving works about the lives of children, Ruth situates herself in direct relationship with her participants. Readers of her stories will know why she became fascinated with the athletic life of children with physical disabilitites and how she discovered the concept of "bodiedness." Anthony will use the third person to tell the history of arts in the community, but his voice will not be that of an abstract disembodied observer; he will use the words of the artists and community members, spoken to him, to tell the story.

The trick is to balance the various voices, not allowing your own voice to take over so that the story is about you rather than your subject. We caution you not to "bare your soul" in an autobiographical or confessional piece (Van Maanen, 1988). You name yourself, but you are not at the center; you are not the focal point of the story: As Dara Tomlin Rossman (personal communication, March 3, 1997) notes, "the 'I' of your writing is the sun illuminating the object; it is not the object itself." You want the reader to engage with what you have learned, not an egocentric revelation of your learning process.

Voice is especially important because authorship gives power. Although power lies in the knowledge produced by the study, the mode of representation chosen by the author augments that power. For example, people who read Ruth's story or watch the documentary will vividly recall Amanda and her triumphs *as Ruth has represented them.* For many people, Amanda will come to symbolize *all* children in wheelchairs. The author's version of reality is powerful, but power also lies in how the participants speak through the authorial voice. The author has to be vigilant that she is accurately and ethically representing the voice she has chosen. Marla and her research team hope to use the power of their learnings to precipitate change. Because they speak *for* the women they have studied, they must be extra careful. To avoid misrepresentations, they rely on the fact-filled newsletters about the health problems they have identified as common to women in the barrio. Their oral report is filled with direct quotes. If they write a book, it will be coauthored and will enable the women to tell their own stories.

Finding the right balance of voice can take several drafts. An example comes from a painful memory of writing the portrait of the principal of a restructuring school (Rallis, 1992). The first draft was overly focused on the author and what she saw; it told more about her than about the principal. Early critiques of the manuscript pointed out that she dominated the text,[3] so she was able to shift the focus. Several drafts later, she captured the "self" of the principal she had shadowed and learned about, keeping her "self" in the background. The following provides an example:

> Ken seems to belong in his school. Whether we walk into the building during the day or for an evening concert, whether we join a group of teachers in a meeting or passing through the halls, Midway High is Ken's domain. The atmosphere reflects his personality: calm and orderly and enthusiastic. Like most comprehensive high schools, Midway is a large and complex organization whose operations are shaped by multiple agendas and constantly reshaped by immediate and arising needs. Yet, Ken is not a slave to these agendas and needs. In my week with Ken, I have seen him balance emerging needs with existing priorities, without breaking the natural momentum of school life. (p. 5)

By knowing your audience and having decided on a format and voice, you can organize an engaging presentation of what you have learned.

ORGANIZING THE REPORT

Despite the alternatives presented previously, many researchers must still produce formal reports. In the report, you synthesize your discoveries for public consumption. The report is the culminating stage in the transformation of data into knowledge, so the organization is a reflection of your analysis and interpretations. Metaphorically, if, during analysis, you organized your closet (data) by fabric, your report is likely to be organized by fabric (recall Chapter 7). Several models for organizing your report exist; your report may be any of the following:

- A chronology of events or descriptive life history of an individual
- Thematic
- A composite ("day in the life of")
- Critical episodes
- Miniportraits

Each model is not exclusive; you may find that overlapping the models works for you. All require thick description and serve to generate theory.

Chronology

A common organizational strategy is to present events chronologically—that is, in the order they happened. This strategy is especially powerful if the story lies in its history. Anthony chooses to describe the development of the community arts program chronologically because he has discovered that the community has a rich history of artistic expression, beginning with community murals drawn on sidewalks outside a building that housed an after-school program. The core of local artists behind these early works has remained in the community and recently initiated the effort to establish the center. Anthony's history of arts in the community culminating in the current activities is a compelling story of community activism and involvement.

Life History

The chronology strategy may also be useful if your focus is an individual. A phenomenologic study, an ethnography, or a case study may result in a descriptive life history. Here you present an account of one person's life, framing the description with analytic points about the significance of that life in light of your questions and the genre. Ruth could write life histories about the children she has studied.

Thematic

Another common organizational strategy is thematic. Meaningful themes that have emerged from your data form the backbone—or structural framework—of your report. The bullets in the executive summary that Marla and her partners offer the board of directors of the clinic are the themes that dominated their interviews and observations. It was shown in Chapter 7 that one theme was *being ignored*. Marla's oral presentation, and a full report were she to write one, would define the themes, providing rich details, examples, and quotations. We organized our report on inclusive schools around themes such as *supports for and barriers to professional development*. This general theme was broken down into subthemes, such as principal activities, central office attitudes, available resources, community involvement, and others.

Composite

Sometimes, findings are best presented as a composite or "day in the life of . . ." The portrait of Ken, the principal of a restructuring school, follows Ken through meetings and interactions of what is called a typical day for him. The day described is actually a composite of the several days during which he was shadowed. All the events around which the day in the report was organized actually occurred but not necessarily during the same day. On balance, however, the day described seems typical— and real.

You may also present a composite individual drawn from data about several different people. The principal, Lee (Goldring & Rallis, 1993), and the teachers, Maggie and Don (Rallis & Rossman, 1995), are composite characters. Their every act and thought are drawn from real principals and teachers in our data sets, but no one principal or teacher was exactly like Lee or Maggie or Don in everything they said, thought, or did. We present these composites as real because they represent the actual teachers we interviewed, observed, or surveyed.

When Marla and the women on the research team collaborate to write a book about women's health issues, they might create composite women from their case studies. The strategy is effective because readers could be overwhelmed by the number of cases necessary to cover all the issues poor women encounter when dealing with health services.

Critical Events

Critical episodes in the life of a person, event, or program provide another organizational structure. Ruth organizes her journal article around critical episodes because each of her children has experienced at least one event that defined their relationship to athletics and sports. She tells the stories of her wheelchair children around these critical episodes. For example, she depicts Amanda by describing the afternoon she and another friend in a wheelchair were left alone in a gymnasium to wait for one parent to pick them up. The parent was delayed. To avoid boredom, the two girls started "fooling around" with a basketball, and Amanda "discovered her talent." Ruth relates a comparable crucial episode for each of her participants.

Portraits

Multiple cases, critical episodes, and composites may be organized and presented as portraits (see Lightfoot & Davis, 1997) or miniportraits of individuals or institutions. Like their painted counterparts, written portraits yield a rich and textured impression of the subject over an extended but limited period of time. Ruth's stories of the children, organized around critical episodes in their lives, are actually miniportraits of each child. The reader can *see* the children and can *touch* their development through the pages on which Ruth describes their experiences.

In summary, writing is an active part of the learning process; it stimulates thinking and is part of the analysis. Through writing, you construct knowledge. Findings gain clarity when you articulate them in writing. Writing up your findings is a process itself: You write, you revise, you rewrite—and then you write again. You make discoveries along the way as you continue to unravel the mysteries in your data. The process of writing draft after draft helps you find your voice and refine your message. At best, the process is interactive: You read and work with the text to produce successive drafts; you seek feedback from colleagues, mentors, and clients; and you leave it and return with revisions (remember the discussion of the creative process in Chapter 7). In short, writing is not simply sitting down at your word processor and tapping on the keyboard.

As a final word about presenting your contribution, we suggest that you be sure to tell people what you are writing about and why, and how you did the study. Give your audience sufficient background about the context of the study but do not drown them in details. Also provide enough grounding in the body of the report to support your conclusions and interpretations. We urge you to create new metaphors: Swim with the dolphins; leap into the unknown; open your eyes to see in the dark; and hold onto the safety bar and enjoy the roller-coaster ride. Finally, trust the process: Discoveries emerge.

USING THE HABITS OF MIND AND
HEART TO GENERATE USEFUL KNOWLEDGE

However organized and however represented, what you have learned can be used by others to generate new knowledge. Your challenge is to write or present something that is true to what you have discovered and that also appeals to a specific audience. Beginners are often concerned about the number of research reports that sit on shelves gathering dust. They are also dismayed, however, at what seems like the crass "packaging" of their work necessary to enhance its potential usefulness to various audiences. Remember that the habits of mind and heart free you to consider multiple and alternative ways to present what you have learned; your goal is to communicate so that others may use what you have discovered.

Audiences might use your work to solve problems, enlighten, legitimize, empower, or all of these. Your reporting can provide information that is *instrumentally useful* in decision making or program redesign, as in Anthony's and maybe Marla's case. Your work may also *enlighten* as you consciously decide to contribute to theory. For example, you may directly stipulate links between practice and theory. Sometimes your contribution happens less planfully, as with Ruth's study. In addition, your work may serve *symbolically*, expressing and legitimizing new understandings for the way things are. Ruth's vivid images of children in wheelchairs playing basketball have high symbolic value. Finally, your work may serve to *empower or emancipate*. Marla and colleagues hope their action research will change women's lives and improve the health services available to them.

You anticipate and plan for certain uses for your work, but do not be surprised at the number of unexpected potential uses—some that you might not be comfortable with. Someone might find a way to misuse the information that you generate. Although mindful of potential negative uses, you understand that you cannot control them all. You let go, knowing that, because your research has been conducted thoughtfully, ethically, and systematically, your contribution sheds light on some small corner of the world.

NOTES

1. The Jasper series is produced by the Learning Technology Center, Peabody College, Vanderbilt University, Nashville, Tennessee. The interactive videos introduce a character—Jasper—who encounters specific problems (such as whether he has enough gas or how to get an injured bird to the veterinarian) he must solve. Sufficient information to solve the problem is embedded in the body of the video; students are asked to advise Jasper.

2. A doctoral student, Gary Rademaker, whose dissertation is comparing periods of transition in schools when principals change to change of command in the military. He is working on a video capturing change of leadership ceremonies to accompany his written material.

3. I thank Carolyn Evertson, Ted Sizer, Pat Wasley, and Paula Evans, among others, for their critique of the early manuscript (Rallis, 1992).

Epilogue

The new semester is well under way, and Marla, Ruth, and Anthony have met for lunch in the student union.

"I guess we're with a celebrity? Can we have your autograph?" Ruth kidded Marla.

"Ay Diós! I didn't think the newspaper would quote me," sighed Marla. "But I'm glad we're getting publicity. It was so good that reporters were there when we presented to the board of the clinic. I didn't expect the women would rally such a big group to come with us to the meeting. And I certainly was surprised when I saw the story on the first page of the neighborhood section."

"Did you have any idea you were going to be such a rabble-rouser, such a troublemaker, when you started the qualitative research class?" Anthony joked.

"I hoped I could make a difference. I just never realized how powerful knowledge can be—as Kent would say," answered Marla. "I mean, the board listened to us this time because we had data—evidence."

"Seriously, I think Kent's class changed our lives, at least a little bit," interrupted Ruth. "Well, I can only speak for myself, but I know I'll never look at a person in a wheelchair the same way again."

"Neither will a lot of other people. I saw the article you wrote for Education Views. I couldn't put it down," said Marla. "It really made me think about the different kinds of challenges each person faces."

"You guys make me feel inferior. I'm not even sure anybody read my report. True, the center did get funded for another year. But I don't feel like I moved mountains or anything," groaned Anthony.

"What makes you think nobody read it?"

"Oh, I made some recommendations for program improvement, but I don't see anything changing," said Anthony.

"Well, you changed, just from doing the study. Remember after the first class, when you thought all you'd do was to hang around, talk, and write something up?" chided Ruth. *"You became the most reflexive one of us."*

"Yeah. This process did get me thinking. And I'd like to believe that all the conversations I had with Nanette—you know, the director—did influence her thinking," mused Anthony. *"Change doesn't happen overnight—look how long it took just to get this center going. I wonder . . . maybe I can meet with her, and we can figure out some way we can use the evaluation findings to get more permanent funding."*

"See. What did I tell you? Always reflecting reflexively!" laughed Ruth.

"I don't think we can ever know for certain what effect—or all the effects—our research has had," said Marla. *"I only know that I've learned a lot and . . . and that those 'habits' have really become habits!"*

•◆•

Appendixes:
Introduction

The three appendixes pull together data gathered by Ruth, Marla, and Anthony for their small-scale qualitative research projects. We include descriptions of the characters and their projects and some data presented earlier. We have also added new data—field notes from observations and transcriptions of interviews. We show how each student begins the process of analyzing, interpreting, and presenting what he or she has learned. In Ruth's case, the analysis process entails reading and reread-ing the data, noting broad themes that emerge through that work. Her sample field notes and transcripts are reformatted with broad right-hand margins in which she writes a term to indicate a theme. She then writes a brief analytic memo in which she develops the theme of *agency*. Writing analytic memos, as indicated in Chapter 7, is an important part of developing insights about the topic; in Ruth's case, this memo is very much work-in-progress.

Marla's process is collaborative. She and the women in her study read and reread and discuss possible themes that have relevance for their lives. Marla then takes these insights and does some preliminary coding of field notes and transcripts. She shares these with the women; they make revisions. On the basis of those revisions, she writes a preliminary summary of what they have learned. This, too, is in the form of an analytic memo. This becomes a "working document" for the women to read, discuss, and revise. Because of her commitment to collaborative work, Marla's process is more iterative and complex than either Ruth's or Anthony's. Therefore, we include a second memo that reflects on the participation of and changes in the team members themselves.

With his focus on the culture of the arts program, Anthony relies on his three guiding questions to analyze the data. He has data from multiple sources: observations, interviews, surveys, and documents. He elaborates subquestions from the guiding questions and codes the data with terms for these subquestions. He then develops a summary of one guiding question for his analytic memo.

We begin each appendix with a reminder about the student's study: its strategy and genre and how it evolved and changed over the course of the project. We comment throughout on the quality of the data gathered and make suggestions for improvement. The text of the interviews and field notes is formatted in regular type; the comments of Ruth, Marla and her team members, and Anthony are in **bold** type. In all instances, our characters have word-processed these excerpts, elaborating points where necessary and adding observer comments at the end of several. You will also find our comments interspersed throughout the interviews, field notes, and analysis; these are in *italic* type. In these, we make suggestions for improvement, we applaud a particularly skillful or effective example, and we discuss alternatives our characters might have considered. At the end of each excerpt, we also comment on the overall quality of the work and how it links to their emerging insights and interpretations.

Appendix A

"Children in wheelchairs can jump."

• ◆ •

Ruth's Data and Analysis

Ruth is an undergraduate student majoring in psychology. She is an avid athlete. At the university, she has been goalie for the lacrosse team and often works out in the gym early in the morning. For the past several years, she has worked at a summer camp for children with disabilities. She enjoys working with children, especially through athletics, and helped design a 3-day wilderness course for deaf children. She volunteers one afternoon a week in a local elementary school and, through her qualitative research project, at the Culverton After School Center. She has found that her qualitative research, linked to phenomenological traditions, has deepened her understanding of the lived experienced of students with disabilities. When designing her study, she anticipated doing some observing at the center but wanted to focus her data gathering on in-depth interviews. She has found that interviewing children can be challenging and exciting, as noted in Chapter 5.

Recall that the purpose of Ruth's phenomenological study is to uncover the deep inner meaning of *bodiedness* for children with physical handicaps. She hoped that her study would produce rich cultural description through stories of these children's relationships with sports. The central concept of bodiedness would be explicated through the children's words and her interpretations of the meaning they express. Her initial design has changed during the course of her research. She began by volunteering at the Culverton After School Center, where she knew children with physical disabilities attended regularly. While observing at Culverton's pick-up basketball games, she noticed that one of the "regulars" is an early adolescent girl—Katrine—who is profoundly deaf. Her skills in basketball are quite impressive. Ruth, because of her experience with the wilderness program for deaf students, becomes fascinated with this young woman and asks her to participate in the study. At this point, she has conducted two in the series of three interviews recommended by phenomenologic methodologists with Mark, a boy who uses a wheelchair, and one of the three with Katrine. She has also interviewed one parent and one teacher.

In this appendix, we offer sample transcripts of Ruth's interviews and field notes and show some preliminary analysis that she undertakes toward the end of the course. As part of an assignment, she writes a brief analytic memo trying to draw together important themes that she has identified in her study. Recall that the text of the interviews and field notes is formatted in regular type; Ruth's comments as the researcher are in **bold** type; our comments are in *italic* type. Ruth has word-processed all the excerpts, elaborating points where necessary and adding observer comments at the end of each. These observer comments are indicated by OC. Some of Ruth's comments were added while transcribing and word-processing her interviews and observations; other notes were made at the time. In some cases, it is unclear. The following are selections from the field notes Ruth has taken while observing at the center two afternoons a week. These are followed by excerpts from interviews she has conducted with Katrine, who is in the eighth grade, and Mark, a fifth grader.

9/24. Field notes at Culverton After School Center. I got there at about 3:00. Took some notes then wrote these afterwards. Tried to take myself back into the scene, like Kent said.

Culverton After School Center is housed in an old reconverted elementary school building. The entrance looks like the entry to almost any old school you know: linoleum tiles underfoot; yellowish lighting; coats hanging on wall hooks; boots and shoes strewn across the floor; backpacks dropped in piles. I enter soon after the children, so their noise and chaos linger. Patsy, one of the aides, makes a futile attempt to push the droppings toward the walls so the pathway is clear. I can see hand smudges on the cream-green walls. Already, I feel the familiar warmth and moderate grime of a place where children are moving too fast to be orderly and too busy to wash. *[excellent description]*

I enter the large room to the left where snacks are spread out on a table. I estimate about 25-30 kids from about 2nd grade to middle school age. One group has already gobbled up their snacks and are heading to the closets that held the gym equipment. I see one boy squirt a juice box all over the wall and floor in the corner. Nobody but me catches his act. He giggles and sprints away. **[I wondered how much juice—and other foodstuff coated these walls! Yuck!]** Actually, only half of them are going to the gym. The other half are going to the art room. A few are carrying books. Later I found out that they probably went to the "quiet room" to read. There is also a game room.

I look for the kids in wheelchairs. I know there are eight in all. Three (Amanda, Mark, and Jill) are with the group going to the gym. Another (Winnie) is in the art room. Sammy usually goes to the reading place so he's probably there. I can't see **[and didn't find out]** where the other three are. So far, the ones I see seem to be part of the crowd of kids. I can pick them out, but they don't stand out. I decide to follow the kids going to the gym. **[Already I'm thinking about how I can get to talk to the girls and boys in wheelchairs. I don't want to be too formal, at least not at first. Right now, I'm just standing there.]** A boy throws a ball at me, nearly hitting me in the nose. He calls to me, "We need another person on our side. Wanna play?" So I drop my notebook and join in. I see that Amanda is on the other team. She's in the middle of their players. Jill is off to the side: She doesn't go onto the court. She looks like she's going to cheer. I see that Mark is on our team. I start to watch Amanda play, but the ball comes to me, and I get into the game. I do notice that she makes two baskets. *[Ruth captures actions and some dialogue here]*

After the game, I get talking to the kids. They ask me who I am. I tell them I'm a student at the university, and I want to see what they do at the center. They ask a dozen questions **[most I can even answer!]**. Then I ask them to introduce themselves **[their identities are on the attached sheet]**. We talk about playing basketball, and they tell me about the league they belong to. One laughs about how it's the only league where kids do wheelies on the floor. **[I'm surprised that Amanda is their captain. I want to find out about that. And I wonder how she learned to play.]** The talk is moving fast so I can't get it all. Then we play some more.

When it's time for parents to come, I walk to the entrance with Amanda. She is kidding me about my team losing. I hand her her coat from its hook, and she wheels out.

OC: This was my first try at observing and recalling afterwards what I saw. I took some notes while there, but it seemed real awkward to be writing in a notebook all the time. I just wanted to get involved with the kids, like at the elementary school. But I really had fun. The kids are terrific and seemed to like having another adult around. *[Ruth is being reflexive about her role at the Center.]* **I am already fascinated by how these kids manage to get a basketball game going. I don't know what data these notes are, but I think I'm getting a sense of the Center and the kids.**

Ruth's field notes are very well done. She describes the setting so that the reader can picture it, she notes actions and movement from setting to setting, and she is able to note some of the conversation that occurs as the children go about their activities. Recall that her initial field notes, taken at the center, have been word-processed and elaborated after the observation. In part, her ability to create rich field notes comes from this discipline of allocating time after an observation to fill in remembered details of action and dialogue.

10/3. Culverton After School Center. I arrive a bit later than usual, so the entry hall is empty except for the backpacks and jackets. That familiar school smell is in the air—salty food, mustiness, floor wax, all mixed with a hint of cleanser. The kids are already in their activities. I can hear the basketball game in progress; I'm told there's one nearly every afternoon. I head for the gym. The game is in full swing. I can sit on the side and take these notes.

Everyone is so engaged in the game that it takes me a minute to realize again that two of the players are in wheelchairs **[they look so at home on the court!].** I recognize Amanda—she's wheeling to guard a large (bulky, not tall) boy who just missed getting the ball. Curtis got it and takes off. Suddenly, a tall—I mean, really tall, nearly six feet—girl streaks in from nowhere and steals it. She's lovely. *[What does she mean by "lovely"?]* **[Jill has wheeled over next to me and whispers, "That's Katrine. Isn't she wonderful?"]** She passes it to Mark (he's in a wheelchair and was on my team both times I played before). Mark takes the ball and, holding it cradled in his lap, wheels down the court after Amanda, Katrine, and the other two. He pats his head three times. **[I find out later this means that Amanda will set up a pick for Katrine who will cut to the basket.]** He passes the ball to Joey, who feeds the ball to Katrine. She grabs the ball, nearly fouling Curtis, dribbles once, and puts it in for two. **[Wow! I'm out of breath.]**

The large boy (I think he's called Diego) walks over and says something to Mark, who is off by the wall now. Mark wheels his chair around and bangs into the wall—vehemently. **[What's going on here?]** Amanda calls out, "Mark, get over here!" so he quickly wheels back in place. He's ready to take a pass again from Katrine. And—it happens all over again: Mark's "carry" down the court, the signals, the set up, the basket by Katrine. This time Diego calls out something **[I cannot make it out]** and Mark wheels over and bumps him. They nearly scuffle, but Joey and Curtis break it up. Joey actually wheels Mark away from Diego. Both Joey and Curtis give Diego "the cold shoulder." *[Again, specifics of body language would help describe "the cold shoulder."]* Diego struts off.

Almost as if there had been no interruption, the court action starts again. Curtis has the ball. He dribbles through Amanda's blocking and passes to another boy. I do not remember who shoots. He misses, and Joey gets the ball. This time Joey carries it down the court and passes to Mark. **[Did I catch a signal from Katrine? I think she touched her shoulder twice, but I'm not sure it was a signal.]** Mark shoots and gets two! Katrine steals the ball on the in-bounds pass and drops it into the basket again. Again, Jill whispers to me about how she admires Katrine. **[The action is so fast I'm sure I'm missing a lot.]** I notice that Mark "carries" the ball a lot and that Katrine makes a lot of baskets. They are almost partners. In fact, their team seems to be a tight unit. Jill has interpreted some of their signals for me. **[Do they know each other well? play a lot together? I see them use hand signals a lot—it seems part of their play. Have they worked this out before?]**

After about 20 minutes of action, they take a break. Most of the kids get their water bottles from the side near where I'm sitting. Jill tells them how good the game is and asks one of the girls **[I don't recognize her]** if she is feeling better **[I guess she was sick last week]**. Joey and Mark are laughing together about some shared amusement. Then Joey goes over to Amanda and Katrine and the other girl and begins to bother them. I can't catch what he is saying but they seem annoyed. *[How does she know this?]* I hear Amanda say, "Oh, grow up, will you." Mark wheels over to the wall and rams it with his wheelchair. Joey grabs the back of his chair and wheels him onto the court again, calling out, "Come on, let's get started." Curtis says he has to go home now, so Amanda asks me if I want to play. I put down my pad and pencil and join them.

We play for about another 45 minutes. I am amazed with how fast they all are. Amanda truly seems to enjoy herself. Mark is always in motion—whether there is court action or not. And he's noisy—he's always calling out to the other kids. That's one way I learned their names. But I noticed that he still uses the hand signals. That tall girl, Katrine, is sooooo good; she really knows basketball and knows how to keep things moving. She's fascinating. When the session is over, I stay behind with Jill and Joey to put away the balls while the others walk to the front. They are talking about how Katrine played last Friday on the middle school team.

OC: I need to find out more about Katrine. Who is she? I also need to find out about how they came to use those hand signals. Another follow-up: Mark and that large boy—Diego?—seems to be some tension there.

Ruth's field notes are exceptionally "alive." They take the reader into the action of the basketball court, as if we were in the gym with her. Her descriptions capture the actions—what people are doing and how it looks. As we have commented in this set of notes, however, Ruth needs to work on providing more specific detail: What does she mean by "lovely," "the cold shoulder," and "annoyed"? These terms clearly mean something to her but are open to various interpretations by others. As she gets feedback from Kent, her skills will grow.

10/5. Second interview with Mark. At his home in the Heights section. Early evening. Only his aunt is at home. In the first interview, I got to know him pretty well. Seems like a neat kid but sometimes a real pain at the Center—teasing the girls, bumping his wheelchair into the walls (I think on purpose), yelling out a lot. Need to focus on what he likes about playing in that pick-up team after school.

Ruth: Good game, today, eh?

Mark: Yeah, not bad.

Ruth: How do you think you played?

Mark: Sometimes I do better. I didn't make any baskets today.

Ruth: I noticed you banging your wheelchair sometimes.

Mark: Oh, that. Yeah.

Ruth: What's going on when you do that?

Mark: I got pretty mad at Diego today.

Ruth: Why? What did he do?

Mark: Aw, he thinks he's so big.

Ruth: What do you mean "big"?

Mark: Big! He's older than me—and he's always letting me know.

Ruth: So you mean older, not taller? *[asking for clarification]*

Mark: Nope. . . . Not really. . . . I guess I mean both.

Ruth: Talk to me about that.

Mark: Naw. . . . (pause). Well, you know, I bet I'm taller than he is but he doesn't know that . . . because of *this* (bangs arms of wheelchair).

Ruth: But I've seen you play. *I've* been on your team and you make a lot of baskets.

Mark: Yeah, more'n Diego.

Ruth: So who's the better player?

Mark: No contest! I am! (laughs)

Ruth: Do you really think so?

Mark: Yeah, most of the time, I'm better.

Ruth: Say I were sitting in the stands watching the game and you're playing better than Diego. What would I see you doing? *[excellent probing strategy]*

Mark: Silly! I'd make more baskets!

Ruth: Oh, come on. You know basketball is much more than making baskets, Mark. Give me a break! What else would I see you doing? *[another excellent probing question]*

Mark: I have the ball more often—that's Diego's problem—he's all over the place so he never gets the ball.

Ruth: So how do you get the ball?

Mark: I use my wheels. I can move faster. I'm The Dominator! *[she could have probed here asking him how]*

Ruth: So your wheelchair actually helps?

Mark: Well, I don't know. I just know that I use it. *[sense of agency????]*

Ruth: What's it feel like being better than him? *[awkwardness here; she should have asked him to elaborate]*

Mark: Cool!

Ruth: Yeah, I'll bet. *[she is assuming that she knows what he means by "cool"]* You're better than Diego but are you the star?

Mark: No! I said I'm The Dominator!

Ruth: But what does that mean? *[here she asks him to elaborate]*

Mark: I told you: I control the ball on the floor.

Ruth: Then you're really the Floor General, right?

Mark: Yeah, man.

Ruth: How do the other kids feel about that?

Mark: That's the problem with Diego; he doesn't want me to be. He wants it all for himself. But the other kids? . . . I guess they've figured that that's how to use me. And anyway, it's only an after-school league; it's not like it's the high school team.

OC: Interviewing Mark was tough. He's bright and cute but bounces all over in his wheelchair. Seems a bundle of energy all the time. It was hard getting him to be more reflective. I wonder if I should continue this with him. He talks better when we're doing something together, like hanging out around the Center practicing lay-ups. Maybe this idea of three long interviews won't work with him. Frustrating.

Interviewing 10- and 11-year-olds has real challenges. Ruth is learning that she will have impressions about Mark's life and worldview, but these are only glimpses into a complex life experience. When an interview does not go as well as a beginning researcher hopes, he or she may be inclined to doubt the whole process. Ruth's reflections about whether she has chosen a genre and design that make sense for research with children are important for her to ponder and consider. This is part of her learning in the field: learning not only about the children and their experiences with bodiedness but also about qualitative research methods and assessing the usefulness of specific techniques for exploring her topic. Although not aware of it yet, Ruth is beginning to understand that what we learn in a study is always partial and incomplete. Learning to live with that ambiguity will become a habit of heart and mind.

10/9. First interview with Katrine. She _is_ the star! Her interpreter's here. I know some sign but not a lot. Katrine has some oral language; that helps, but Joanie makes it easier.

Ruth: Thanks for agreeing to talk to me. You know that I'm real interested in how you feel about basketball and how you got to be so good. I've talked with Mark some and been around the Center.

Katrine: Yeah, I've seen you. You don't play too bad yourself. **[I'm trying to keep eye-contact with K rather than her interpreter. Not as hard as I thought because K speaks ok.]**

Ruth: Thanks. So what started you in basketball?

Katrine: Well, I've got four older brothers and they'd take me outside to the driveway where our dad put up a hoop. We'd shoot for hours. That started when I was real little . . . like around 4.

Ruth: So this was a way you hung out with your brothers?

Katrine: Yeah. That was about the only time they'd pay attention to me. And it was neat! I loved it. I had my four big brothers all to myself!

Ruth: I've got a brother, but he never played basketball with me!

Katrine: Oh, but I was really good!

Ruth: When did you know you were really good?

Katrine: I guess I've always known. They wouldn't have played with me if I couldn't have kept up with them. At least after they taught me the basics.

Ruth: Do you remember how they taught you? *[good question; asking her to recall early experiences]*

Katrine: Boy, it seemed like a lot of drill but . . . they were pretty patient with me.

Ruth: Do you remember anything specific? *[another good question; asking for details]*

Katrine: They were bigger than me so they always had the ball. I got tired of them always having it. So they had to teach me how to steal the ball. That worked pretty well when I was little and could wiggle in between them. Now I'm nearly 6 feet and it's not so easy! (laughs)

Ruth: Other ways you knew you were good? *[Ruth has shifted away from exploring how Katrine's brothers taught her; she could have probed more here]*

Katrine: Well, my mom talked to me about basketball camp when I was 10. That was a clue. You know, I just play here because I like the other kids. It's not like playing over at the middle school.

Ruth: I wondered because I've seen you here a lot, and you're really much better than the others.

Katrine: Well, I got to know Amanda and Mark and some of the others because my mom works, and I have to come here when I don't have practice over at the school.

Ruth: So you see this as practice?

Katrine: Yeah . . . maybe. I think it's a different kind of drill. Some of the kids are in wheelchairs so it's all different. And sometimes I know I'm teaching them too, but I try not to let it show.

Ruth: When I watch you on the court, it seems like you really enjoy playing. Is that true?

Katrine: (big smile) Yeah. Here it's ok to be tall. Other places people stare at me or make jokes. Sometime, if I'm not looking, I don't get the jokes but I can see it in their faces.

Ruth: I was wondering about your hearing. *[a delicate topic to bring up]*

Katrine: It's ok to call me deaf! I am, just like I'm tall.

Ruth: **[this felt weird to me; embarrassing]** Ok. Ok. Sorry. . . . Are there any times when being deaf is a problem on the basketball court?

Katrine: Well, sure! You've got kids out there in wheelchairs—they can't move around too well—and you've got me—I don't hear so well!! Somehow we make it work. (big smile)

Ruth: What about on the middle school team? *[not being specific enough; unclear exactly what Ruth means here]*

Katrine: I'm just as good there, too. **[K sounds defensive; not a good question]**

Ruth: Oh, I know. What I meant is . . . on the school team, how do the other kids signal you when they're passing and you're not looking? What do they do?

Katrine: It depends. Actually, I've got pretty good peripheral vision so I can keep my eye on everyone else. That's one of the things that makes me a good player; I know how to pick up signals. My brothers taught me and my mom says it's easier for me because I'm deaf. And you know, she told me about hearing a couple of girls sitting on the risers during a game. My mom was right in front of them and heard one say to the other something about how did my being deaf make me a better player. When she told me, I hooted.

Ruth: Do you think it does?

Katrine: Well, you know, I'm not sure. . . . It sure isn't a handicap.

Ruth: Do you think of yourself as having a disability?

Katrine: I'm not sure. That word is pretty weird and deaf people don't like it much. I just don't think of myself that way. **[need to probe how she feels about being deaf]**

OC: Interviewing K was a pleasure! She seems poised and confident. I wonder if some of that comes from being so good at basketball. *[beginnings of analysis here; trying to make connections]* **It felt awkward when I asked about playing on the middle school team; she got defensive and it was a bad question.** *[good critical reflection]* **Sometimes it was slow, with the interpreter going back and forth, but it worked ok. I'm glad I could keep eye contact with K rather than Joanie . . . hard at times. The idea of agency keeps coming to mind.** *[important analytic insight]*

There are real differences in the reflectiveness and openness of Mark and Katrine. Katrine is mature and articulate; Mark is less interested in and able to reflect on his lived experience. This makes phenomenological interviewing particularly challenging with younger children. Should Ruth pursue a more substantial study on this topic, she might well decide to focus on older children or to alter her methods of gathering data.

ANALYSIS

Phenomenologic studies are open-ended, searching for the themes of meaning in participants' lives. Broad categories are sought, with sub-themes to elaborate the topography of meaning. Phenomenologic analysis requires that the researcher approach the texts with an open mind, seeking what meaning and structures emerge. The first step in reducing text is to read the interview transcripts (and related observation field notes, if gathered) and mark those passages that stand out as interesting. Through his growing understanding of the phenomenon, the researcher develops an intuitive sense of what is "interesting." An essential part of the process is to examine those passages to discern and identify what prompted this initial interest. The researcher might then check with the participant to see if he or she agrees with the emerging analytic themes. Each transcript is unique; the meaning of the experience of interest will emerge from that transcript. The identified important passages of interest are then assigned codes that represent themes. Using these words to organize the data, the researcher generates a profile, a narrative, depicting the meaning of the phenomenon for the individual.

Ruth's study has focused on the meaning of *bodiedness* for children who have physical disabilities. As the study has evolved, Ruth has identified the concept of *agency* to capture the children's feelings about their lives, particularly in terms of participating in sports activities. Related themes focus on how their families support their independence and the meanings associated with differentness. These themes are broad and provide preliminary categories for Ruth to rely on as she begins to analyze the data.

Ruth's preliminary organization is very simple. Because she is relying primarily on interviews, she keeps her transcripts in files identified by the children's names. As she becomes more confident about the salient themes, however, she reorganizes segments of data into those themes. She then creates folders containing copies of relevant quotes for each theme. As she writes the final report, she relies on this thematic organization, which pulls together data about the children and their families. Tables A.1, A.2, A.3, and A.4 show Ruth's preliminary coding and analysis about the theme of agency.

The following is an example of the preliminary analysis Ruth does with her data. Kent has asked the students to write analytic memos periodically. These help organize the data, provide insights into the topic, and identify areas for further data gathering. Ruth wrote this memo after several observations at the center and four of the planned-for six interviews. She develops the theme of *agency*, pulling together snippets of data and elaborating her interpretations. She is well aware of her partial understanding of the complexities of the children's lives.

ON AGENCY

Mark is the point guard—the floor general—of an after-school basketball team. Katrine is the star center. Both have what society calls "disabilities."

TABLE A.1 Preliminary Coding: Agency (Mark's Interview, 10/5)

Mark: I use my wheels. I can move faster. I'm The Dominator!

Ruth: So your wheelchair actually helps?

Mark: Well, I don't know. I just know that I use it.

Ruth: What's it feel like being better than him?

Mark: Cool!

Agency: sense that he can be good despite using a wheelchair

Ruth: Yeah, I'll bet. You're better than Diego but are you the star?

Mark: No! I said I'm The Dominator?

Ruth: But what does that mean?

Mark: I told you: I control the ball on the floor.

Ruth: Then you're really the Floor General, right?

TABLE A.2 Preliminary Coding: Agency (Katrine's Interview, 10/9)

Ruth: When did you know you were really good?

Katrine: I guess I've always known. They wouldn't have played with me if I couldn't have kept up with them. At least after they taught me the basics.

Ruth: Do you remember how they taught you?

Katrine: Boy, it seemed like a lot of drill but . . . they were pretty patient with me.

Agency: sense of being strong and powerful; relationships with brothers (acceptance???)

Ruth: Do you remember anything specific?

Katrine: They were bigger than me so they always had the ball. I got tired of them always having it. So they had to teach me how to steal the ball. That worked pretty well when I was little and could wiggle in between them. Now I'm nearly 6 feet and it's not so easy! [laughs]

Ruth: Other ways you knew you were good?

Katrine: Well, my mom talked to me about basketball camp when I was 10. That was a clue. You know, I just play here because I like the other kids. It's not like playing over at the middle school.

TABLE A.3 Preliminary Coding: Agency (Field Notes)

We talk about playing basketball, and they tell me about the league they belong to. One laughs about how it's the only league where kids do wheelies on the floor.

Agency: sense of the value of their "differentness" (???)

TABLE A.4 Agency: Acceptance

K's interview (10/9)
"They were pretty patient with me." (p. 3)
"It [being deaf] sure isn't a handicap." (p. 5)

M's interview (10/5)
"I guess they've figured out how to use me." (p. 4)

Field notes (10/3)
"Mark takes the ball and, holding it cradled in his lap, wheels down the court after Amanda, Katrine, and the other two. He pats his head three times. I find out later this means that Amanda will set up a pick for Katrine who will cut to the basket." (p. 9)

Mark uses a wheelchair and has to be helped to use the bathroom. Katrine is profoundly deaf and has been since birth. Mark has been called "crippled"; Katrine has been told that she daydreams and is stupid. Both have survived the cruelty of their peers and adults and built lives that are strong and powerful. How? Through a sense of *agency*.

Agency is defined as action, as having an effect, as being able to influence events. Children with physical disabilities, living in an able-bodied world, can feel marginalized, different, weird. Some cannot get into a building because there are no ramps; others do not hear the bells ring announcing the end of a class. The hearing and ambulatory world is indifferent to their differences. Within this indifferent or down-right hostile world, Mark and Katrine have come to feel they are accepted and have power as individuals. Power to shape events, to have an effect, to be accepted in the world. They have a sense of agency.

This preliminary analytic memo develops the theme of *agency* that I have identified in the data gathered up to now. Using quotes from interviews and observation field notes, as well as my own interpretations, I elaborate on the concept of agency as Mark and Katrine have taught me about it.

Sense of Efficacy

Integral to the meaning of disability to both Mark and Katrine is a *sense of efficacy*—the capacity to act upon the world in positive ways. Katrine was taught in her early years that she could compete with her brothers. They drilled her in the basics of basketball, developing her natural talents. As she grew (both in height and in skill), she could play nearly evenly with them.

She could steal the ball and hit jump shots playing two-on-two with them. All these early experiences helped build a sense of efficacy.

Mark has learned that his quickness with his arms and his ability to see opponents' moves make him quite effective as a point guard, even using a wheelchair. He calls himself "the dominator," which suggests that he relishes this leadership role on the court.

Acceptance

For both Mark and Katrine, a sense of agency comes in part from being *accepted and valued* by their peers. This is played out (no pun intended) on the basketball court where both feel they have important roles to play that are recognized and valued by others on the team. Mark describes his role on the team as setting up plays and controlling the movement of the ball. He calls himself "the dominator," suggesting that his role is a powerful one. He notes that the other kids "have figured out how to use me"—he feels like he's a valuable contributor. In an observation (10/3), I wrote that Mark decides the plays and works the ball from player to player, calling out their names as he passes:

> Mark takes the ball and, holding it cradled in his lap, wheels down the court after Amanda, Katrine, and the other two. He pats his head three times. **[I find out later this means that Amanda will set up a pick for Katrine who will cut to the basket.]** He passes to Joey, who feeds the ball to Katrine. She grabs the ball, nearly fouling Curtis, dribbles once and puts it in for two.

The team has decided that plays will be signaled using hand gestures—a mark of respect for Katrine. In the first interview with her, Katrine mentioned this: "That's one of the things that makes me a good player; I know how to pick up signals. My brothers taught me, and my mom says it's easier for me because I'm deaf." Katrine has turned what society calls a disability into a strength; the team honors and values this capacity in her.

Next Steps

These ideas are just now coming together. I have become fascinated with Katrine and Mark and how they view their worlds. It is difficult to get Mark to elaborate on how he feels about his role on the court as someone who uses a wheelchair; it has been easier with Katrine. I plan to do one more interview with Mark (at the Center) and two more with Katrine. She is quite open about her deafness and how it has shaped her life; Mark is less so.

Ruth's preliminary analytic memo brings together her insights about these two children and data that support these insights. She will have to tease out more fully what she means (and what she infers Mark and Katrine mean) by agency, efficacy, and acceptance. Is efficacy distinct from agency? What is the role of a sense of acceptance in the development of Mark and Katrine's worldviews? These are questions for Ruth to consider as her study and analysis proceed.

Appendix B

"We can change the system."

•◆•

Marla's Data and Analysis

Marla is an experienced health care professional who, early in her career, helped build a clinic in a Central American village. She sees herself as an activist and hopes to improve the U.S. health care system for poor women; therefore, she has come to the university for a master's degree in public health. Although she is not certain about the specific aspect of health care that she wants to attack, she is sure that the recipients of the care should take part in posing the questions. Her greatest concern has been how the people in her study are affected by it, so she has involved the study participants in seeking answers and determining how the answers could be used. Her experiences as a Latina in the United States have taught her that collaboration is more effective than competition for changing any system. Also, she is intrigued by the experiences of poor women but does not want to impose her views on them. She has chosen, therefore, a participatory action research strategy. Through volunteer work at the clinic where she used to work, Marla has identified a small group of women who live in the neighborhood and are committed to discovering ways to improve health services and to take action. The possibility that research can be coupled with action appeals to her proactive nature. Self-assured and optimistic, she believes the world can be changed for the better.

As it has unfolded over the semester, Marla's study has two purposes: (a) to facilitate a team of women who engage in participatory inquiry about health care services and (b) to summarize the processes of this inquiry and what the women discover and then to report it to Professor Kent for the course requirements. As often occurs with participatory action research, Marla feels torn between activism with the community and the demands of the academic world.

As the study has evolved, she and her team have focused on three women whose experiences in obtaining health services are problematic. To satisfy the requirements of the course at the university, the study results in mini descriptive case studies of these three women collaborators. For Marla's personal work in the clinic and with the community, she hopes the study will lead to action intended to change the clinic to better meet poor women's needs. Midway through the study, several possible courses of action have been identified by the women and Marla.

Early on in this participatory action research, in dialogue with one another, Marla and her team identified failure to return for follow-up visits as a major problem—one shared by the women and by clinic staff. They decided to identify three women who live in the community, had visited the clinic within the past 6 months, and were willing to share their experiences with health services. Together, the team talked about strategies for dialogue with the women and developed an initial set of guidelines. They practiced interviewing with one another as a preliminary step. The following interview excerpts include one interview conducted by Marla and one conducted by a team member, Julia. The observation notes were taken at the health clinic by Julia and Aida, another team member. Marla, as a volunteer, has been doing informal participant observation. She makes notes about these experiences when she returns home in the evening. The team members have shared their interview transcriptions and observation notes with one another, seeking each other's input and comments. You will see the researcher's comments and our comments throughout the excerpts. As a reminder, the team members' comments are in **bold** type; our comments are in *italics*.

10/22. Interview with Teresa, woman who used clinic but didn't come back. Done in Spanish and translated. Open-ended questions. M means

me (Marla); T means Teresa; MC means my comments added while transcribing. About one-half hour.

M: You've heard about the group of women I am with? We're talking with women like you who've lived in the neighborhood for a year or more. We want to know about what kind of services are important to you. Especially health services. Tell me a little bit about yourself. Do you like living here? *[good beginning; acknowledges that Teresa has recently moved here from the Island]*

T: It's not so bad. I mean, I have a job. There's food. And the kids. There's lots for them to do. You know, they aren't always hanging around.

M: So . . . life's maybe a little better here . . . for you?

T: Oh yeah, it's better. Not the weather, but you know, we have more. I never had a wash machine before.

M: So taking care of the clothes is easier?

T: Yes, I even iron the girls' dresses. **[MC: I want to get to health, but I'd rather she brought it up.]**

M: What else do you have here that is important, that maybe you did not have before?

T: Oh . . . things . . . you know . . . like . . . um . . . oh! Supermarkets! So many choices. You don't have to get just what is at the little market. I don't know if that's so good (laugh). . . . The kids, you know, eat not so good: lots of potato chips and stuff.

M: Do you ever worry about their health? or yours?

T: Yeah, but what can I do? I take them to the clinic when I have to. You know, I have to for the school, with all those shots. And the dentist clinic.

M: What about you? Your health?

T: Oh, I don't get sick. **[MC: I know she used the clinic once. Doesn't she remember that? Maybe she doesn't consider that to be sick?]** *[Marla's observer comment is a bit judgmental]*

M: So you're pretty tough?

T: (smiles) Maybe so! I don't get so sick.

M: If you did, what would you do?

T: I guess I'd call my cousin. She lives the block over. She'd come help me with the children. **[MC: I wonder if she just doesn't see the clinic and doctors as an option.]**

M: Do you think you'd ever need a doctor? Would you ever use one?

T: Oh, I don't know about doctors. I just don't know. **[MC: I wait here for a few seconds. I'm hoping she will tell me what she means.]** *[Wait time is often needed to allow the person being interviewed to collect his or her thoughts]* I think the kids need them for the shots. But I just don't know about doctors. **[MC: Not sure if she means she doesn't trust them or if she doesn't know about doctors . . . what they are for?]**

M: Do you know anything a doctor could do for you? How to use one?

T: Umm . . . no.

M: But you used the clinic yourself once. Did a doctor help you then?

T: The clinic.. . . Yes. But I didn't see a doctor. I mean you don't see a *doctor* at the clinic. Do you?

M: Do you remember who treated you? What they said? What they did?

T: I remember. I had red spots on my skin. A nice woman looked at it. She gave me cream. It went away.

M: Did you ever go back? Did they tell you to come back?

T: Maybe. But I had the cream. The red came back once, so I used what was left. Why should I go back?

M: Did the woman who treated you seem to know what she was doing? Did she explain everything to you? **[MC: I should not have asked her both of these questions at once, but I want her to talk in general about the experience at the clinic.]** *[Marla's politics are showing here; she could have asked a more neutral question about the service]*

T: I guess so. She told me how to use the cream. I didn't ask her anything else.

M: Can you think back to the whole visit to the clinic. . . and tell me why you came, what you were thinking about as you were there, as you waited, how you explained your problem, how you were treated? Just kind of tell me the whole story. *[excellent question]*

T: I didn't have to wait too long. And it was pretty comfortable. I was kinda scared, 'cause I didn't know what the place was like. I came because my boss noticed the red. He told me to come. I didn't know. They were real nice, but they acted like I should of known what to do. I didn't know how to fill out the papers they gave me. **[MC: I realize how much she does not know, does not know, does not know. I guess we need to let people know!]** Yolanda, she's my oldest daughter, she was with me. She helped me. I got called into a room. Everything was real clean. The woman in the blue blouse came in. Asked me so many questions. She was real smart. I don't think she was a doctor. She said her name was Sara, not doctor somebody. I didn't understand all that she said. But I liked her. And the cream worked. **[MC: Ah, she's talking. It sounds as if the clinic is not an integral part of the community. She would not have come if her boss had not told her to. Now I have specific questions. Let's see if she would go back.]**

This is a good preliminary, getting-to-know-you interview. Marla has asked about Teresa's experiences and probed to discover her knowledge about the clinic's services. She has also asked some leading questions, ones that indicate where her political interests lie. Because Marla's work is explicitly oriented toward political action, such questions are consistent with her paradigm. She might want to consider if she is allowing Teresa to fully express her own views, however. From this interview, Marla has developed some insights into how the clinic is perceived by Teresa and identified strands to follow-up on in subsequent interviews.

10/23. Interview with Yvette, young woman who visited clinic about six weeks ago with some breathing problems. Didn't come to scheduled follow-up visit. Researcher = me (Julia); Woman = Yvette.

Researcher: Tell me about the first time you went to the clinic. *[good beginning question]*

Woman: Well, I had to walk over from the bus stop and it was raining. . . really pouring. I had two bags of groceries and it felt like they weighed a ton! It was hard. . . so hard. That stupid girl behind the desk—she acted like I wasn't even there. Looked right through me. Just gabbed on the phone.

Researcher: Yeah, getting to the clinic isn't very easy. I had to take two buses to get here.

Woman: So what do you want to talk with me about?

Researcher: Well, all about the clinic and how you feel about it. Seems like when you first went, you didn't feel too welcome when you got there, right? *[This could be a "leading question," but Julia is asking for corroboration of an impression she has]*

Woman: Yeah, it was pretty uncomfortable.

Researcher: Tell me about that some more. *[excellent elaboration question]*

Woman: Well, that stupid girl.. . . You know. If I wasn't having so much trouble breathing I think I would have left.

Researcher: What happened? What'd she do?

Woman: When she finally got off the phone—and it was her boyfriend, I think—she asked me a million questions and typed them into her stupid computer. Then she had me sit back down and fill out one of those long information sheets—you know, the ones that ask you if you sleep at night, how often you have a glass of water—questions that don't have anything to do with my breathing.

Researcher: Did you fill it out?

Woman: Most of it. Some of it seems pretty stupid. Then I had to sit there and wait. Seemed like forever. I almost got to see a whole episode of *As the World Turns*! Then the nurse called me in.

Researcher: So you finally got to see a doctor?

Woman: No! I changed into one of those little white things and sat in an examining room but there was no TV in there! (laughs)

Researcher: Well, what did you do?

Woman: There was a magazine with recipes that was lying there. Something about eating "light and healthy."

Researcher: And then the doctor came in?

Woman: No, it was one of those. . . what do they call them? Physicians' assistants?

Researcher: And what did he do? *[This series of questions assumes a linear story-telling mode; the woman might respond more fully if she could structure the narrative herself]*

Woman: Oh, it was a "she" and she was ok.

Researcher: What did she do?

Woman: She examined me and asked me some questions about my "lifestyle."

Researcher: What did she mean?

Woman: Kinds of foods I eat, about my apartment, alcohol, where I work.

Researcher: Did she help you? *[She has asked a series of yes-no questions; she could ask for more elaboration]*

Woman: She said she thought it might be asthma but because it's not really bad, she wanted to try something to prevent it. So she gave me an inhaler.

Researcher: Did she tell you how to use it?

Woman: Yeah, I was supposed to breathe it four times a day.

Researcher: Did she give you any special instructions?

Woman: Just that I had to be sure to do it regularly.

Researcher: Did it help?

Woman: No. I finally gave up. It seemed more trouble than it was worth. I did it for about a week. You know, I'd carry it in my pocketbook to work, and I'd pull it out, and I'd puff on it. People around me would laugh. The supervisor asked me to go into the back when I had to do it. He didn't like it; thought it might make the customers nervous. It just got to be more trouble. And, I wasn't breathing any better.

Researcher: Did you ever think about going back to the clinic again to get something else?

Woman: Naw, it's so far, and it take so much time. It just didn't seem worth it.

Researcher: What could the clinic do to make it better? *[excellent question to elicit her hopes for the clinic]*

Woman: Sure! Open a branch right next to where I work. And cut down on all the wait time. Maybe hire more people or get more efficient. I don't even have any kids yet, and I can't find time. How do they think they can serve people with big families? It's gotta be easier. Oh yeah, one more thing: Hire people to work behind the desk who are nice. People like us. People from the neighborhood. You know, I tried to call them once, but I got put on hold forever—and when I finally got a real person, she made me feel ignorant, like I shouldn't have been asking the question.

Researcher: Well, this has been real helpful. I might come and talk with you again. Would that be ok? And we'd like to ask you if you'd be interested in joining a group of women who meet once every two weeks—right near here—to talk about the ways the clinic can serve them better. Think you might be interested?

Woman: I'll think about it.

This interview helps Marla and her team to establish more fully what the experience of being placed in the impersonal bureaucracy of the clinic with its "wait time" and requests for information. It also depicts how this woman left the clinic with insufficient understanding about her asthma and the use of the inhaler. This is important information for the team to probe into more deeply to explore the reasons why women do not feel comfortable returning to the clinic for follow-up care. In a subsequent team meeting, they hypothesize that (a) the woman was not told sufficiently explicitly that she should return (information), and (b) that she may have felt depersonalized there because of her class, gender, ethnicity, or all three (institutionalized oppression).

10/10. 6:46 p.m. Clinic. Observation by Julia.
Waiting area is about 12' × 15' with colorful (red, blue, orange, black) plastic-covered chairs arranged in groups around the room. TV hanging from ceiling in north corner. Piles of magazines around. Smell of overbrewed coffee coming from the dispenser in the corner mixed with smell of Vicks' cough drops and cheap perfume. Receptionist sitting behind counter; working at her computer. It's quiet. Three groups here. One's a mother, father, and three kids. Talking Spanish. Father's arm is around mother; little

girl on mother's lap. Other two playing with puzzle on floor. Kids look close together in age; maybe 4-6? One on lap about 2? Little girl is coughing, sneezing, looks like she's got a fever. *[What does it mean to look feverish?]* Two old men, unshaven, drab-colored baggy clothes. One is dozing off; the other is smiling at the little kids. Both drinking coffee from dispenser in the corner **[here to see a doctor or just to watch TV? may be homeless]**. Young girl obviously pregnant wearing short, tight dress, lots of jewelry and makeup. Long hair pulled back in a clip. Guy with her is much older, dressed flashy (polyester suit, earrings, long, stringy hair in pony tail, cowboy boots).

7:01 p.m.—Nothing's really happened.

7:03 p.m.—Door opens from back and tall woman with arm in sling walks out; stops at reception desk, makes another appointment, leaves.

7:06 p.m.—Middle-aged man comes out; dressed in jeans and sweatshirt; talks with receptionist, appears to pay bill, leaves.

7:10 p.m.—Nothing happening. **[These people have been here waiting for at least a half an hour! I'm going to have to leave soon; I hope something happens soon.]**

7:15 p.m.—Two PAs wearing blue jackets come out from room behind counter. One calls for the Ariaga family; the other for Lucy. Father stays with two kids playing with puzzle; mother carries little girl into back area. Father pats mother's arm as she leaves. Lucy pushes herself up; her man continues his reading, pays no attention at all. *[focus is on interaction between clients rather than clinic staff and clients; might want to redirect or refocus based on this interest]* **[People seem comfortable here: reading, watching TV, playing with games; almost like a hotel lobby]** *[excellent descriptions: positive, neutral, and nonjudgmental]*

7:21 p.m.—Still quiet; we're just sitting here!

7:23 p.m.—Woman comes in; 30-something; curly brown hair, dark eyes; drags in resistant preadolescent girl; register with receptionist and take seats. Girls eyes are sullen; mother touches her arm, she jerks it away. Mother picks up *Good Housekeeping*; girl picks up *People*.

7:30 p.m.—No changes; I have to leave.

OC: [added later] I continue to wonder what the old men were there for and what the interactions in the examining rooms were like, especially for the mother and her little girl and the pregnant girl. Seemed like a long time to wait; I wonder if that's typical. I'm also curious about the receptionist: She seemed ok with the men (a little flirty?) but was cool with the women. Wonder what's going on there.

There is strong detail in these field notes, specifically around the passage of time. Because the team knows that clinic visits can entail seemingly endless waiting, these field notes are useful as data describing waiting. They also identify gender issues as having a potential role in the experiences of women who use the clinic.

11/3. Clinic observation. Early evening (5:30). Observation by Aida.

The place is buzzing. Three people waiting for receptionist. She's tied up with one of the PAs—he's trying to explain something to her. Moving around the room clockwise I see three guys—late teens, early 20s—wearing jeans and leather jackets. They're talking together—complaining about how there's no smoking allowed. Next is a woman whose photo I've seen in the community newspaper. She's really attractive *[Who defines attractive? What does it mean? is it culturally defined?]*, in her 40s, tall, and has on a charcoal gray tailored suit, high heels, earrings, and a bracelet. **[I think she is principal of the school.]** Beyond her chair are two old men. They are pretty creepy: mesmerized by the TV, grubby clothing. All I hear from them is an occasional grunt or chuckle. *[Again, note the use of "creepy"; does Aida define this?]* One spills coffee on his already-stained pants.

Two kids are sitting doing puzzles. They keep arguing softly and every now and then break into laughter. **[Are they alone or waiting for someone else—parent?]**

Bang! the door to the back rooms is thrown open. Short middle-aged woman with wild hair comes storming out. She's yammering away, a mile a minute, but I can't understand. What language is that? A man in one of those blue shirts comes out with her **[I think this one is a doctor; he's an Anglo]**, trying to calm her down and be patient, but he's not having much luck. Turns to receptionist, asks her something. I see them roll their eyes. Receptionist brings up something on the computer screen; PA shows it to the woman. She yells at him and turns to leave, charging out through the doors. He shrugs and walks back into the examining rooms. **[Who does he think he is? She really seemed upset, and I'm not sure he tried all that hard.]**

Everyone was really quiet listening to this and watching. After she leaves, a couple of people exchange looks and shrug their shoulders. The two old men lean over and whisper to each other; then they go back to their TV show. **[I can't really hear what the old men say but guess it has to do with the woman.]**

Woman in her 30s, looking really tired, carrying two shopping bags from Food Lion. Waits at receptionist's desk for several minutes. Looks exasperated. I can hear her hacking cough all the way across the room. Woman taps her foot. **[impatient?]** Finally talks with receptionist; her tone is belligerent. Receptionist is "all business." *[What does this mean?]* **I've been here 45 minutes, no halt in the action. Gotta go now.**

These notes focus on interactions and capture some of the action that takes place in the clinic. There are lots of terms used that will need to be fleshed out for the field notes to be more concrete and detailed—for example, "attractive" and "creepy." They also further identify potential issues of role, class, gender, and ethnicity as important analytic insights. These will be focused on more fully as the study progresses.

ANALYSIS

Case studies are uniquely intended to capture the complexity of a particular event, program, individual, or place. They focus holistically on an organization or individual. The conceptual framework and research questions help narrow a broad focus more closely into categories of interest. These categories then provide the initial ways for thinking analytically and for a first cut on coding the data. In Marla and her team's case, they have assumed a critical stance, focusing on oppression and domination in specific ways. They assume a feminist and class-based perspective, examining ways that clinic services are structured to depersonalize poor women and their choices in health care.

Marla and her team's strategy is similar to Ruth's, although it is more iterative and collaborative. Marla has assumed responsibility for organizing and managing the data. She initially organizes the data by source: observations, field notes of team meetings, and interviews with women. She and her team meet regularly for dialogue and analysis. They read the data independently and then bring their insights to the team meetings. As their understanding evolves, they reorganize the data into salient themes. They also develop files for data about the three women on whom they focus in-depth. These files contain the team's notes, transcriptions of interviews, and excerpts from the women's journals. Marla, as "chief scribe" of the group, creates a set of tables that summa-

TABLE B.1 "Waiting"

"That stupid girl behind the desk—she acted like I wasn't even there. Looked right through me. Just yammered on the phone." (Int w/Yvette, 10/23, p. 1)

"When she finally got off the phone—it was her boy friend, I think—she asked me a million questions and typed them into her stupid computer." (Int w/Yvette, 10/23, p. 3)

"Then I had to sit there and wait. Seemed like forever. I almost got to see a whole episode of *As the World Turns!*" (Int w/Yvette, 10/23, p. 3)

"These people have been waiting here for at least a half an hour!" (OC, Obs, 10/10, p. 2)

"Still quiet; we're just sitting here!" (OC, Obs, 10/10, p. 2)

---

rize data around emerging themes; one such table is presented in Table B.1. For her first analytic memo, she writes about the theme as well as the team's process in analyzing these data collaboratively; this first memo follows.

MEMO #1: COLLABORATIVE ANALYSIS: THE PROCESS AND SOME PRELIMINARY INSIGHTS

Analyzing data together is hard work. My team and I have met weekly for the past seven weeks. We have read over the data we are gathering before these meetings, and then come into the meeting ready to talk about what we discover. After that, we go home, read through the data again, and come back to share those insights. The team has been terrific! They are really committed to doing this work, even though it means lots of reading and thinking. And they are also continuing to interview the three women and do some observations at the clinic.

We've had some interesting discussions. One centered around the theme of *waiting*. We all agreed that the data we had from the women, our own experiences, and what we observed show that there are lots of ways that people who use the clinic are made to wait. Take Yvette, for example. She talked about how the girl at the desk made her wait while she was on a personal phone call. And she talked about sitting watching TV for a long time before she was called in to see one of the PAs or doctors. In the field notes, we have mentioned several times when people had to sit and wait and wait and wait.

The discussions we've had about this have to do with "why" questions. We've disagreed about the reasons that women have to wait. We all have our own hypotheses, but we haven't really explored this deeply with the three women. Aida says that she thinks it has to do with race. I think it has to do with class and gender. For example, we have all seen that the receptionist responds differently to men than women, and she always listens to the PAs. Julia believes it is that the doctors are so busy that they can't see the patients sooner. It is just in the nature of health clinics to not be able to see people quickly. We are all concerned about this waiting, because it may be one of the reasons that the women don't come back to the clinic. The next steps in our process will be to discuss these possibilities with the three women in some depth.

This early memo describes the preliminary data analysis done by Marla and her team and identifies next steps, as asked for in Kent's course requirements. The team has focused on "waiting" as a persistent issue for the women. This insight comes from their own previous experiences in clinics, the data from the women, and their observations. They are beginning to hypothesize that this expectation of several lost hours at the clinic might be a deterrent for the women to return for follow-up care. Although not providing much supporting data (in the form of quotes from interviews and field notes), this memo hints at the complexity of collaborative data analysis: the need for full involvement, balancing alternative insights and perspectives, and honoring the views of all team members. The next memo Marla writes shows the evolution of the team's process from inquiry and reflection to a commitment to take action, an essential element of participatory action research.

MEMO #2: TAKING ACTION

We have come a long way, my team and I. We have gathered data and involved the three women in the process of reflecting on their experiences, identifying possible reasons, and discussing various courses of action that we, as committed women, can take.

One idea that has become very important is how the three women feel like they are not real people when they come into the clinic. Some of this has to do with all the time they spend waiting; some has to do with having a man examine them; some has to do with speaking English. We have discussed all this with them in two sessions where we talked through what we were collectively learning and asked them what actions they might take. The three women all commented on how, going through this process with us has made them feel like they could take some action. They talked about the need to change the clinic, in small ways at first, to make it *their* clinic. In one of these meetings, Yvette talked about her oldest daughter who goes to the Eastside Community College for a degree in human services. One of her instructors talked about the need for bilingual workers in community health clinics to serve as a liaison and interpreter with clinic patients. Her instructor is committed to changing social service agencies to better meet the needs of the people they are supposed to serve. One idea that came out of this discussion was to ask the instructor to work with the manager of the clinic to have people like Yvette's daughter placed there for some of their internship work. We agreed that this kind of action might make the clinic more responsive to the needs of poor people, especially women.

Another idea that has come out of these meetings is to ask for an appointment with the Director of Health Clinics for the city. His office is downtown, and he may not agree, but the women—Yvette, Teresa, and Maria—and all the members of our team feel that, as a group and based on our action research, he might listen to us. We want to talk with him about what we have learned and see if he can develop a plan for assigning staff to the neighborhood clinics. We talked about how this might be a good time to try to meet with him because of the big grant that the city just got to help rebuild poorer neighborhoods.

We also are planning to meet with the *Healthy Women/Healthy Children* group that has formed in The Heights. They are an advocacy group that is trying to change health care services to women and children and are close to us. We can join forces with them and learn what their strategies are for getting bureaucracies to listen.

I am feeling a bit overwhelmed by all the work ahead of us. But I'm really pleased that the women continue to be as involved as they are. They are coming to learn that the clinic is *their* clinic. They understand now how it works and want to take action to make it work for them.

Marla's second memo describes the process of determining to take action that is central to participatory action research. It might have turned out otherwise:

The women might have continued to feel distant and marginalized from the clinic; they might have felt that taking action would come to nothing. Through the process of dialogue, research, and reflection, however, they have come to a place of commitment to action. Although Marla's work for the qualitative research course will soon end, her work with these women, and others like them, will continue for a long time.

Appendix C

"A community brings
the arts to everyone."

•◆•

Anthony's Data and Analysis

Anthony is returning to the university for an advanced degree in public policy. Upon graduation from college, he volunteered as a community development worker dealing with issues of water quality and housing. When funding for this project was cut, he applied for a legislative internship in Washington, D.C., to serve as staff on a joint committee on arts and education. His interest in evaluation and policy studies springs from these experiences: He learned firsthand, when his project's funding was cut, the effects of policy decisions on community members and their advocates. He hopes that his work will inform the policy-making process through the provision of more effective, thoughtful, and detailed information.

The purpose of his study is to describe and evaluate the effectiveness of a program designed to bring arts to members of the community; he uses a miniethnographic design to describe the culture of the program. As part of his responsibilities to the funding agency, Anthony will write an evaluation report to inform the agency and decision makers concerned with the arts. Bringing arts to the community means providing actual, usable opportunities for people who live in the neighborhood to both appreciate and create various forms of art.

The elements of a community-based program are many and complex. As Anthony has explored his topic and problem, he has decided to focus on specific elements of the program: participation at center events, staff and participant attitudes toward the activities, and views of nonparticipating community members about the program. His overarching question is, "How is *participation* defined through the culture of the program?" He documents participation through his observations and logs kept by staff members. Attitudes toward the program are being obtained through two techniques: in-depth interviews and a survey. Anthony has made some preliminary decisions about how many participants and nonparticipants to interview and survey. He decided, given the resources available, to survey participants as they attend activities and to invite active participants to be interviewed. He further decides that interviewing 10 to 15 "actives" would give him an in-depth portrait of their involvement and views about the program—their views on participation.

Interviewing and surveying nonparticipating community members has been more difficult. To date, he has surveyed seven households within five blocks of the arts center by walking around the neighborhood on Saturday mornings, leaving surveys and inviting household members to sit for a brief interview. He is not sure how many of these nonparticipating member interviews he will ultimately be able to do, but he will stop after he has approximately 10.

10/10. 12:15-1 p.m.
Community Arts Center Office.

I'm sitting in the office of the Center because I want to get a sense of the "culture" of the Center and its community, so I figured here is a good place to start. I chose the noon hour because I thought people might stop by during their lunch hours. The Center is housed in a three-story commercial building—it used to be some kind of store. The first floor is an open space so they use it for large classes and the gallery. The office is at the back of this space. I ask Dionne *[Who is this person?]* what is upstairs and she tells me there are several smaller rooms used for classes and storage. The third floor is a dance studio—she says it is also used for rehearsals *[Anthony might have asked what kind of rehearsals]*.

The room seems to be overflowing with papers. On the side walls are file cabinets. A big table is pushed up against the wall next to the door—it's spread with papers. On the wall above it is a cork board. Schedules and such are tacked on it. The room has two desks. Dionne—late 30s?—is sitting at one. She is the assistant director/secretary. She answers phones, knows the schedules. Welcomes people when they enter. The door is open. A somewhat balding man enters. He is carrying a brown paper bag.

[What kind of papers? Documents can often reveal important aspects of the culture.]

She is a jack-of-all trades to this organization— knows everybody and where everything is.

D: "Hey there, Gene. So how did the gum work go? Was the dentist gentle?"

Is she just nosy or does she care?

G: "I survived. Got some catching up to do. Thought I'd see what's happening and if I can help on anything." He opens the bag, takes out two steaming cups of soup and a loaf of bread. "It's their version of minestrone today."

Is this a regular routine? His bringing her lunch?

D: "Smells good. Thanks. Actually, you can do the registrations for Heather's class." Gestures to the computer on the other desk.

[Who is Heather? What does she teach?]

Gene begins working on the computer. Both sip soup and tear off chunks from the loaf. It's quiet until two women enter.

D: "About time you two came by. You need to try on your costumes. They're in the back room—way upstairs."

W1: "I got a job! Aren't you going to ask me what it is?"

[Anthony might want to note what the job is— to give an idea about the kind of folks who use the center; give more of a description of these women—age? ethnicity? clothing?]

W2: "Yeah, she's part of the labor force now. Wonder if she'll have time for us anymore."

D: "Well, congratulations! But don't forget you're still Stella to us."

Is Stella her name or the role she has in the play?

There are now five of us in the relatively small office. Stella perches on Gene's desk; her friend takes the other folding chair. Conversation turns to what happened over the weekend in the neighborhood.

[Can he capture any of this conversation?]

They seem really comfortable with each other.

Enter an elderly man. He looks a little timid. "I understand you have some drawing classes."

D: "You're just in time to sign up for Barney's watercolor class. It'll meet in the late afternoon. How does that sound?"

EM: "I don't know. Do I need experience?"

D: "Now, honey, you've got all the experience you need for this class. You can fill out this paper—and try some of this bread. What brings you to us?"

She is really a master at making people feel comfortable.

EM: "My granddaughter keeps telling me I need to get what she calls 'an interest.' I think she's worried about me. Always wanted to paint. . . ."

D assures him he is in the right place. He takes a chunk of bread and joins us. He tells us his name is Leo. D starts telling him how important it can be to learn to paint. She tells him about the Center.

Food may play a part in this culture.

[This a chance to hear the values and beliefs of the center]

A tall artsy-looking woman comes in. Everyone's attention turns to her and she sort of "takes over" the room. She's babbling on about getting ready for her afternoon class of kindergartners. She says something to the two women and to Gene. She helps herself to a gulp of D's soup. She opens the closet and gets materials—finger paints today. Another gulp of soup. She tosses instructions to D and leaves.

[What is "artsy"?] **I find out later that she does a mixed-methods class for 5- and 6-year-olds. They are in a morning kindergarten in the nearby elementary school. Their mothers bring them to the group while they go to Heather's pot throwing class. How can she teach the class? She seems so disorganized herself?** *[Anthony's comment is a bit judgmental]*

The woman who teaches the pottery class, Heather, comes into the room. She brings a large bag filled with various equipment—including her lunch. She joins us, turning the talk to the outdoor craft show planned for this month.

[What kind of materials does she bring? Does she provide her own or does the center?]

Time's up. I thank everyone for letting me listen and take notes. I talk to D for a minute arranging to observe a class. She also gives me some advice on the survey. *[Elaborating on this advice would be helpful]* **I may follow up today by interviewing Gene.**

OC: There seems to be a lot of interaction and joking around with one another in the office. I was particularly impressed with how much Dionne knows about everyone and how, without skipping a beat, she greeted the Elderly Man and made him feel welcome there. There's something intriguing that goes on around food here.

Anthony's early field notes provide strong detail and capture dialogue well. As with many beginners, however, the field notes are uneven. Anthony is learning that "paying attention" with the level of focus and concentration necessary for excellent field notes is hard work. Although comments at the end of the field notes are astute: He has important insights into the culture of the program very early on. This is often the case, although the researcher may not realize it at the time. As Anthony reviews these early field notes and his commentary on them, the insights become more clear.

11/3. 4-6:15 p.m. Watercolor class.

The class is a watercolor workshop. The 12 students (5 males; 7 females) have been together for 3 weeks (this is their 4th lesson). The instructor (Barney) signaled it was time to begin class by turning on a slide that showed an impressionist painting. He explained that they were going to learn a new technique, but he wanted to talk about impressionist painting first. He asked the class to give their "impressions" of the painting. I could hardly hear him, even though the room is not large. Class members responded: "old-fashioned"; "shadows"; "soft"; "bright colors"; "people look like they are going to move."

I'm not sure who it was. Maybe a Seurat.

Not sure the class knew what he wanted. Were enthusiastic but seemed mildly confused.
[Anthony is having some difficulty sorting out what are descriptions and what are his comments on the actions he is observing; note that he includes in his field notes, "I could hardly hear him"; this might be better bolded as an observer's comment]

B: "Yes, that's all true. He accomplished that effect by using quick, short brushstrokes—almost like little dots." Barney spoke a few sentences about the brushstrokes and colors the painter used. He stood at the front of the room with his arms immobile at his side, stiff and dull.

Can this guy paint, let alone teach painting?

S: "Yeah, I heard Monet did that. But this doesn't look like Monet."

I think it would have been better if he had used a large print of the original or a poster. Anything but a slide. i can't tell what he's trying to demonstrate. I wonder if this is part of a curriculum and he is just using it because he thinks he is supposed to. He doesn't seem to have a handle on the point he's trying to get across.

B: "OK, let's get to work. Today, you'll need the fat brushes, sponges, and a cup of water next to your colors." Suddenly Barney loosened up and became an artist. He began to demonstrate a technique with sponges and water. He didn't talk a lot, but his hands flew across the paper and between the paper and the materials. The class gathered around. Almost as quickly as he began, he turned away from the easel and told them to try it.

He was almost dancing!

He didn't even ask the group if anyone had questions about what he just did, but he wandered among them, pointing out things, making suggestions, and answering individual questions. *[Observer comments on pedagogy; could lead to important insights; detail is good]*

People worked at their easels. The room was quiet. Not much talking except with Barney. People seemed absorbed in their painting. *[how does he infer "absorbed"?]*

The behavior norms must be established already. Everyone knows what they are supposed to do, where the materials are, and how to interact with each other and Barney. The atmosphere is very ordered but comfortable. Industrious is the word.

After sitting at the side of the room, I wandered around looking at the painting. Finally, I whispered a few questions about how they learned to do certain procedures, if this was their first watercolor class, and how many paintings they had worked on in this class. With one exception, this was everyone's first class. They practice different techniques, but they are each working to complete one full watercolor.

I felt as if I'd seen two different people in Barney. What was that attempt to teach about impressionism at the beginning of the class?

OC: Barney is an enigma to me! He seems to be an effective instructor but I'm just not sure. I wonder what he thinks about participation in this class. He's gotten people to come to take it, but do they really relate to the stuff about Impressionism? I'll have to follow up on that when I interview him.

These field notes were difficult for Anthony to take, although he is able to capture details and the flow of action. He is a bit judgmental, however, in his observer's comments. With feedback from Kent and other class members, he will reflect on this, seeking to understand what was difficult about Barney and the class for him. This process is important for Anthony's growing skills in being reflexive. His notes to himself at the end of the field notes identify areas for further investigation; this helps keep him on track with his questions.

11/8. Interview with an active participant. Gene is a writer in his 50s; works out of his own home; was selected because he is very active

in Center activities. Director mentioned that they want to get him on the advisory board. Q = interviewer's question; A = respondent's answer; OC = researcher's comments added after transcribing the interview.

Q: Gene, thanks so much for agreeing to the interview this afternoon. You know I'm interested in the programs at the Center and how participants feel about those programs. You're pretty active, which is why I wanted to talk with you. Tell me about why the arts are important to you. *[good "grand tour" question]*

A: Oh, there are lots of reasons. For one thing, it's my life—I'm a writer, you know. People need ways to express themselves, to communicate. The arts provide such an alternative to the boob tube! And a way for different generations to relate to one another.

Q: Can you give me an example of that?

A: One that comes to mind right away is the outdoor crafts show that was here last month. Did you see the pot-throwing demonstration that my friend Heather had? At one point, she let people come up and try it and all ages were interested. A couple of those punk teenagers really got into it! It was wonderful!

Q: Yes, I sa . . .

A: What I was going to add was about the clothesline art show where my sister took her daughter who's 24 and our father who's in his 80s. They had a great time talking about the scenes of the neighborhood and city that the local artists had painted. That, to me, is one of the great values of the arts—seeing families together appreciating or doing.

Q: Doing? . . . Talk about doing. *[asking for elaboration]*

A: There was Heather's pottery booth, but there's always some sort of class at the Center that teaches you how to do—the painting, pottery, silversmithing. Oh, I almost forgot! Once a season we have a play. There's this marvelous stockbroker—a guy who just split up with his wife—who comes and acts, and it's *so* important for him.

Q: Why is *doing* important in the arts? *[good probing question]*

A: Because it's a way to express yourself. I write, but I need other ways too. That's why I take the painting. Oh, and another reason arts are so important is because we learn through them; we learn to do things we hadn't done before.

Q: It would be helpful if you could give me some specific examples. *[excellent question for detail]*

A: Take my friend Jack, the stockbroker. He had done some acting in high school and college but never really taken a class or studied it. So what did he really know? He was a natural, that's all. But in preparing the play each year, we bring in a professional actor to work with our community actors. Jack's told me several times how much he learns from these sessions.

Q: You've been telling me some ways that people participate. What are other ways people participate in the Center? *[too vague]*

A: I'm not sure I know what you mean.

Q: Well, if they don't want to paint or throw a pot or act in a play, what else can they do?

A: Don't you know? They come to activities like the clothesline art show or the crafts show. Or, once we had a dance group give a performance—people came to that. I've even been asked to read some of my poetry . . . but I'm not sure I'm ready yet.

Q: Why not?

A: Well, these are my neighbors and I'm not sure I want them to. . . .

Q: Do you think they may not value it as much as you?

A: You mean value my writing? Yeah, maybe that's it. Poetry's really personal.

Q: I've learned from interviews with other community members that it matters a lot to them to have people like you and Heather right here—they say it's uplifting. I think it makes them feel good about their community. What do you think?

A: Well, I can understand that, but when it comes to sharing my poetry in a public forum, it makes me feel a little strange.

Q: I've also heard that many parents appreciate having the after-school classes for their kids. *[asking for corroboration of a perspective he has heard from others]*

A: Yes, I think it is important. Some of these kids might not get exposure to art without them.

Q: Why is that?

A:　Well, you know art isn't that important in schools any more . . . and parents are so busy too. It's hard to find a place for the arts in lots of people's lives.

Q:　And you feel the Center provides a place?

A:　Definitely! It's wonderful for *all* of us.

OC: I think I'm beginning to get some insights into the various ways of participation in the arts program. This was great! I'll need to flesh out "ways of participation" in some kind of concept map to help me understand it better. Then I might share it with someone like Gene.

We agree with Anthony's impression of this interview. He asked for elaboration and specific, concrete details from Gene. This will help him build a typology of "ways of participation." The discussion about Gene reading his poetry aloud was a bit delicate; something Anthony had not anticipated, but he handled it with tact.

11/15. Interview with nonparticipant community member. Sal is in his 30s and married. He and his wife both work in a local company. Two nights a week Sal goes to night school so it was tough scheduling this interview. I had met him when I brought around the surveys last Saturday. He was outside repairing the front steps.

Q:　So how's that loose riser doing?

A:　I think I've got it fixed. I hope so 'cause I wouldn't have a chance to get back to it for a couple of weeks. So what questions do you have for me?

Q:　You know I'm doing a study of the Arts Center. I've talked with both participants and nonparticipants. You told me you've never really done anything there. Is that right?

A:　Yeah. I don't really have time. I hardly had time to fill out that questionnaire you left! Boy, was that long!

Q:　Sorry! but I appreciate it. . . . So you really don't have much free time?

A:　Hell no! I do a lot of overtime at work, and then there's these classes I'm taking . . . my wife's taking one, too. I'm really busy.

Q:　When you do have some free time, what do you do?

A:　Well, there's some other couples that me and my wife are friends with, and we might go to a movie on a Saturday night. I visit my folks; they live down by the shore. I *love* to go to ballgames . . . but I only got to one this summer. Guess I don't have time even for that anymore, what with the upkeep on this place and everything else.

Q: Well, I've been noticing that you've got an incredible CD collection and it's all different kinds. Some Jazz; some New Age; some rock; some classical; some blue-grass. That's quite impressive! *[picking up on some aspect of the arts that clearly has value to Sal]*

A: Aw, well, you know. . . . I used to play the guitar a bit. Ah, the classical guitar. I really miss it sometimes.

Q: You must miss it. When did you last do anything with your music?

A: Well, it's been a long time since I played. The wife and I used to go to some clubs when we were first married. But . . . no time, no money now. You know, sometimes I wish I could've played my guitar for a living rather than trying to be what everybody else says I should be. Ah, but that's just a dream.

Q: Do you ever get a chance to talk to musicians, professional or otherwise? *[asking for elaboration on the place of music in Sal's life]*

A: There was a time when my friends were all musicians, so we'd talk about it a lot. Now, our friends are from work. I don't know what happened to those old guys who played.

Q: You know, the arts center had a concert in the early summer. I don't remember the details on it but, did you hear about that? Did you go?

A: I didn't know they had concerts. *[This is important data; information about the program may not reach some community members]* You mean like, somebody came and played the piano or guitar or some instrument? You don't mean some symphony?

Q: Well, no. It would have to have been one or two people because it's a small room.

A: Hmmm. That's cool.

Q: If you'd know about it would you have gone?

A: I don't know. There's the time thing.

Q: What might help you learn about offerings at the Center—assuming that some day you might have time?

A: Oh, I don't know. I don't even really read my mail these days. Judy takes care of all that. Does the Center send out announcements?

Q: Yes, it does.

A: Well, she must throw them away, because I never see them. But she's busy too.

Q: Again, is there any way the Center could get to you?

A: When I finish my degree, that's a different story. Right now, I'm not sure I'd even want to know if Andres Segovia himself were playing!

OC: Clearly, the Center and its program of offerings are not part of Sal's everyday life. This interview felt difficult, but we did establish that Sal loves music. I also learned that he doesn't get information about the Center's activities. If he knew about some of the offerings, he might take advantage of them. I'll have to check up on how they disseminate information about what's happening. Obviously, Sal is not one of the "drop-ins."

Anthony is learning that interviewing people who do not participate and have little knowledge about the community arts program is, indeed, difficult. He did well to pick up on Sal's interest in music, however. This may be an important insight for the program staff to consider. Also, Anthony should pursue this idea of "drop-ins."

ANALYSIS

Ethnographies usually begin with broad domains for gathering data that then shape analysis; they are balanced between structure and openness. Central to ethnographic studies is the concept of culture. Although vague and ambiguous, the concept focuses attention on widely shared and deeply held beliefs extant in a cultural group. Anthony's study focuses on program staff's and community members' beliefs about the arts, participation in events and activities, and the value to the community of the program. These categories—arts, participation, and value—are guides for his analysis.

Anthony initially organizes his data by the various data gathering techniques he uses: He has one folder for interviews and others for the survey returns and observations. As he gets more deeply into the analysis, however, he reorganizes the data into themes, based on the original

TABLE C.1 Actions at Pottery Exhibit (10/17)

Time	# around wheel	Interactions	Actions
9:00-9:30 a.m.	/ / / /	Questions: / / Comments: / / /	Touching pots Picking up glazes
9:30-10:00 a.m.			

TABLE C.2 Participation

Theme	Data Source
Types of participating	
Watching and asking questions	Obs notes, pottery exhibition (10/17)
Attending classes	Obs notes, watercolor class (11/3)
Giving readings	Int trans, Gene (11/8)
Attending concerts (wanting to)	Int trans, Sal (11/5)
Helping out at office	Obs notes, office (10/10)
Value of participating	
Brings families together	Int trans, Gene (11/8)
Lets people experiment and take risks	Obs notes, office, Elderly Man (10/10) Obs notes, watercolor class (11/3)
Gets teenagers off the streets	Int trans, Gene (11/8)
Expressing self	Int trans, Gene (11/8) Obs notes, office, Elderly Man (10/10)

evaluation questions about the extent of participation by community members; ways of participating; and the value of the program to staff, local artists, and both participating and nonparticipating community members. His observations at events and in the program office, the surveys he has administered, and his interviews with participants and nonparticipants are brought together to help him respond to the evaluation questions. Anthony identifies an overarching theme—a culture of inclusion—to depict the ways the program is integrated into the community.

As presented in Chapter 7, Anthony has used checklists to document interactions at events; Table C.1 shows his checklist constructed while observing interactions between potters and community members at an outdoor crafts show. He recorded the number of times community members went to the potter's wheel and the interactions between potter and community members. He has made hash marks (/) for each person

Table C.3 Culture of Inclusion: Knowing and Being Known

Knowing and Being Known	
Observ, 10/10	
D: "Hey there, Gene. So how did the gum work go? Was the dentist gentle?"	**Details of life**
G: "I survived. Got some catching up to do. Thought I'd see what's happening and if I can help on anything." He opens the bag, takes out two steaming cups of soup and a loaf of bread. "It's their version of minestrone today."	**Sharing food**
D: "Smells good. Thanks. Actually, you can do the registrations for Heather's class." Gestures to the computer on the other desk. Gene begins working on the computer.	**Helping out**
Observ, 10/10	
W1: "I got a job! Aren't you going to ask me what it is?"	**Details of life**
W2: "Yeah, she's part of the labor force now. Wonder if she'll have time for us anymore."	
D: "Well, congratulations! But don't forget you're still Stella to us."	
Observ, 10/10	
EM: "I don't know. Do I need experience?"	
D: "Now, honey, you've got all the experience you need for this class. You can fill out this paper—and try some of this bread. What brings you to us?"	**Reassurance** **Sharing food**
EM: "My granddaughter keeps telling me I need to get what she calls 'an interest.' I think she's worried about me. Always wanted to paint. . . ."	
D assures him he is in the right place. He takes a chunk of bread and joins us.	**Sharing food**

or interaction as a running tally of presence, interactions, and actions. He also records instances of data that describe perspectives on *ways of participating* (Table C.2). For his analytic memo, Anthony presents and interprets some of these data to depict participation.

Anthony will elaborate these data with details from interviews with active participants and those less active, seeking to build a grounded understanding and explanation for his central concept—participation—and how that is fostered by a *culture of inclusion*. A summary table of Anthony's preliminary analysis of this concept is presented in Table C.3.

ANALYTIC MEMO:
WHAT PARTICIPATION MEANS

The community arts program office buzzes with people and ideas. Located in an aging storefront building just across from the little park, it sits at the center of the community. People are in and out all day long and well into the evening. Attendance at events and enrollment in classes is high. How has this program succeeded in building such strong links to its community? Three critical elements of the program stand out: (1) There is a strong belief in involving community members in all aspects of the program; (2) a variety of activities and events are offered; and (3) it is staffed by community members and the location is ideal. This analytic memo begins with detailing attendance and enrollment, then elaborates on the *culture of inclusion* that characterizes the program.

Attendance

Records from the program office and results from the survey of instructors indicate that most classes offered by the center are fully enrolled: 82% of all classes this year have enrolled at least 10 people (the minimum number needed). Instructors indicated that attendance in classes is generally good (the exception being the class on "WomanPause" which had 100% each session). Observations (crafts show, classical guitar concert, clothesline art exhibit, indigenous dance) indicate that community members attend regularly and in high numbers. Estimates ranged from 175 to over 200 in attendance.[1]

From the interviews, the ways people participate and the value of it to them are being documented. Community members have mentioned that they are able to watch closely an artist at work and to ask him questions or comment; they particularly mention that this casual atmosphere makes asking questions easy. Many talk about the classes they or their children have attended. A few help out in the office, but several noted how they feel they can "drop in" to the office to see what is happening. A few even mention that there is always a cup or a bite of something available for them when they do.

The value to them of the program is that the variety of activities give them ways to express themselves or appreciate the work of others. Some mentioned that they can take risks and try out new things. In the case of a man who came into the program office, he mentioned that he had always wanted to paint (ON, 10/10),[2] and the class in watercolors would let him try this out. One artist who teaches poetry writing said that the program brings families together and even involves youth in important ways (I, 11/8).

A Culture of Inclusion

The program is clearly successful, although not without challenges. Program staff, instructors, and community members have built a *culture of inclusion* that makes the community feel that the program belongs to them. This is accomplished through actions and interactions that suggest that people feel known and welcomed in all program activities. Ways of *being known and welcomed* include: (1) the accessibility of the Center and its office (dropping-in is easy); (2) program staff and "regulars" in the program office know details of their lives (to drop in is to belong); (3) food is shared regularly, including offering it to "newcomers" who come in ("come eat with us"); and (4) everyone is asked to help out in small and large ways (ON, 10/10). For example, two women from the community came into the office to share the good news about one of them getting a job. Others there were congratulatory but suggested that the woman would be missed if she no longer dropped in regularly. When an elderly man entered the program office to ask about a painting class, the staff person reassured him that he needed no prior experience, invited him to share a large loaf of bread on the table, and facilitated his signing up for the watercolor class. These observations suggest that those who are integral to the program's functioning (staff and community members alike) take quite seriously the notion that the program is to welcome and serve *all* the community.

Next steps are to continue gathering data about attendance; complete the surveys of community members; and locate additional people (participants and non-participants) for interviews. The interviews with less-active people are proving to be especially useful for identifying ways the Center can reach out more effectively; these will be incorporated in the final report under Recommendations.

This in-process memo by Anthony is well-done. He provides sufficient evidence to support his themes, but at times his points are a bit unclear—for example, when he discusses attendance. He indicates the broad themes for his subsequent data gathering and analysis and is beginning to flesh out the concept of culture of inclusion. This may well be the most insightful aspect of Anthony's evaluation. He will have to continue to document participation, however, to satisfy the requirements of the evaluation contract.

NOTES

1. Estimates were obtained by counting rows and numbers of seats in rows for the concerts. For the outdoor shows, estimates were obtained by counting people around an exhibit and multiplying by the number of exhibits with some estimate of "large" or "small" groups. This is a crude, but qualitatively effective, way to estimate; the estimates were corroborated by program staff.

2. ON means observation notes; I indicates an interview.

References

Adelman, C., Jenkins, D., & Kemmis, S. (1983). Rethinking case study: Notes from the Second Cambridge Conference. In *Case study: An overview,* Case Study Methods 1. Victoria, Australia: Deakin University Press.

Ball, S. (1990). Self-doubt and soft data: Social and technical trajectories in ethnographic fieldwork. *Qualitative Studies in Education, 3*(2), 157-171.

Bargar, R. R., & Duncan, J. K. (1982). Cultivating creative endeavor in doctoral research. *Journal of Higher Education, 53,* 1-31.

Berelson, B. (1952). *Content analysis in communication research.* Glencoe, IL: Free Press.

Blumer, H. (1969). *Symbolic interactionism.* Englewood Cliffs, NJ: Prentice Hall.

Bogdan, R. C., & Biklen, S. K. (1992). *Qualitative research in education: An introduction to theory and methods* (2nd ed.). Boston: Allyn & Bacon.

Bolman, L. G., & Deal, T. E. (1991). *Reframing organizations: artistry, choice, and leadership.* San Francisco: Jossey-Bass.

Bolman, L. G., & Deal, T. E. (1993). *The path to school leadership.* Newbury Park, CA: Corwin Press.

Bolman, L. G., & Deal, T. E. (1994). *Becoming a teacher leader.* Thousand Oaks, CA: Corwin Press.

Bolman, L. G., Deal, T. E., & Rallis, S. F. (1995). *Becoming a school board member.* Newbury Park, CA: Corwin Press.

Booth, W. C., Colomb, G. G., & Williams, J. M. (1995). *The craft of research.* Chicago: University of Chicago Press.

Bredo, E., & Feinberg, W. (1982). *Knowledge and values in social and educational research.* Philadelphia: Temple University Press.

Brown, L. (Ed.). (1993). *The new shorter Oxford English dictionary,* Vol. 1. Oxford, UK: Clarendon.

Brown, L. M., & Gilligan, C. (1990, August). Listening for self and relational voices: A responsive/resisting reader's guide. In M. Franklin (chair), *Literary theory as a guide to psychological analysis.* Symposium presented at the annual meetings of the American Psychological Association, Boston, MA.

Burrell, G., & Morgan, G. (1979). *Sociological paradigms and organisational analysis*. London: Heinemann.

Chase, S. E. (1996). Personal vulnerability and interpretive authority in narrative research. In R. Josselin (Ed.), *Ethics and process in the narrative study of lives* (pp. 45-59). Thousand Oaks, CA: Sage.

Chatman, R. (1990). *Fresh roses*. Unpublished doctoral dissertation, Vanderbilt University, Nashville, TN.

Chelimsky, E., & Shaddish, W. R. (Eds.). (1997). *Evaluation for the 21st century: A handbook*. Thousand Oaks, CA: Sage.

Creswell, J. W. (1994). *Research design: Qualitative and quantitative approaches*. Thousand Oaks, CA: Sage.

Cronbach, L. J. (1975). Beyond the two disciplines of scientific psychology. *American Psychologist, 30*, 116-127.

Delamont, S. (1992). *Fieldwork in educational settings: Methods, pitfalls, and perspectives*. London: Falmer.

Demerath, P. W. (1997). *The social cost of acting "extra": Dilemmas of student identity and academic success in post-colonial Papua New Guinea*. Unpublished doctoral dissertation. University of Massachusetts at Amhurst.

Denzin, N. K. (1989). *Interpretive interactionism*. Newbury Park, CA: Sage.

Denzin, N. K. (1994). The art and politics of interpretation. In N. K. Denzin & Y. S. Lincoln (Eds.), *Handbook of qualitative research* (pp. 500-515). Thousand Oaks, CA: Sage.

Douglas, J. D. (1976). *Investigative social research: Individual and team field research*. Beverly Hills, CA: Sage.

Eisner, E. W. (1991). *The enlightened eye: Qualitative inquiry and the enhancement of educational practice*. New York: Macmillan.

Eisner, E. W., & Peshkin, A. (Eds.). (1990). *Qualitative inquiry in education: The continuing debate*. New York: Teachers College Press.

Elliot, J., & Keynes, M. (1991). *Action research for educational change*. Philadelphia: Open University Press.

Erickson, F. (1986). Qualitative methods in research on teaching. In M. C. Whittrock (Ed.), *Handbook of research on teaching* (3rd ed., pp. 119-161). New York: Macmillan.

Evertson, C. M., & Green, J. L. (1986). Observation as inquiry and method. In M. C. Wittrock (Ed.), *Handbook of research on teaching* (3rd ed., pp. 162-213). New York: Macmillan.

Fisk, D. B. (1996). *Empowerment through place: Participatory architecture and education at Concord Academy*. Unpublished doctoral dissertation, University of Massachusetts at Amherst.

Flinders, D. J. (1992). In search of ethical guidance: Constructing a basis for dialogue. *Qualitative Studies in Education, 5*(2), 101-115.

Freire, P. (1970). *Pedagogy of the oppressed*. New York: Seabury.

Gaardner, J. (1994). *Sophie's world*. New York: Farrar, Strauss, & Giroux.

Gage, N. L. (1989). The paradigm wars and their aftermath: A "historical" sketch of research on teaching. *Educational Researcher, 18*(7), 4-10.

Geertz, C. (1973). *The interpretation of culture: Selected essays*. New York: Basic Books.

Geertz, C. (1983). "From the native's point of view": On the nature of anthropological understanding. In C. Geertz (Ed.), *Local knowledge: Further essays in interpretive anthropology* (pp. 55-70). New York: Basic Books..

Gilligan, C., Brown, L. M., & Rogers, A. (1990). Psyche embedded: A place for body, relationships, and culture in personality theory. In A. Rabin, R. Zucker, R. Emmons, & S. Frank (Eds.), *Studying persons and lives.* New York: Springer.

Gleick, J. (1987). *Chaos: Making a new science.* New York: Viking.

Goldring, E. B., & Rallis, S. F. (1993). *Principals of dynamic schools: Taking charge of change.* Newbury Park, CA: Corwin Press.

Green, J. C. (1990). Knowledge accumulation? Three views of the nature and role of knowledge in social science. In E. G. Guba (Ed.), *The paradigm dialogue.* Newbury Park, CA: Sage.

Guba, E. G. (Ed.). (1990). *The paradigm dialogue.* Newbury Park, CA: Sage.

Hammersley, M., & Atkinson, P. (1983). *Ethnography: Principles in practice.* London: Routledge.

Hertz, R., & Imber, J. B. (1995). *Studying elites using qualitative methods.* Thousand Oaks, CA: Sage.

Heshuius, L. (1994). Freeing ourselves from objectivity: Managing subjectivity or turning toward a participatory mode of consciousness. *Educational Researcher, 23,* pp. 15-22.

Hodder, I. (1994). The interpretation of documents and material culture. In N. K. Denzin & Y. S. Lincoln (Eds.), *Handbook of qualitative research* (pp. 393-402). Thousand Oaks, CA: Sage.

Holstein, J. A., & Gubrium, J. F. (1994). Phenomenology, ethnomethodology, and interpretive practice. In N. K. Denzin & Y. S. Lincoln (Eds.), *Handbook of qualitative research* (pp. 262-272). Thousand Oaks, CA: Sage.

Johnson, J. M. (1975). *Doing field research.* Beverly Hills, CA: Sage.

Jorgensen, D. L. (1989). *Participant observation: A methodology for human studies.* Newbury Park, CA: Sage.

Kahn, A. (1992). *Therapist initiated termination to psychotherapy: The experience of clients.* Unpublished doctoral dissertation, University of Massachusetts at Amhurst.

Kahn, R., & Cannell, C. (1957). *The dynamics of interviewing.* New York: Wiley.

Kaye, W., & Rallis, S. F. (1989). Educational aspects: Resuscitation training and evaluation. In W. Kaye & N. Bircher (Eds.), *Cardiopulmonary resuscitation.* New York: Churchill Livingstone.

Kidder, T. (1993). *Old friends.* Boston: Houghton Mifflin.

Kincheloe, J. L. (1991). *Teachers as researchers: Qualitative inquiry as a path to empowerment.* New York: Falmer.

Kozol, J. (1995). *Amazing grace: The lives of children and the conscience of a nation.* New York: Crown.

Krieger, S. (1985). Beyond "subjectivity": The use of the self in social science. *Qualitative Sociology, 8,* 309-324.

Lareau, A. (1989). *Home advantage: Social class and parental intervention in elementary education.* New York: Falmer.

Lightfoot, S. L. (1983). *The good high school: Portraits of character and culture.* New York: Basic Books.

Lincoln, Y. S., & Guba, E. G. (1985). *Naturalistic inquiry.* Beverly Hills, CA: Sage.

Lindblom, C. E., & Cohen, D. K. (1979). *Usable knowledge.* New Haven, CT: Yale University Press.

Marshall, C., & Rossman, G. B. (1995). *Designing qualitative research* (2nd ed.). Thousand Oaks, CA: Sage.

Maslowe, A. (1970). *Motivation and personality.* New York: Harper & Row.

Mehrabian, A., & Ferris, S. R. (1967). Inference of attitudes from non-verbal communication in two channels. *Journal of Consulting Psychology, 31.*

Merriam, S. B. (1988). *Case study research in education.* San Francisco: Jossey-Bass.

Patton, M. Q. (1990). *Qualitative evaluation and research methods* (2nd ed.). Newbury Park, CA: Sage.

Patton, M. Q. (1996). *Utilization-focused evaluation* (3rd ed.). Thousand Oaks, CA: Sage.

Peshkin, A. (1988). In search of subjectivity—One's own. *Educational Researcher, 17,* 17-21.

Phillips, D. C. (1990). Subjectivity and objectivity: An objective inquiry. In E. W. Eisner & A. Peshkin (Eds.), *Qualitative inquiry in education: The continuing debate* (pp. 19-37). New York: Teachers College Press.

Polanyi, M. (1962). *Personal knowledge.* Chicago: University of Chicago Press.

Popkewicz, T. S. (1984). *Paradigm and ideology in educational research: The social functions of the intellectual.* London: Falmer.

Punch, M. (1994). Politics and ethics in qualitative research. In N. K. Denzin & Y. S. Lincoln (Eds.), *Handbook of qualitative research* (pp. 83-97). Thousand Oaks, CA: Sage.

Rallis, S. F. (1980). *Different views of knowledge use by practitioners.* Unpublished qualifying paper, Harvard University, Cambridge, MA.

Rallis, S. F. (1990). *Learning disabilities identification process: Final evaluation report.* Providence, RI: Department of Education, Office of Special Needs.

Rallis, S. F. (1992). *Connecting the conversations about change: Portrait of a principal as a leader.* Providence, RI: Brown University, Coalition of Essential Schools.

Rallis, S. F., & Rossman, G. B. (with Phlegar, J. M., & Abeille, A.). (1995). *Dynamic teachers: Leaders of change.* Thousand Oaks, CA: Corwin Press.

Reichardt, C. S., & Rallis, S. F. (Eds.). (1994). The qualitative-quantitave debate: New perspectives. *New Directions for Program Evaluation, 61.*

Rein, M. (1970). *Social policy: Issues of choice and change.* New York: Random House.

Reissman, C. K. (1991). When gender is not enough: Women interviewing women. In J. Lorber & S. A. Farrell (Eds.), *The social construction of gender* (pp. 217-236). Newbury Park, CA: Sage.

Reissman, C. K. (1993). *Narrative analysis.* Newbury Park, CA: Sage.

Richards, T. J., & Richards, L. (1994). Using computers in qualitative research. In N. K. Denzin & Y. S. Lincoln (Eds.), *Handbook of qualitative research* (pp. 445-462). Thousand Oaks, CA: Sage.

Richardson, L. (1994). Writing: A method of inquiry. In N. K. Denzin & Y. S. Lincoln (Eds.), *Handbook of qualitative research* (pp. 516-529). Thousand Oaks, CA: Sage.

Rossman, G. B., Corbett, H. D., & Firestone, W. A. (1988). *Change and effectiveness in schools: A cultural perspective.* Albany: State University of New York Press.

Rossman, G. B., Rallis, S. F., & Uhl, S. (1996). *Final report to the Boston Public Schools: Formative evaluation of the Boston Public Schools' Inclusion Initiative.* Boston: Office of Special Education.

Rossman, G. B., & Wilson, B. L. (1994). Numbers and words revisited: Being "shamelessly eclectic." *Quality and Quantity: International Journal of Methodology, 28,* 315-327.

Rubin, H. J., & Rubin, I. S. (1995). *Qualitative interviewing: The art of hearing data.* Thousand Oaks, CA: Sage.

Sadker, D. M., & Sadker, M. (1994). *Failing at fairness: How America's schools cheat girls.* New York: Scribner.

Schatzman, L., & Strauss, A. L. (1973). *Field research: Strategies for a natural sociology.* Englewood Cliffs, NJ: Prentice Hall.

Seidman, I. E. (1991). *Interviewing as qualitative research: A guide for researchers in education and the social sciences.* New York: Teachers College Press.

Silverman, D. (1993). *Interpreting qualitative data: Methods for analyzing talk, text, and interaction.* Newbury Park, CA: Sage.

Siskin, L. (1994, October). *Seduction and desertion: Implicit promises in qualitative research.* Unpublished speech given at the Spencer Hall Conference on Teacher Development, London, Ontario.

Soltis, J. F. (1990). The ethics of qualitative research. In E. W. Eisner & A. Peshkin (Eds.), *Qualitative inquiry in education: The continuing debate* (pp. 247-257). New York: Teachers College Press.

Spradley, J. S. (1979). *The ethnographic interview.* New York: Holt, Rinehart & Winston.

Strauss, A. L., & Corbin, J. (1990). *Basics of qualitative research: Grounded theory procedures and techniques.* Newbury Park, CA: Sage.

Stringer, E. T. (1996). *Action research: A handbook for practitioners.* Thousand Oaks, CA: Sage.

Taylor, S. J., & Bogdan, R. (1984). *An introduction to qualitative research: The search for meanings* (2nd ed.). New York: J. Wiley.

Tesch, R. (1990). *Qualitative research: Analysis types and software tools.* New York: Falmer.

Thorne, B. (1983). Political activist as political observer: Conflicts of commitment in a study of the draft resistance movement in the 1960s. In R. Emerson (Ed.), *Contemporary field research: A collection of readings* (pp. 216-234). Prospect Heights, IL: Waveland.

Van Maanen, J. (1988). *Tales of the field: On writing ethnography.* Chicago: University of Chicago Press.

Van Maanen, J. (Ed.). (1995). *Representation in ethnography.* Thousand Oaks, CA: Sage.

Van Manen, M. (1990). *Researching lived experience: Human science for an action sensitive pedagogy.* Albany: State University of New York Press.

Weiss, C. H. (1998). *Evaluation methods for studying programs and policies.* Upper Saddle River, NJ: Prentice-Hall.

Weiss, C. (1979, September/October). The many meanings of research utilization. *Public Administration Review.*

Weiss, C. (1980). Knowledge creep and decision accretion. *Knowledge: Creation, Diffusion and Utilization, 1*(3), 381-404.

Whyte, W. F. (1981). *Street corner society.* Chicago: University of Chicago Press. (Original work published 1943)

Wolcott, H. F. (1995). *The art of fieldwork.* Walnut Creek, CA: AltaMira.

Index

Access:
    introduction and invitations, 102-104, 105
    time needed to establish, 101-102, 104
    to elite individuals, 134
    written permission, 103-104
Action research, 17, 18
    data analysis, 235-239
    field notes, 225-235
    generating research questions, 83
Adelman, C., 70, 258
Adolescents, interviewing, 136
African Americans, interviewed by
    whites, 127, 128
Agency:
    acceptance, 223
    defined, 222
    nature of, 31-32, 36
    phenomenologic study, 220-223
    sense of efficacy, 222-223, 252-255
Analytic memo, 207-208, 236-238, 255-257
Anonymity, 49-50, 106, 161
Aristotle, 6
Atkinson, P., 38, 90, 94, 109, 260

Ball, S., 94, 166, 258
Bargar, R. R., 176, 258
Berelson, B., 146, 258
Betrayal, 51-52
Bias, 42
Biklen, S. K., 116, 147, 258

Bilingualism, 161-163
Blumer, H., 121, 123, 258
Bogdan, R., 98, 262
Bogdan, R. C., 116, 147, 258
Bolman, L. G., 14, 196, 258
Booth, W. C., 76, 78, 258
Breadth, qualitative research study, 118
Bredo, E., 56, 258
Brown, L. M., 38, 39, 116, 133, 147, 184, 198, 258, 259
Burrell, G., 28, 33, 34, 36, 37, 55, 56, 89, 258

Cannell, C., 124, 260
Case studies, 68, 70-72
    data anlaysis, 175
    data collection, 87, 153
    generating research questions, 83
    interviewing, 132
Change:
    research resulting in, 17, 18, 66
    See also Action research
Chaos theory, 31
Chase, S. E., 57, 259
Chatman, R., 196, 259
Chelimsky, E., 22, 259
Children, interviewing, 135-136
Coauthorship, qualitative research study, 108
Codes of ethics, 48
Cohen, D. K., 22, 260
Colomb, G. G., 76, 78, 258

Comembership, 110, 154
Conceptual framework, qualitative
 research study, 64, 74-84, 95
Confidentiality, 49-50, 106, 161
Consent, qualitative research, 50-51
Content analysis, 145
Context, qualitative research, 8, 19, 46
Contrast questions, 132
Coparticipation, 96, 112n2
Corbett, H. D., 67, 101, 261
Corbin, J., 90, 189, 262
Cover terms, cultural domain, 183
Creswell, J. W., 79, 90, 259
Critical case study, data collection, 153
Cronbach, L. J., 47, 259
Cultural domains, 183
Culture of inclusion, 252, 256-257

Data, 5
 coding, 180-181
 organizing, 177-178
 transformation into knowledge, 5, 6, 11
Data analysis, 88, 168-172
 action research, 235-239
 analytic memo, 207-208, 236-238,
  252-255
 category generation, 179-180, 181-182
 coding, 180-181
 defined, 176
 ethnographic design, 252-257
 ethnographic interview, 183-184
 genre and, 174-176
 interview data, 183-186
 management tasks, 173
 material culture, 187-188
 modifying, 173
 narrative data, 184-186
 observations, 186-187
 ongoing vs. analysis at the end, 172-173
 organizing data, 173, 177-178
 phenomenologic study, 174-175, 184,
  219-220
 procedures, 176-181
 research proposal, 88
 structured or open-ended, 174
Data collection, 8, 21, 40, 113-117, 149-151
 bilingualism, 161-163
 case study, 87, 153

 decisions about, 117-120
 depth or breadth, 118-119
 ethnography, 153
 interviewing, 8, 116-117, 121, 122, 124-136
 language of, 161-163
 material culture, 145-146, 147n1
 modifying, 163
 observing people and actions, 117, 121,
  136-139
 phenomenologic study, 153
 prefigured or open-ended, 119-120
 preparation for, 151-153
 questions about, 152
 reflexivity, 163-165
 relevance of data, 157-159
 research proposal, 87-88
 standardized instruments, 122-123
 systematic inquiry, 120-124
 tape recorders, 159, 160-161
 transcripts, 160-161
 unsolicited information, 158-159
 See also Field notes
Data interpretation, 27, 88, 171, 181-182
Davis, J. M., 202, 261
Deal, T. E., 14, 196, 258
Deception, qualitative research, 50-51
Deductive reasoning, 10, 11, 21n5
Delamont, S., 40, 112, 147, 166, 194, 259
Demerath, 98
Denzin, N. K., 7, 138, 197, 198, 259
Depth, qualitative research study, 118-119
Descriptive cultural studies:
 coauthorship, 108
 defined, 17
 depth, 118
 generating research questions, 83
Design and methodology section,
 research proposal, 64, 65, 84-88
Dialogic interviews, 125
Douglas, J. D., 125, 259
Duncan, J. K., 176, 258

Eisner, E. W., 22, 57, 259
Elite individuals, interviewing, 134
Elliot, J., 18, 259
Emancipatory use, qualitative research,
 12, 15-16
Emic perspective, 38, 42, 115, 132, 179

Empiricism, 6
Empowerment:
    from qualitative research, 15-16, 107
    as goal of research, 79
Enlightenment use, qualitative research,
    12, 13-14
Entrance process, 93-112
    approach and negotiations, 101-104, 108
    expectations and relationships, 104-111
    gatekeepers, 54, 108-111
    intended involvement, 96-101
    introduction and invitation, 102-103
    preparation, 94-96
    reciprocity, 105-108
    relationship with participants, 104-111,
        155-156
    time, 101-102, 104
    touring facility, 154-155
    written permission, 103-104
Erickson, F., 22, 47, 259
Ethical codes, 49, 52
Ethical standards, qualitative research, 43,
    48-52, 56n10
Ethnographic interviewing, 132-133,
    183-184
Ethnographies, 67-70, 83, 87, 89n5, 240-241
    data analysis, 185, 252-257
    data collection, 153
    field notes, 241-252
Etic perspective, 38, 132, 179
Evaluation research, 17-18, 83
Evertson, C. M., 121, 259
Expert individuals, interviewing, 134

False consciousness, 36
Feinberg, W., 56, 258
Ferris, S. R., 147, 261
Field notes, 121, 122
    action research, 225-235
    bilingualism, 161-163
    ethnographies, 241-252
    examples, 139-145
    language fluency, 161
    language of, 161-163
    observer comments, 137
    phenomenological study, 209-219
    raw field notes, 137, 138
    running record, 137

tape recorders, 159, 160-161
thick descriptions, 138
transcripts, 160-161, 209-219
Firestone, W. A., 67, 101, 261
First person voice, 76, 198
Fisk, D. B., 196, 259
Flinders, D. J., 57, 259
Focus group interviewing, 134-135
Formative information, 17, 22n8
Freire, P., 16, 259

Gaardner, J., 6, 259
Gage, N. L., 53, 259
Gatekeepers, 54, 108-111
Gathering data. See Data collection
Geertz, C., 10, 35, 138, 259
Genre, 66-74
    critical and postmodern assumptions,
        66-67
    data analysis and, 174-176
    data collection, 117
    generating research questions, 83
Gilligan, C., 133, 147, 184, 198, 258, 259
Gleick, J., 31, 260
Goldring, E. B., 201, 260
Grant proposal, research proposal, 53, 81
Green, J. C., 22, 260
Green, J. L., 121, 259
Guba, E. G., 56, 57, 260
Gubrium, J. F., 72, 90, 260

Habits of mind and heart:
    data analysis, 166-167
    data collection, 111-112, 147
    data interpretation, 188, 193
    defined, 18-20
    knowledge and discovery, 54-55
    planning, 88-89
    report writing, 203
Hammersley, M., 38, 90, 94, 109, 260
Hermeneutics, 7, 19
Hertz, R., 148, 260
Heshuius, L., 57, 260
Heuristic process, qualitative research,
    18-19
Hodder, I., 148, 187, 260
Holstein, J. A., 72, 90, 260

Huberman, A. M., 189

Imber, J. B., 148, 260
Included terms, cultural domain, 183
In-depth interviewing:
    as conversation, 126, 130
    dialogic interview, 125
    ethnographic interviewing, -133, 132,
        183-184
    follow-up questions, 128-131
    informal, 124, 126
    phenomenological interview, 133-134
    phenomenologic in-depth
        interviewing, 72
    social group identities, 126-128
    standardized open-ended interview,
        124
    voice-centered interviewing, 133,
        147n5, 184
In-depth studies, 118-119
Individual rights, theories of, 48-49
Inductive analysis, 179
Inductive logic, 10, 11, 21n5
Informal interviews, 124, 126
Informant role, 112n6
Information:
    formative information, 17, 22n8
    summative information, 17, 22n8
    transformation to knowledge, 5, 6
Instrumental use, qualitative research,
    12-13
Integrity, qualitative research, 43-44, 94
Interpretivist paradigm, 35-36, 55n5, 66, 79
Intervention effects, 8
Interviewers, qualities of, 125
Interview guide approach, 124-125
Interviewing, 8, 116-117, 121
    adolescents, 136
    body language, 117
    children, 135-136
    as conversation, 126, 130
    cultural differences, 126-128
    as data collection, 7, 116-117, 121,
        124-136
    "elites" or experts, 134
    follow-up questions, 128-131
    in-depth interviewing, 124-136

prefigured or open-ended techniques,
    119-120
voice-centered interviewing, 133,
    147n5, 184
Interview record, 122

Jenkins, D., 70, 258
Johnson, J. M., 104, 260
Jorgensen, D. L., 94, 260
Justice, 49

Kahn, A.,,, 86, 268
Kahn, R., 124, 260
Kant, I., 48
Kaye, W., 100, 260
Kemmis, S., 70, 258
Keynes, M., 18, 259
Kidder, T., 14, 260
Kincheloe, J. L., 22, 260
Knowing, nature of, 29-32, 55
Knowledge:
    critical and postmodern assumptions,
        66
    heuristic aspect, 18-19
    information transformed into, 5, 6, 11
    nature of, 29-32
    subjectivist view of, 30, 66
Kozol, J., 166, 198, 260
Krieger, S., 112, 260

Laboratory research, 8
Lareau, A., 27, 260
Lightfoot, S. L., 108, 202, 260
Lincoln, Y. S., 56, 57, 260
Lindblom, C. E., 22, 260
Literature review, research proposal, 74

Mandated reporter, 52
Marshall, C., 60, 89, 90, 147, 260
Marx, K., 36
Maslowe, A., 14, 261
Material culture, 145-146
    data analysis, 187-188
    data collection, 145-146, 147na
Mehrabian, A., 147, 261

Member checks, 45
Merriam, S. B., 46, 90, 261
Micropolitics, 53, 54
Miles, M. B., 189
Morgan, G., 28, 33, 34, 36, 37, 55, 56, 89, 258

Narrative data, data analysis, 184-186
Note taking. *See* Field notes

Objectivity, 28-32, 40, 46
Observation notes. *See* Field notes
Observations, data analysis, 186-187
Observing, 8, 116, 121, 136-139
  prefigured or open-ended techniques, 119-120
Open-ended techniques, qualitative research study, 119, 174

Paradigm, 28
Participants, 21n2, 38
  collaborative relationship with, 104-111, 155-156
  interaction with, 117
  observing, 118
  relationship with researcher, 104-111, 155-156, 166
Passive voice, use of, 76
Patton, M. Q., 12, 22, 89, 99, 106, 112, 124, 129, 133, 148, 179, 189, 193, 261
Permission, 103-104
Perspective, 9, 26-37
  establishing, 40-43
  writing about, 45
Peshkin, A., 22, 57, 259, 261
Phenomenological interviewing, 133-134
Phenomenologic study, 68, 72-74, 83, 87
  agency, 220-224
  data analysis, 174-175, 184, 219-220
  data collection, 153
  field notes, 209-219
Phenomenology, 7, 72, 133
Phillips, D. C., 57, 261
Polanyi, M., 18, 261
Policy, 13
Policy studies, 17-18, 81, 83

Politics, qualitative research, 53-54
Popkewicz, T. S., 55, 56, 261
Population selection, qualitative research study, 86
Positivist paradigm, 35, 55n5
Postmodernism:
  authorship, 56n8
  material culture, 146
  qualitative research, 53-54, 66, 67, 89n3
Power dynamics, 54, 108-111, 134
Prediction, as goal, 35
Prefigured techniques, qualitative research study, 119, 174
Prejudice, 42
Privacy, qualitative research, 49-50, 106, 161
Proposal. *See* Research proposal
Punch, M., 51, 52, 57, 261

Qualitative research:
  action research, 17, 18, 83, 225-239
  anonymity, 49-50, 106, 161
  applicability to other situations, 47
  approaches to, 7
  bias, 42
  characteristics, 7-11
  comembership, 110, 154
  consent, 50-51
  context, 8, 19, 46
  deception, 50-51
  defined, 5-7, 20
  descriptive cultural studies, 17
  emancipatory use, 12, 15-16
  emergent nature of, 10
  empiricism, 6
  enlightenment use, 12, 13-14
  ethical standards, 43, 48-52, 56n10
  evaluation research, 17-18
  functions of, 43, 79
  heuristic process, 18-19
  holistic approach to, 8, 120
  inductive logic, use of, 10
  instrumental use, 12-13
  integrity, 43-44
  interactive nature of, 26
  interpretive nature of, 10
  as learning, 1-21

participants, 21n2, 97-99, 104-111,
155-156, 165-166
personal perspective in, 40-43, 45, 67
politics, 53-54
postmodern assumptions, 66-67, 89n3
power dynamics, 54, 108-111, 134
prejudice, 42
reflexivity, 9, 26-37, 38-40, 67, 163-165
seduction and abandonment, 51-52, 106
sensitivities needed, 19-20
as social action, 16
standards, 44-48
strategies, 16-18, 20
study, policy studies, 17-18
study coauthorship, 108
study confidentiality, 49-50, 106, 161
symbolic use, 12, 14-15
trust, 51-52, 104
trustworthiness, 43-54, 56n9
truth, 45-46
uses of, 11-16, 21n1
See also Research proposal
Qualitative research study:
access, 102-104
assumptions, 27-37, 66-67
breadth, 118
case studies, 68, 70-72
coauthorship, 108
comembership, 110, 154
conceptual framework, 64, 74-84, 95
content analysis, 145
covert, 98-100
data analysis. See Data analysis
data collection. See Data collection
depth, 118-119
designing, 20-21, 58-89, 97-98
empowerment from, 15-16, 79, 107
entrance process, 93-112
ethnographies, 67-70, 89n5
field notes. See Field notes
gatekeepers, 54, 108-111
genres, 66-74, 117
getting comfortable in the field, 153-157
limitations and delimitations, 84
material culture, 145-148
open-ended techniques, 119
overt, 98-100
overview questions and subquestions,
81-84

phenomenological studies, 68, 72-74
planning, 58-89
population selection study, 85-86
prefigured techniques, 119
privacy, 49-50, 106, 161
reciprocity, 105-108
research log, 43
research questions, 81-84
site selection study, 85-86
social group identities, 126-128
standardized instruments, 122-123
statement of research problem, 77-78
strategy, 85, 95
topic statement, 76-77
"the underground," 156-157

Rademaker, G., 204
Radical change, of society, 33-34
Radical objectivist paradigm, 35, 37, 55n5
Radical subjectivist paradigm, 35, 36, 55n5
Rallis, S. F., 14, 41, 56, 100, 166, 196, 199,
201, 204, 258, 260, 261
Randomization, as goal, 35
Reality, nature of, 31
Reciprocity, qualitative research study,
105-108
Reflexivity:
data collection, 163-165
defined, 9, 38
qualitative research, 26-37, 67
of researcher, 38-40
Reichardt, C. S., 56, 261
Rein, M., 13, 261
Reissman, C. K., 122, 189, 261
Relationships:
collaborative, 104-111, 155-156
during entrance process, 104-111
terminating, 165-166
Report writing, 67, 190-193
audience and purpose, 194-195
chronological format, 200
composite organization, 201-202
critical events format, 202
cultural domains, 183-184
data analysis, 182-183
formats, 195-197
life history format, 200-201
new formats, 197

organization, 200-203
   portrait format, 202-203
   thematic organization, 201
   voice, 75-76, 89n8, 89n9, 197-199
Research:
   applied research, 6
   basic research, 6
   bias, 42
   defined, 3
   interpretivist paradigm, 35-36, 55n5,
      66, 79
   laboratory research, 8
   limitations and delimitations, 84
   overview questions and subquestions,
      81-84
   positivist paradigm, 35, 55n5
   postmodern assumptions, 53-54, 56n8,
      66-67, 89n3, 146
   prejudice, 42
   purposes of, 79, 99
   radical objectivist paradigm, 35, 37,
      55n5
   radical subjectivist paradigm, 35, 36,
      55n5
   research questions, 81-84
   standards, 44-48
   status quo vs. radical change, 33-37
   subjectivity vs. objectivity, 28-32, 40,
      46, 198
   See also Qualitative research;
      Qualitative research study; Research
      proposal
Researcher, 7-8, 20, 21n4
   as active agent, 6, 8-9
   charasteristics, 8-11
   entrance process, 93-112
   intended involvement, 96-101
   as learner, 6, 23-55
   as participant, 97-99
   perspective, 9, 26-37, 40-43, 45, 67
   reflexivity, 9, 26-37, 38-40, 67, 163-165
   relationship with participants, 104-111,
      155-156, 165-166
   self-awareness, 37-38, 67
   temrinating relationship with
      participants, 165-166
Research log, 43
Research problem, stating in research
   proposal, 77-78

Research proposal, 63-66
   conceptual framework, 64, 74-84, 95
   data collection, 87-88
   data management and analysis, 88
   design and methodology section, 64,
      65, 84-88
   grant proposal, 53, 81
   introduction section, 75-76
   limitations and delimitations, 84
   literature review, 74
   overview questions and subquestions,
      81-84
   research questions, 81-84
   significance of the statement, 80-81
   statement of purpose, 78-80, 99
   statement of research problem, 77-78
   topic statement, 76-77
   "voice," 75-76, 89n8, 89n9
Research report, 67, 190-204
   as chronology, 200
   composite organization, 201-202
   critical events format, 202
   data analysis, 182-183
   Internet formats, 197
   as life history, 200-201
   portrait format, 202-203
   thematic organization, 201
   video to supplement, 197
   See also Report writing
Richards, L., 177, 189, 261
Richards, T. J., 177, 189, 261
Richardson, L., 194, 197, 261
Rogers, A., 147, 259
Rosenau, P. M., 90
Rossman, D. T., 198
Rossman, G. B., 41, 60, 67, 89, 90, 100, 101,
   147, 166, 187, 201, 260, 261
Rubin, H. J., 148, 262
Rubin, I. S., 148, 262

Sadker, D. M., 51, 262
Sadker, M., 51, 262
Schatzman, L., 93, 262
Seduction and abandonment, 51-52, 106
Seidman, I. E., 72, 90, 126, 133, 148, 184,
   262
Semantic relationships, cultural domain,
   183

Shaddish, W. R., 22, 259
Silverman, D., 189, 262
Siskin, L., 51, 106, 166, 262
Site selection, qualitative research study, 86
Social action, qualitative research as, 16
Social group identities, qualitative research, 126-128
Social sciences, positivist paradigm, 35, 55n5
Society:
    critical and postmodern assumptions, 66
    four paradigms, 34-36, 55n5
    status quo vs. radical change, 33-37
    subjectivity vs. objectivity, 28-32, 40
Sociology of regulation, 55n4
Soltis, J. F., 57, 262
Sponsor, as gatekeeper, 110
Spradley, J. S., 132, 189, 262
Stake, R. E., 90
Standardized instruments, data collection, 122-123
Standardized open-ended interviews, 125
Standards, research, 44-48
Statement of purpose, research proposal, 78-80, 99
Status quo, of society, 33
Strauss, A. L., 90, 93, 189, 262
Stringer, E. T., 22, 262
Structural questions, 132
Subjectivity, 28-32, 198
Summative information, 17, 22n8
Symbolic use, qualitative research, 12, 14-15

Tape recorders, data collection, 159, 160-161
Taylor, S. J., 98, 262

Tesch, R., 177, 189, 262
Thick descriptions, 138
Third persion voice, 76, 89n8, 198
Thorne, B., 112, 262
Topic statement, research proposal, 76-77
Transcripts, 160-161, 209-219
Trust, qualitative research, 51-52
Trustworthiness, qualitative research, 43-54, 56n9
Truth:
    objectivity vs. subjectivity, 28-32
    qualitative research, 45-46

Uhl, S., 41, 261
Unit of analysis, 79
Utilitarianism, 48

Van Maanen, J., 10, 14, 22, 90, 198, 262
Van Manen, M., 72, 89, 262
"Voice":
    research proposal, 75-76, 89n8, 89n9
    research report, 197-199
Voice-centered interviewing, 133, 147n5, 184

Web of praxis, 16
Weiss, C., 13, 14, 262
Whyte, W. F., 102, 262
Williams, J. M., 76, 78, 258
Wilson, B. L., 187, 261
Wolcott, H. E., 112, 148, 262
Written permission, 103-104

Yin, R. K., 90

About the Authors

Gretchen B. Rossman is Professor of Education at the University of Massachusetts at Amherst, where she teaches qualitative research design and methods, education policy, and leadership. She has served as visiting professor at the Harvard University Graduate School of Education. Prior to assuming her responsibilities at the University of Massachusetts, she was director of field studies at Research for Better Schools in Philadelphia and has been an elementary school teacher. She received her PhD in education from the University of Pennsylvania. Her recent books include *Mandating Academic Excellence* (with Bruce Wilson) and *Designing Qualitative Research* (2nd ed.) (with Catherine Marshall; Sage).

Sharon F. Rallis is Lecturer on Education at the Harvard University Graduate School of Education, where she teaches courses in qualitative research and where she received her EdD. She has been associate professor at Vanderbilt University. Previously, she directed the *Designing Schools for Enhanced Learning* initiative for the Regional Laboratory for Educational Improvement of the Northeast and Islands in Andover, Massachusetts. She has also been a teacher, counselor, and principal. Her books include *Principals of Dynamic Schools* (with Ellen Goldring) and *Becoming a School Board Member* (with Lee Bolman and Terry Deal), both published by Corwin Press.

Rossman and Rallis have also coauthored *Dynamic Teachers* (Corwin Press) and are currently writing *Collaborative Inquiry: Evaluator as Critical Friend* (Sage). They have found collaborative work intellectually stimulating, creative, and thoroughly rewarding.